WHO *IS* ***BLACK?***

WHO **IS BLACK?**

ONE NATION'S DEFINITION

F. JAMES DAVIS

THE PENNSYLVANIA STATE UNIVERSITY PRESS
UNIVERSITY PARK, PENNSYLVANIA

Excerpt from the poem "Cross" by Langston Hughes copyright © 1926 by Alfred A. Knopf Inc. and renewed 1954 by Langston Hughes. Reprinted from *Selected Poems of Langston Hughes,* by permission of Alfred A. Knopf Inc.

Excerpts from *Drylongso: A Self-Portrait of Black America* by John Langston Gwaltney copyright © 1980 by John Langston Gwaltney. Reprinted by permission of Random House Inc.

Excerpt from *Nobody Knows My Name* copyright © 1961 by James Baldwin. Copyright © renewed 1989 by Gloria Karefa-Smart. Used by arrangement with the James Baldwin Estate.

Library of Congress Cataloging-in-Publication Data

Davis, F. James (Floyd James), 1920–
Who is black? : one nation's definition / F. James Davis.

p. cm.
Includes bibliographical references and index.
ISBN 0-271-00739-7 (cloth)
ISBN 0-271-00749-4 (paper)
1. Afro-Americans. 2. Miscegenation—United States.
3. Mulattoes—United States. 4. United States—Race relations.
I. Title.
E185.62.D29 1991
0305.896′073—dc20 90-47971
CIP

Fourth printing, 1993

Copyright © 1991 The Pennsylvania State University
All rights reserved
Printed in the United States of America

It is the policy of The Pennsylvania State University Press to use acid-free paper for the first printing of all clothbound books. Publications on uncoated stock satisfy the minimum requirements of American National Standard for Information Sciences—Permanence of Paper for Printed Library Materials, ANSI Z39.48–1984.

CONTENTS

to those students, colleagues, and friends, and especially to my wife, Lucy, who encouraged me to pursue this topic

PREFACE

The way a person gets defined as black in the United States has occasionally been the subject of fiction, such as *Kingsblood Royal* by Sinclair Lewis or *Pudd'nhead Wilson* by Mark Twain, and also of portions of biographies or essays, but nonfiction treatments of how the definition developed, and of its implications and consequences, are rare and generally quite brief. And seldom has this topic been emphasized in scholarly research and writing on race relations, black history, or civil rights. It has certainly been unusual to stress that other countries define who is black in different ways, or that we define no other ethnic population as we do blacks. The present effort, written for the general reader as well as for scholars, is the first book-length treatment of the subject.

My aim has been to write a book that is objective, that is based on what we know about race relations and that points up the problems and policy issues related to defining who is black. Many observers have written as though America's definition of a black person is the only conceivable one, but this implies that the status of racial hybrids is everywhere the same, even though up to four types of status have been noted (Berry, 1965; Blalock, 1967). Using cross-cultural comparisons (Chapter 5), I discuss seven different ways societies have defined the status of racially mixed people. This book has many implications for conflict theories, as well as for phenomenological, symbolic interactionist, structural, or other interpretations, but I chose to set these formal theoretical tasks aside and highlight the significance of the definition of who is black.

My first course in race relations, just before World War II, was with Professor Edward B. Reuter, a formidable authority on the American mulatto. During the war, I participated in military forces that were segregated in the North and overseas, as well as in the South. Returning to academic life for doctoral study in sociology and law after the war, I was greeted by Gunnar Myrdal's *An American Dilemma* (1944). This monumental study of race relations emphasized the uniqueness and consequences of the definition of who is black in the United States, but that aspect of the study received little attention from other scholars. Later this question of definition seemed to get lost in the civil rights, black power, and black history movements, a notable exception in the 1950s and 1960s being the work of Brewton Berry (1963, 1965). Also, a few excellent treatments of miscegenation became available, such as those by Lerone Bennett, Jr. (1962), James Hugo Johnston (1970), and John W. Blassingame (1972, 1973).

I managed to teach about minorities often during my career, even before I was able to specialize in the subject. At the end of the turbulent 1960s, at a time when many white sociologists and other white scholars abandoned race relations as a major specialty, I chose to concentrate on minority groups more than ever. I am grateful to my department at Illinois State University for making this possible. The fullest knowledge of minority issues requires the talents and perspectives of contributors from the minority community and the dominant community both. It is the nation's problem, and the world's.

To compensate for the lack of published material on how blacks are defined, I developed the topic for my classes and emphasized it in my textbook on minorities (Davis, 1978). Some other recent textbooks address this question of definition too. Student interest in the definition of a black person seemed strong, on the part of black and white students alike, and my colleagues and friends also showed interest. The publication of Joel Williamson's *New People* (1980) was most encouraging. So I began work on this book, and, after retiring from teaching, found the time to complete it.

I acknowledge my reliance on generations of writers and scholars in many fields, a debt that is only partly reflected in the works cited. I am also indebted to a large number of students who helped me improve the analysis and keep learning. Responses of black students have been especially valuable. Most of my students in courses on minorities have been at Illinois State University, California State University at Fullerton, and Hamline University (Minnesota), but some were at The College of Wooster (Ohio) and Western State College of Colorado.

Many colleagues and friends encouraged this effort, often helping more than they knew with timely questions or suggestions, and some provided help with specific problems. I want to thank all who have been supportive and to acknowledge by name some of the most helpful:

Sociologists: James E. Blackwell, Ernest Q. Campbell, Anthony J. Cortese, Delbert J. Ervin, Barbara Sherman Heyl, Dorothy Lee, Wilbert M. Leonard II, the late Arnold M. Rose, Raymond L. Schmitt, Atlee L. Stroup, William L. Tolone, Noriko Omori Tsuya, Robert H. Walsh, William J. Wilson

Anthropologists: Robert T. Dirks, Edward B. Jelks, Martin K. Nickels, Charlotte Otten

Biologists: Kenneth L. Fitch, Harry Huizinga, Robert D. Weigel

Historians: Joseph A. Grabill, John D. Heyl, Frederick W. Kohlmeyer, Mark Plummer, Stephanie Shaw, L. Moody Sims, Walker D. Wyman, Jr.

Political Scientists: Richard G. Browne, George C. Kiser, Richard J. Payne, Hibbert Roberts, Thomas D. Wilson

Other Fields: Brian Bégué, Roger R. Cushman, Jr., Douglas A. DeLong, Carl Esenwein, William Frinsko, Gary A. Hoover, Scott D. King, Charles E. Morris, Jr., Keith E. Stearns

Helpful criticisms and suggestions were offered by three sociologists who read the manuscript for the Pennsylvania State University Press: Mary C. Waters, Roy Austin, and Robert Blauner. Comments and support provided by Sanford G. Thatcher, director of the Press, proved invaluable. For reading all or substantial parts of the manuscript, I am indebted to Stephanie Shaw, Elizabeth Oggel, and Barbara S. Heyl; daughters Elinor Davis, Miriam Davis, and Sarah Davis Platt; Daniel Platt; and the kindest critic of all, my wife, Lucile Anderson Davis.

ONE

THE NATION'S RULE

In a taped interview conducted by a blind, black anthropologist, a black man nearly ninety years old said: "Now you must understand that this is just a name we have. I am not black and you are not black either, if you go by the evidence of your eyes. . . . Anyway, black people are all colors. White people don't look all the same way, but there are more different kinds of us than there are of them. Then too, there is a certain stage [at] which you cannot tell who is white and who is black. Many of the people I see who are thought of as black could just as well be white in their appearance. Many of the white people I see are black as far as I can tell by the way they look. Now, that's it for looks. Looks don't mean much. The things that makes us different is how we think. What we believe is important, the ways we look at life" (Gwaltney, 1980:96).

How does a person get defined as a black, both socially and legally, in the United States? What is the nation's rule for who is black, and how did it come to be? And so what? Don't we all know who is black, and isn't the most important issue what opportunities the group has? Let us start with some experiences of three well-known American blacks—actress and beauty pageant winner Vanessa Williams, U.S. Representative Adam Clayton Powell, Jr., and entertainer Lena Horne.

For three decades after the first Miss America Pageant in 1921, black women were barred from competing. The first black winner was Vanessa Williams of Millwood, New York, crowned Miss America 1984. In the same year the first runner-up—Suzette Charles of Mays Landing, New Jersey—was also black. The viewing public was charmed by the television images and magazine pictures of the beautiful and musically talented Williams, but many people were also puzzled. Why was she being called black when she appeared to be white? Suzette Charles, whose ancestry appeared to be more European than African, at least looked like many of the "lighter blacks." Notoriety followed when Vanessa Williams resigned because of the impending publication of some nude photographs of her taken before the pageant, and Suzette Charles became Miss America for the balance of 1984. Beyond the troubling question of whether these young women could have won if they had looked "more black," the publicity dramatized the nation's definition of a black person.

Some blacks complained that the Rev. Adam Clayton Powell, Jr., was so light that he was a stranger in their midst. In the words of Roi Ottley, "He was white to all appearances, having blue eyes, an aquiline nose, and light, almost blond, hair" (1943:220), yet he became a bold, effective black leader—first as minister of the Abyssinian Baptist Church of Harlem, then as a New York city councilman, and finally as a U.S. congressman from the state of New York. Early in his activist career he led 6,000 blacks in a march on New York City Hall. He used his power in Congress to fight for civil rights legislation and other black causes. In 1966, in Washington, D.C., he convened the first black power conference.

In his autobiography, Powell recounts some experiences with racial classification in his youth that left a lasting impression on him. During Powell's freshman year at Colgate University, his roommate did not know that he was a black until his father, Adam Clayton Powell, Sr., was invited to give a chapel talk on Negro rights and problems, after which the roommate announced that because Adam was a Negro they could no longer be roommates or friends.

Another experience that affected Powell deeply occurred one summer during his Colgate years. He was working as a bellhop at a summer resort in Manchester, Vermont, when Abraham Lincoln's aging son Robert was a guest there. Robert Lincoln disliked blacks so much that he refused to let them wait on him or touch his luggage, car, or any of his possessions. Blacks who did got their knuckles whacked with his cane. To the great amusement of the other bellhops, Lincoln took young Powell for a white man and accepted his services (Powell, 1971:31–33).

Lena Horne's parents were both very light in color and came from black upper-middle-class families in Brooklyn (Horne and Schickel, 1965; Buckley, 1986). Lena lived with her father's parents until she was about seven years old. Her grandfather was very light and blue-eyed. Her fair-skinned grandmother was the daughter of a slave woman and her white owner, from the family of John C. Calhoun, well-known defender of slavery. One of her father's great-grandmothers was a Blackfoot Indian, to whom Lena Horne has attributed her somewhat coppery skin color. One of her mother's grandmothers was a French-speaking black woman from Senegal and never a slave. Her mother's father was a "Portuguese Negro," and two women in his family had passed as white and become entertainers.

Lena Horne's parents had separated, and when she was seven her entertainer mother began placing her in a succession of homes in different states. Her favorite place was in the home of her Uncle Frank, her father's brother, a red-haired, blue-eyed teacher in a black school in Georgia. The black children in that community asked her why she was so light and called her a "yellow bastard." She learned that when satisfactory evidence of respectable black parents is lacking, being light-skinned implies illegitimacy and having an underclass white parent and is thus a disgrace in the black community. When her mother married a white Cuban, Lena also learned that blacks can be very hostile to the white spouse, especially when the "black" mate is very light. At this time she began to blame the confused color line for her childhood troubles. She later endured much hostility from blacks and whites alike when her own second marriage, to white composer-arranger Lennie Hayton, was finally made public in 1950 after three years of keeping it secret.

Early in Lena Horne's career there were complaints that she did not fit the desired image of a black entertainer for white audiences, either physically or in her style. She sang white love songs, not the blues. Noting her brunette-white beauty, one white agent tried to get her to take a Spanish name, learn some Spanish songs, and pass as a Latin white, but she had learned to have a horror of passing and never considered it, although Hollywood blacks accused her of trying to pass after she played her first bit part in a film. After she failed her first screen test because she looked like a white girl trying to play blackface, the directors tried making her up with a shade called "Light Egyptian" to make her look darker. The whole procedure embarrassed and hurt her deeply. Her long struggle to develop a clear sense of self, including a definite racial identity, is explored further in Chapter 7.

Other light mulatto entertainers have also had painful experiences because of their light skin and other caucasoid features. Starting an acting career is never easy, but actress Jane White's difficulties in the 1940s were compounded by her lightness. Her father was NAACP leader Walter White. Even with dark makeup on her ivory skin, she did not look like a black person on the stage, but she was not allowed to try out for white roles because blacks were barred from playing them. When she auditioned for the part of a young girl from India, the director was enthusiastic, although her skin color was too light, but higher management decreed that it was unthinkable for a Negro to play the part of an Asian Indian (White, 1948:338). Only after great perseverance did Jane White make her debut as the educated mulatto maid Nonnie in the stage version of Lillian Smith's *Strange Fruit* (1944).

In Southern California in the 1960s, my family and I had a surprising experience with a couple not so well known to the general public as the above three celebrities. We began attending an almost all-white church served by an interim minister who had retired and who was apparently white. Both he and his wife were gentle, intelligent, soft-spoken people who inspired trust. After several weeks, during one of a series of orientation meetings for new members, we were startled to hear our minister call himself black and refer to the black neighborhood in Chicago where he and his family had lived. When we inquired what he meant, he quietly explained that although they did not like to make a fuss about it, he and his wife also did not want to keep their backgrounds a secret and pass as white. When he was recruited, members of the church must have known this, but it was never mentioned. This couple appeared to be white, biologically, yet our minister insisted on their blackness.

THE ONE-DROP RULE DEFINED

As the above cases illustrate, to be considered black in the United States not even half of one's ancestry must be African black. But will one-fourth do, or one-eighth, or less? The nation's answer to the question "Who is black?" has long been that a black is any person with *any* known African black ancestry (Myrdal, 1944:113–18; Berry and Tischler, 1978:97–98; Williamson, 1980:1–2). This definition reflects the long experience with slavery and later with Jim Crow segregation (see Chapters 3 and 4). In the South it became known as the "one-drop rule," meaning that a single drop of "black blood" makes a person a black. It is also known as the "one black ancestor rule," some courts have called it the "traceable amount rule," and anthropologists call it the "hypo-descent rule," meaning that racially mixed persons are assigned the status of the subordinate group (Harris, 1964:56). This definition emerged from the American South to become the nation's definition, generally accepted by whites and blacks alike (Bahr, Chadwick, and Stauss, 1979:27–28). Blacks had no other choice. As we shall see, this American cultural definition of blacks is taken for granted as readily by judges, affirmative action officers, and black protesters as it is by Ku Klux Klansmen.

Let us not be confused by terminology. At present the usual statement of the one-drop rule is in terms of "black blood" or black ancestry, while not so long ago it referred to "Negro blood" or ancestry. The term "black" rapidly replaced "Negro" in general usage in the United States as the black power movement peaked at the end of the 1960s, but the black and Negro populations are the same. The term "black" is used in this book for persons with any black African lineage, not just for unmixed members of populations from sub-Saharan Africa. The term "Negro," which is used in certain historical contexts, means the same thing. Terms such as "African black," "unmixed Negro," and "all black" are used here to refer to unmixed blacks descended from African populations.

We must also pay attention to the terms "mulatto" and "colored." The term "mulatto" was originally used to mean the offspring of a "pure African Negro" and a "pure white." Although the root meaning of mulatto, in Spanish, is "hybrid," "mulatto" came to include the children of unions between whites and so-called "mixed Negroes." For example, Booker T. Washington and Frederick Douglass, with slave mothers and white fathers, were referred to as mulattoes (Bennett, 1962:255). To whatever extent their mothers were part white, these men were more than half white. Douglass was evidently part Indian as well, and he looked it (Preston, 1980:9–10). Washington had reddish hair and gray eyes. At the time of the American Revolution, many of the founding fathers had some very light slaves, including some who appeared to be white. The term "colored" seemed for a time to refer only to mulattoes, especially lighter ones, but later it became a euphemism for darker Negroes, even including unmixed blacks. With widespread racial mixture, "Negro" came to mean any slave or descendant of a slave, no matter how much mixed. Eventually in the United States, the terms mulatto, colored, Negro, black, and African American all came to mean people with any known black African ancestry. Mulattoes are racially mixed, to whatever degree, while the terms black, Negro, African American, and colored include both mulattoes and unmixed blacks. As we shall see, these terms have quite different meanings in other countries.

Whites in the United States need some help envisioning the American black experience with ancestral fractions. At the beginning of miscegenation between two populations presumed to be racially pure, quadroons appear in the second generation of continuing mixing with whites, and octoroons in the third. A quadroon is one-fourth African black and thus easily classed as black in the United States, yet three of this person's four grandparents are white. An octoroon has seven white great-grandparents out of eight and usually looks white or almost so. Most parents of black American children in recent decades have themselves been racially mixed, but often the fractions get complicated because the earlier details of the mixing were obscured generations ago. Like so many white Americans, black people are forced to speculate about some of the fractions—one-eighth this, three-sixteenths that, and so on.

BLACK LEADERS, BUT PREDOMINANTLY WHITE

Many of the nation's black leaders have been of predominantly white ancestry. During slave times, Robert Purvis was the son of a wealthy white Charleston merchant and a free mulatto woman. His father sent him north to be educated at Amherst College and then to live a life of leisure near Philadelphia. He could have passed as white, but instead helped form the American Anti-Slavery Society and became an effective abolitionist leader (Bennett, 1962:252). During the Reconstruction period after the Civil War, all but three of the twenty black congressmen and two black senators in Washington, D.C., were mulattoes, and some were very light. W.E.B. Du Bois—sociology professor, critic of Booker T. Washington's view that change toward racial equality had to be gradual, and founder in 1910 of the National Association for the Advancement of Colored People (NAACP)—had French, Dutch, and African ancestors (Bennett, 1962:279).

James Augustine Healy was born in 1830 to a mulatto slave and an Irish planter and taken north to a Quaker school on Long Island in 1837. He graduated from Holy Cross College in 1849, and in 1854 was ordained a priest at Notre Dame Cathedral in Paris, France. He became the first black bishop in the United States, serving in that capacity in Portland, Maine. One of his younger brothers, Patrick Francis Healy, became a Jesuit priest. Later, as Monsignor Healy, Patrick served as president of Georgetown University from 1873 to 1882 and has often been called the "second founder" of that institution (Bennett, 1962:253–54).

Walter White, president of the NAACP from 1931 to 1955, was estimated by anthropologists to be no more than one sixty-fourth African black. Both his parents could have passed as white (White, 1948:13; Cannon, 1956:13). When he told whites he was black, they would often say "Are you sure?" They could not understand why a white man wanted to be black (White, 1948:3–4). He had fair skin, fair hair, and blue eyes, yet he chose not to pass as white. He had been raised as a segregated Negro in the Deep South and had experienced white discrimination and violence. Ottley characterized Walter White as "one of the shrewdest negotiators of the race" (1943:244). The "race" for which White negotiated was the ethnic group with which he identified—his community—certainly not his correct genetic classification.

In a biography of Walter White, his second wife, a brunette white, reveals their experiences as an "interracial couple" (Cannon, 1956:14). When they toured the world with an American goodwill mission and were referred to as an interracial couple, puzzled people often asked White how he happened to marry a "colored" woman. The black press was outraged by this marriage (Cannon, 1956:12–13), as it had been decades earlier by the marriage of Frederick Douglass to a white and by the second marriage of Lena Horne. Although the genetic crossing in White's marriage was minute at most, he had married across the social group barrier, outside the black community.

Another major black leader of the twentieth century, A. Philip Randolph, was predominantly white. His mother and his mother's father both could pass as white (Anderson, 1972:31). As a boy, Randolph shared his minister father's outrage when the Jim Crow laws were passed in Jacksonville, Florida, depriving blacks of political participation and segregating the library, streetcars, and other public facilities. In New York, Randolph became a leading black editor and head of the small but influential Brotherhood of Sleeping Car Porters. He was chiefly responsible for pressuring President Franklin Roosevelt into signing the World War II order against racial segregation in war industries and for getting President Harry Truman to sign the order in 1948 to desegregate the U.S. armed forces. He also organized marches on Washington, D.C., including the gigantic rally in 1963 at which the Rev. Dr. Martin Luther King, Jr., gave his "I have a dream" speech. We may note also that King had an Irish grandmother on his father's side and apparently some American Indian ancestry (Bennett, 1965:18).

PLESSY, PHIPPS, AND OTHER CHALLENGES IN THE COURTS

Homer Plessy was the plaintiff in the 1896 precedent-setting "separate-but-equal" case of *Plessy v. Ferguson* (163 U.S. 537). This case challenged the Jim Crow statute that required racially segregated seating on trains in interstate commerce in the state of Louisiana. The U.S. Supreme Court quickly dispensed with Plessy's contention that because he was only one-eighth Negro and could pass as white he was entitled to ride in the seats reserved for whites. Without ruling directly on the definition of a Negro, the Supreme Court briefly took what is called "judicial notice" of what it assumed to be common knowledge: that a Negro or black is any person with any black ancestry. (Judges often take explicit "judicial notice" not only of scientific or scholarly conclusions, or of opinion surveys or other systematic investigations, but also of something they just assume to be so, including customary practices or common knowledge.) This has consistently been the ruling in the federal courts, and often when the black ancestry was even less than one-eighth. The federal courts have thus taken judicial notice of the customary boundary between two sociocultural groups that differ, on the average, in physical traits, not between two discrete genetic categories. In the absence of proof of a specific black ancestor, merely being known as a black in the community has usually been accepted by the courts as evidence of black ancestry. The separate-but-equal doctrine established in the Plessy case is no longer the law, as a result of the judicial and legislative successes of the civil rights movement, but the nation's legal definition of who is black remains unchanged.

State courts have generally upheld the one-drop rule. For instance, in a 1948 Mississippi case a young man, Davis Knight, was sentenced to five years in jail for violating the anti-miscegenation statute. Less than one-sixteenth black, Knight said he was not aware that he had any black lineage, but the state proved his great-grandmother was a slave girl. In some states the operating definition of black has been limited by statute to particular fractions, yet the social definition—the one-drop rule—has generally prevailed in case of doubt. Mississippi, Missouri, and five other states have had the criterion of one-eighth. Virginia changed from one-fourth to one-eighth in 1910, then in 1930 forbade white intermarriage with a person with any black ancestry. Persons in Virginia who are one-fourth or more Indian and less than one-sixteenth African black are defined as Indians while on the reservation but as blacks when they leave (Berry, 1965:26). While some states have had general race classification statutes, at least for a time, others have legislated a definition of black only for particular purposes, such as marriage or education. In a few states there have even been varying definitions for different situations (Mangum, 1940:38–48). All states require a designation of race on birth certificates, but there are no clear guidelines to help physicians and midwives do the classifying.

Louisiana's latest race classification statute became highly controversial and was finally repealed in 1983 (Trillin, 1986:77). Until 1970, a Louisiana statute had embraced the one-drop rule, defining a Negro as anyone with a "trace of black ancestry." This law was challenged in court a number of times from the 1920s on, including an unsuccessful attempt in 1957 by boxer Ralph Dupas, who asked to be declared white so that a law banning "interracial sports" (since repealed) would not prevent him from boxing in the state. In 1970 a lawsuit was brought on behalf of a child whose ancestry was allegedly only one two-hundred-fifty-sixth black, and the legislature revised its law. The 1970 Louisiana statute defined a black as someone whose ancestry is more than one thirty-second black (La. Rev. Stat. 42:267). Adverse publicity about this law was widely disseminated during the Phipps trial in 1983 (discussed below), filed as *Jane Doe v. State of Louisiana.* This case was decided in a district court in May 1983, and in June the legislature abolished its one thirty-second statute and gave parents the right to designate the race of newborns, and even to change classifications on birth certificates if they can prove the child is white by a "preponderance of the evidence." However, the new statute in 1983 did not abolish the "traceable amount rule" (the one-drop rule), as demonstrated by the outcomes when the Phipps decision was appealed to higher courts in 1985 and 1986.

The history in the Phipps (Jane Doe) case goes as far back as 1770, when a French planter named Jean Gregoire Guillory took his wife's slave, Margarita, as his mistress (Model, 1983:3–4). More than two centuries and two decades later, their great-great-great-great-granddaughter, Susie Guillory Phipps, asked the Louisiana courts to change the classification on her deceased parents' birth certificates to "white" so she and her brothers and sisters could be designated white. They all looked white, and some were blue-eyed blonds. Mrs. Susie Phipps had been denied a passport because she had checked "white" on her application although her birth certificate designated her race as "colored." This designation was based on information supplied by a midwife, who presumably relied on the parents or on the family's status in the community. Mrs. Phipps claimed that this classification came as a shock, since she had always thought she was white, had lived as white, and had twice married as white. Some of her relatives, however, gave depositions saying they considered themselves "colored," and the lawyers for the state claimed to have proof that Mrs. Phipps is three-thirty-seconds black (Trillin, 1986:62–63, 71–74). That was more than enough "blackness" for the district court in 1983 to declare her parents, and thus Mrs. Phipps and her siblings, to be legally black.

In October and again in December 1985, the state's Fourth Circuit Court of Appeals upheld the district court's decision, saying that no one can change the racial designation of his or her parents or anyone else's (479 So. 2d 369). Said the majority of the court in its opinion: "That appellants might today describe themselves as white does not prove error in a document which designates their parents as colored" (479 So. 2d 371). Of course, if the parents' designation as "colored" cannot be disturbed, their descendants must be defined as black by the "traceable amount rule." The court also concluded that the preponderance of the evidence clearly showed that the Guillory parents were "colored." Although noting expert testimony to the effect that the race of an individual cannot be determined with scientific accuracy, the court said the law of racial designation is not based on science, that "individual race designations are purely social and cultural perceptions and the evidence conclusively proves those subjective perspectives were correctly recorded at the time the appellants' birth certificates were recorded" (479 So. 2d 372). At the rehearing in December 1985, the appellate court also affirmed the necessity of designating race on birth certificates for public health, affirmative action, and other important public programs and held that equal protection of the law has not been denied so long as the designation is treated as confidential.

When this case was appealed to the Louisiana Supreme Court in 1986, that court declined to review the decision, saying only that the court "concurs in the denial for the reasons assigned by the court of appeals on rehearing" (485 So. 2d 60). In December 1986 the U.S. Supreme Court was equally brief in stating its reason for refusing to review the decision: "The appeal is dismissed for want of a substantial federal question" (107 Sup. Ct. Reporter, interim ed. 638). Thus, both the final court of appeals in Louisiana and the highest court of the United States saw no reason to disturb the application of the one-drop rule in the lawsuit brought by Susie Guillory Phipps and her siblings.

CENSUS ENUMERATION OF BLACKS

When the U.S. Bureau of the Census enumerates blacks (always counted as Negroes until 1980), it does not use a scientific definition, but rather the one accepted by the general public and by the courts. The Census Bureau counts what the nation wants counted. Although various operational instructions have been tried, the definition of black used by the Census Bureau has been the nation's cultural and legal definition: all persons with any known black ancestry. Other nations define and count blacks differently, so international comparisons of census data on blacks can be extremely misleading. For example, Latin American countries generally count as black only unmixed African blacks, those only slightly mixed, and the very poorest mulattoes (see Chapter 5). If they used the U.S. definition, they would count far more blacks than they do, and if Americans used their definition, millions in the black community in the United States would be counted either as white or as "coloreds" of different descriptions, not as black.

Instructions to our census enumerators in 1840, 1850, and 1860 provided "mulatto" as a category but did not define the term. In 1870 and 1880, mulattoes were officially defined to include "quadroons, octoroons, and all persons having any perceptible trace of African blood." In 1890 enumerators were told to record the *exact* proportion of the "African blood," again relying on visibility. In 1900 the Census Bureau specified that "pure Negroes" be counted separately from mulattoes, the latter to mean "all persons with some trace of black blood." In 1920 the mulatto category was dropped, and black was defined to mean any person with any black ancestry, as it has been ever since.

In 1960 the practice of self-definition began, with the head of household indicating the race of its members. This did not seem to introduce any noticeable fluctuation in the number of blacks, thus indicating that black Americans generally apply the one-drop rule to themselves. One exception is that Spanish-speaking Americans who have black ancestry but were considered white, or some designation other than black, in their place of origin generally reject the one-drop rule if they can. American Indians with some black ancestry also generally try to avoid the rule, but those who leave the reservation are often treated as black. At any rate, the 1980 census count showed that self-designated blacks made up about 12 percent of the population of the United States.

No other ethnic population in the nation, including those with visibly non-caucasoid features, is defined and counted according to a one-drop rule. For example, persons whose ancestry is one-fourth or less American Indian are not generally defined as Indian unless they want to be, and they are considered assimilating Americans who may even be proud of having some Indian ancestry. The same implicit rule appears to apply to Japanese Americans, Filipinos, or other peoples from East Asian nations and also to Mexican Americans who have Central American Indian ancestry, as a large majority do. For instance, a person whose ancestry is one-eighth Chinese is not defined as just Chinese, or East Asian, or a member of the mongoloid race. The United States certainly does not apply a one-drop rule to its white ethnic populations either, which include both national and religious groups. Ethnicity has often been confused with racial biology (see Chapter 2), and not just in Nazi Germany. Americans do not insist that an American with a small fraction of Polish ancestry be classified as a Pole, or that someone with a single remote Greek ancestor be designated Greek, or that someone with any trace of Jewish lineage is a Jew and nothing else.

It is interesting that, in *The Passing of the Great Race* (1916), Madison

Grant maintained that the one-drop rule should be applied not only to blacks but also to all the other ethnic groups he considered biologically inferior "races," such as Hindus, Asians in general, Jews, Italians, and other Southern and Eastern European peoples. Grant's book went through four editions, and he and others succeeded in getting Congress to pass the national origins quota laws of the early 1920s. This racist quota legislation sharply curtailed immigration from everywhere in the world except Northern and Western Europe and the Western Hemisphere, until it was repealed in 1965. Grant and other believers in the racial superiority of their own group have confused race with ethnicity. They consider miscegenation with any "inferior" people to be the ultimate danger to the survival of their own group and have often seen the one-drop rule as a crucial component in their line of defense. Americans in general, however, while finding other ways to discriminate against immigrant groups, have rejected the application of the drastic one-drop rule to all groups but blacks.

UNIQUENESS OF THE ONE-DROP RULE

Not only does the one-drop rule apply to no other group than American blacks, but apparently the rule is unique in that it is found only in the United States and not in any other nation in the world. In fact, definitions of who is black vary quite sharply from country to country (see Chapter 5), and for this reason people in other countries often express consternation about our definition. James Baldwin relates a revealing incident that occurred in 1956 at the Conference of Negro-African Writers and Artists held in Paris. The head of the delegation of writers and artists from the United States was John Davis. The French chairperson introduced Davis and then asked him why he considered himself Negro, since he certainly did not look like one. Baldwin wrote, "He *is* a Negro, of course, from the remarkable legal point of view which obtains in the United States, but more importantly, as he tried to make clear to his interlocutor, he was a Negro by choice and by depth of involvement—by experience, in fact" (1962:19).

The phenomenon known as "passing as white" is difficult to explain in other countries or to foreign students. Typical questions are: "Shouldn't

Americans say that a person who is passing as white *is* white, or nearly all white, and has previously been passing as black?" or "To be consistent, shouldn't you say that someone who is one-eighth white is passing as black?" or "Why is there so much concern, since the so-called blacks who pass take so little negroid ancestry with them?" Those who ask such questions need to realize that "passing" is much more a social phenomenon than a biological one, reflecting the nation's unique definition of what makes a person black. The concept of "passing" rests on the one-drop rule and on folk beliefs about race and miscegenation, not on biological or historical fact.

The black experience with passing as white in the United States contrasts with the experience of other ethnic minorities that have features that are clearly non-caucasoid. The concept of passing applies only to blacks—consistent with the nation's unique definition of the group. A person who is one-fourth or less American Indian or Korean or Filipino is not regarded as passing if he or she intermarries and joins fully the life of the dominant community, so the minority ancestry need not be hidden. It is often suggested that the key reason for this is that the physical differences between these other groups and whites are less pronounced than the physical differences between African blacks and whites, and therefore are less threatening to whites. However, keep in mind that the one-drop rule and anxiety about passing originated during slavery and later received powerful reinforcement under the Jim Crow system.

For the physically visible groups other than blacks, miscegenation promotes assimilation, despite barriers of prejudice and discrimination during two or more generations of racial mixing. As noted above, when ancestry in one of these racial minority groups does not exceed one-fourth, a person is not defined solely as a member of that group. Masses of white European immigrants have climbed the class ladder not only through education but also with the help of close personal relationships in the dominant community, intermarriage, and ultimately full cultural and social assimilation. Young people tend to marry people they meet in the same informal social circles (Gordon, 1964:70–81). For visibly non-caucasoid minorities other than blacks in the United States, this entire route to full assimilation is slow but possible.

For all persons of any known black lineage, however, assimilation is blocked and is not promoted by miscegenation. Barriers to full opportunity and participation for blacks are still formidable, and a fractionally black person cannot escape these obstacles without passing as white and cutting off all ties to the black family and community. The pain of this separation, and condemnation by the black family and community, are major reasons why many or most of those who could pass as white choose not to. Loss of security within the minority community, and fear and distrust of the white world are also factors.

It should now be apparent that the definition of a black person as one with any trace at all of black African ancestry is inextricably woven into the history of the United States. It incorporates beliefs once used to justify slavery and later used to buttress the castelike Jim Crow system of segregation. Developed in the South, the definition of "Negro" (now black) spread and became the nation's social and legal definition (see Chapter 3). Because blacks are defined according to the one-drop rule, they are a socially constructed category in which there is wide variation in racial traits and therefore not a race group in the scientific sense (see Chapter 2). However, because that category has a definite status position in the society it has become a self-conscious social group with an ethnic identity.

The one-drop rule has long been taken for granted throughout the United States by whites and blacks alike, and the federal courts have taken "judicial notice" of it as being a matter of common knowledge. State courts have generally upheld the one-drop rule, but some have limited the definition to one thirty-second or one-sixteenth or one-eighth black ancestry, or made other limited exceptions for persons with both Indian and black ancestry. Most Americans seem unaware that this definition of blacks is extremely unusual in other countries, perhaps even unique to the United States, and that Americans define no other minority group in a similar way.

In the United States there are still complex, major issues about the opportunities and rights of blacks, but none concerning how we define who is black. The personnel officer, the census taker, the judge, the school admissions staff, the affirmative action officer, and the black political caucus leader all readily classify a predominantly white mulatto as a black person. Spanish-speaking people are often exempted if they are not too dark, and other deviations from the rule are noted in Chapter 6, yet the one-drop rule has generally prevailed. Even so, the rule has its costs, and the attendant ambiguities, strains, conflicts, and traumatic experiences are explored in Chapter 7.

The aim here is to contribute to a greater understanding of the origins, operation, and effects of the American definition of who is black and thus to fuller knowledge about race relations in the United States. To accomplish this, we examine the unique history of black-white relations in American society and observe contrasts with the corresponding rules and experiences in other societies with racially mixed populations. Arbitrary and contradictory as our one-drop rule is, it is deeply embedded in the social structures and cultures of both the black and the white communities in the United States and strongly resistant to change. The final chapter raises basic questions about prospects for the future.

The analysis in this book, although it is based on materials pertinent to a number of theoretical perspectives, has been oriented primarily toward an approach that emphasizes conflict and differences in group power (Davis, 1978:27–31). Latent conflict is common in patterns of accommodation between racial or ethnic groups, because typically these patterns reflect inequalities of group power and include institutionalized discrimination (Blalock, 1967:139; Blackwell, 1975:29–32). When conflicts become overt, they may under the right conditions effect changes in relative power and in patterns of intergroup relations. Only after cataclysmic struggles will dominant groups let go of such extremely unequal and highly institutionalized systems as slavery, Jim Crow segregation, or Apartheid. Rules for intergroup relations, including social definitions of racial categories, are forged and changed in power politics. Both customary and legal classifications of racial and ethnic groups are products of complex cross-pressures brought to bear by interest groups that have different amounts of power (Dominguez, 1986:12, 23–55, 267–73). We now turn to the development of the one-drop rule through the conflicts and changing patterns of black-white relations in the United States.

T W O

MISCEGENATION AND BELIEFS

Much of the rhetoric advanced in the 1950s and 1960s against desegregating the public schools and other public facilities in the American South featured the assertion that racial integration would destroy the purity of the races. In a speech in 1954, U.S. Representative John Bell Williams of Mississippi referred to the day the U.S. Supreme Court announced its decision in the case of *Brown v. Board of Education of Topeka, Kansas* (347 U.S. 483) as Black Monday. Then, in a book called *Black Monday,* Yale-educated Circuit Court Judge Thomas Brady of Mississippi contended that the *Brown* decision would lead to "the tragedy of miscegenation." He wrote fiercely that he and the South would fight and die for the principles of racial purity and white womanhood rather than follow the Supreme Court's decision. He maintained that God opposes racial mixing and that Southern whites had a God-given right to keep their "blood" white and pure (Blaustein and Ferguson, 1957:7–8). It was, of course, centuries too late to keep the races pure in the South.

The concept of "any known black ancestry" implies well over three and a half centuries of truth about racial mixing. The vast majority of Americans defined as blacks are not pure descendants of the slaves from Africa, but racially mixed (Bennett, 1962: chap. 10). Thus, members of the black community, as defined by the one-drop rule, vary all the way from a diminishing number of unmixed African blacks to those who appear to be of purely European origin. At the same time, only traces of the many different tribal cultures of the people captured in sub-Saharan Africa remain. The slaves came from an extensive area of West and West Central Africa from Senegal to Angola, from coastal and inland regions, from many different tribes, from different religions, and speaking a variety of languages. Today's black culture and sense of identity are largely the products of the centuries of experience in the United States, along with a few African survivals. At least by the 1920s, a *new people* had emerged in the American crucible, both in the physical sense and in the sociocultural sense (Williamson, 1980:3).

As Gunnar Myrdal (1944) pointed out, it is the social and legal definition of the black population in the United States that has counted, not its scientific accuracy. However, this socially constructed category has meaning only in relation to the realities of race and miscegenation. Biological realities have social consequences, including the spread of beliefs about race and miscegenation. In order to understand the emergence of the one-drop rule and its implications, then, it is necessary to explore some of the complexities of the process of miscegenation. This requires at least a brief and nontechnical consideration of the scientific criteria used in the physical anthropology of race.

We must first distinguish racial traits from cultural traits, since they are so often confused with each other. As defined in physical anthropology and biology, *races* are categories of human beings based on average differences in physical traits that are transmitted by the genes not by blood. *Culture* is a shared pattern of behavior and beliefs that are learned and transmitted through social communication. An *ethnic group* is a group with a sense of cultural identity, such as Czech or Jewish Americans, but it may also be a racially distinctive group. A group that is racially distinctive in a society may be an ethnic group as well, but not necessarily. Although racially mixed, most blacks in the United States are physically distinguishable from whites, but they are also an ethnic group because of the distinctive culture they have developed within the general American framework.

RACIAL CLASSIFICATION AND MISCEGENATION

The system of racial classification noted for discussion here is based on the measurement of visible traits of human anatomy, an approach that has been supplanted by research on the frequency of certain gene markers. Earlier physical anthropologists found hair form, nose shape, and head shape to be the most dependable criteria for establishing reasonably discrete racial categories, although some other traits were found to be valuable for classifying subraces. If a cross-section of a strand of hair is round, the hair will be straight; if it is flat, the hair will be extremely curly; if it is oval-shaped the hair will be wavy. The nasal index (the ratio of the length of the nose to its width) provides the narrow, wide, and intermediate types. The cephalic index (the ratio of the length of the head to its width) yields round-headed, long-headed, and intermediate types. Lip eversion and the color of hair, eyes, and skin have proven to be only somewhat reliable for racial classification, and still other traits, such as body type, even less reliable. This is illustrated below by the distribution of skin color.

Using mainly hair form, nose shape, and head shape, A. L. Kroeber (1948:140) arrived at three major races: caucasoid, mongoloid, and negroid, commonly referred to as white, yellow, and black. On the average, he found caucasoids to have the longest heads and mongoloids the roundest; mongoloids the straightest hair and negroids the most tightly curled; caucasoids the narrowest noses and negroids the broadest. Comparing just negroids and caucasoids, he found that the former usually have rounder heads, frizzier hair, and broader noses. Negroids have darker skins than caucasoids too, with a very large exception noted below. Other anatomical classifiers have found four or five races, and some have refined the subgroups and ended up with many races (Hooton, 1948; Coon, 1962; Garn, 1965). More recent researchers prefer to focus on the frequency of traits in different human populations and to reject the assumption that there are pure races.

Although negroids are very dark, skin color is poorly correlated with Kroeber's more dependable racial criteria, largely because of the dark-skinned peoples of India, Pakistan, Bangladesh, and some contiguous areas. Kroeber and others have had little difficulty placing these South Asians in the caucasoid category on the basis of their straight hair, relatively long heads, narrow noses, and thin, inverted lips. Physical anthropologists believe the dark skin color is explained by variation and selective adaptation of that trait to climate, not by genetic influence from African populations. Thus, there is wide variation in skin color among Kroeber's subgroups of the caucasoid race, which are Nordic, Alpine, Mediterranean, Hindu (the "dark whites"), and the Ainu of the Japanese island of Hokkaido. Kroeber's subgroups of the mongoloid race are Asiatic, Oceanic, and American Indians (who came from Siberian Asia) and, of the negroid race, African, Oceanic, Negritos (pygmies), and Bushmen (who have some non-negroid traits).

External anatomical traits vary independently rather than being transmitted in genetic clusters (Berry and Tischler, 1978:34–35). Classification is complicated by the existence of many racially mixed populations around the world, and Kroeber was unable to place such groups as Polynesians and the native Australians within one of his three major categories. At best, such anatomical groupings as Kroeber's three races are only rough, statistical categories representing average differences of combinations of traits. Human races are subspecies groups, not completely discrete categories, and were so even before miscegenation. The fact that reproduction occurs across racial lines demonstrates that all human beings belong to the same species.

Albinos occur in all three races and cause particular consternation when they appear among negroid peoples or among Hindu caucasoids. Albinism is the genetic absence or marked weakness of pigmentation, so that the skin is pale and milky, the hair very light, and the eyes pink. A Nigerian sociologist who is also an albino creates wonder wherever he goes in Africa, Europe, or the United States. The first reaction often is shock, since the other visible traits do not match the color characteristics. However, close observers usually are able to conclude that he is of negroid stock. Usually people are so preoccupied with his anomalous appearance that they are unaware of his visual handicap, a concomitant of albinism.

Efforts to improve on racial classification by using blood types have not proved very successful. The major blood types have been found to have different frequencies among Kroeber's caucasoid, mongoloid, and negroid groups. However, all the blood types are found in all of Kroeber's three races, and the differences are not great. Put another way, the correlation between blood type and external anatomical traits is small. Sickle-cell anemia is a genetic, blood-connected factor that illustrates the dubious relationship between blood type and race. This disease is frequent among American blacks and the West African peoples from which slaves came, but it is also frequent among non-negroid populations in Greece, Southern India, and some other areas of the world. In fact, in the past the sickle-cell trait was found in regions that had high rates of malaria, and it appears to have been an adaptive response to that disease (Newman, 1973:266–67).

What are the overall results of centuries of miscegenation in the United States? At least three-fourths of all people defined as American blacks have some white ancestry, and some estimates run well above 90 percent. The blacks with no white lineage are mainly in the more isolated, rural areas of the Deep South, notably in South Carolina. As many as one-fourth of all American blacks have some American Indian ancestry, and a great many people classed as Indians have some black background (Pettigrew, 1975:xiii). Thus, the color spectrum among the black population ranges from ebony to lighter than most whites, and the other racial traits show a similar range of variation. A "new people" indeed, biologically, derived predominantly from African black populations, but with a large infusion of genes from European white peoples and a substantial amount from American Indians.

In terms of gene frequencies, apparently somewhere between one-fifth and one-fourth of the genes of the American black population are from white ancestors. The national estimates by physical anthropologists have ranged from about 20 percent to 31 percent, with recent opinion apparently inclining toward the lower figure. The estimates vary considerably for different regions, with Northern blacks having the larger percentages of "white genes." Keep in mind that most American blacks throughout the nation have some "white genes," but that there are regional and local variations in the estimated amount. For example, it has been estimated that in Detroit 25 percent of the genes in the black population are "white genes"; in Oakland, California, 22 percent; in New York City, 19 percent; in two counties of Georgia, 11 percent; and in Charleston, South Carolina, 4 percent (Reed, 1969:765). The low figure for Charleston may be due in part to the considerable number of mulattoes accepted as white there before and for a time after the Civil War. Also, many Angolan blacks in isolated areas of South Carolina have remained largely unmixed to the present.

It has been estimated that about 1 percent of the genes of the white population of the United States are from African ancestors. Estimates ranging up to 5 percent, and suggestions that up to one-fifth of the white population have some genes from black ancestors, are probably far too high. If these last figures were correct, the majority of Americans with some black ancestry would be known and counted as whites! The peak years for passing as white were probably from 1880 to 1925, with perhaps from 10,000 to 25,000 crossing the color line each year, although such estimates are most likely inflated. By 1940 the annual number had apparently declined to no more than 2,500 to 2,750 a year (Burma, 1946:1822; Williamson, 1980:103). It must be remembered that most of those who pass as white take few "negroid genes" with them, so that today around 99 percent of the genes in the white population are from European ancestors. During slavery and its aftermath, however, some who were legally accepted as white in the South had as much as one-fourth African ancestry. At least since the 1920s, apparently, most mulattoes who could pass have remained in the black population.

A further genetic point is very important and has a bearing especially on the question of passing as white. Genes are randomly distributed in individuals, so, although it is extremely improbable, a mulatto who is half white and half unmixed black might not have inherited any genes from African ancestors (Trillin, 1986:75). The smaller the proportion of any ancestry, the more probable it is that there are no genes from that lineage. In other words, having one or more black ancestors does not prove that an individual has some negroid traits or can transmit genes from African forebears. The widely held belief is that an individual's racial traits and genetic carriers are necessarily in direct proportion to the person's fraction of African black ancestry. Some persons with three-eighths or even one-half African lineage have been known to pass as white, presumably in cases in which the number of "negroid genes" was much less than the proportion of African ancestry. In instances where someone has received no "negroid genes" at all from the known African ancestors, that person not only appears white but is in biological fact white.

It is important to note that miscegenation is a biological process that requires sexual contact but not intermarriage. Many estimates of the extent and effects of miscegenation are based solely on intermarriage data, because good data of other kinds are not easy to find. It is also important to note that the mixing of genes is continuous within a group defined by the one-drop rule, even if sexual contact with the out-group declines or ceases. That is, miscegenation occurs when there is sexual contact between unmixed African blacks and mulattoes, and between mulattoes and other mulattoes, not just when there is mixing between whites and African blacks or whites and mulattoes. In all four of these instances, genes from populations derived from Europe and sub-Saharan Africa are being mixed. In mulatto-mulatto unions, genes are mixed whether the ancestry of one individual is mainly white and the other mainly black, or the ratios are more nearly even. This genetic mixing is not publicly defined as such, and the marriages concerned are certainly not thought of as intermarriages. Yet very often these unions involve much more miscegenation than occurs between whites and near-white "blacks."

RACIST BELIEFS ABOUT MISCEGENATION

Public beliefs about race and miscegenation often bear little or no resemblance to the current conclusions of physical anthropologists. Sets of beliefs—ideologies—provide groups and individuals with needed justifications for patterns of action. Ideologies such as racism and sexism help people rationalize patterns of discrimination, and sometimes even extremely brutal treatment, against racial minorities and women. There is less acceptance of racist beliefs now than there was earlier in the century, particularly among the better educated, and scientific knowledge about race has been fairly widely disseminated in schools and by the mass media. However, racist views have been highly influential in the history of the United States and are held today by many people other than the right-wing extremists who express them openly. The term "racism" is most useful when limited to patterns of discrimination that are consciously rationalized according to the beliefs discussed below. Unfortunately, the term is often used now to mean any systematic discrimination against a group, irrespective of the beliefs used to justify the behavior.

The content of racist ideologies consists of five key beliefs, all of which scientists generally agree are false. The first of these beliefs is that some races are physically superior to others and that they can be ranked from strongest to weakest based on differences in longevity and rates of selected diseases. Actually, a particular group will appear to be strong in some respects but weak in others. Traditionally, American blacks have had higher rates of tuberculosis, infant mortality, and sickle-cell anemia, while whites have had higher rates of cancer and several types of heart disease. Group differences in occupation, income, housing, sanitation, nutrition, medical care, education, and developed group immunities to particular diseases must all be taken into account.

The second key belief in racist ideology is that some races are mentally superior to others and that the races can be ranked from most intelligent to least intelligent. On standardized tests designed to measure intelligence (learning capacity), the average scores for blacks, Indians, and other minorities have often been reported to be well below the national average. However, so-called intelligence (or IQ) tests actually measure an inextricable combination of learning potential and what has been learned. Knowledge of the culture and of the language in which the test is written greatly affects the test scores. Because the most widely used intelligence test, the Stanford-Binet, was standardized on white, middle-class Americans, it is not "culture-free." Other factors shown to be correlated with intelligence test scores are social class background, learning experiences at home, quality of schooling, health, motivation, and learned attitudes toward competition and speed (Loehlin, Lindsey, and Spuhler, 1975:62–71). Many studies have shown that IQ scores rise with improved learning opportunities and with familiarity with the matters tested, as when blacks have moved from the rural South to the urban North (Pettigrew, 1971:95–113). The genetics of physical traits should not be confused with whatever genetic determinants there may be of problem-solving ability, and we have seen that racial traits are not inherited in clusters (Montagu, 1975:1–16).

The third key belief is that race causes culture, that each inbred population has a distinct culture that is genetically transmitted along with its physical traits. Ethnic groups, which in this belief are confused with races, are believed to share certain values and patterns of behavior because it is just "in their blood." Actually, culture is transmitted through the process of socialization, not by the genes. Parental habits and values cannot be passed on genetically. A wide range of cultural patterns can be learned by members of the same race. A Korean orphan child raised from infancy in Iowa has the racial traits of its biological parents but learns English and Midwest American culture.

The fourth key belief is that race determines temperamental dispositions of individuals, a view based on crude stereotypes of the personalities in ethnic groups. Examples are that the English have an inborn reserve, that Italians are by nature gregarious and emotional, and that all blacks are just naturally rhythmic and happy. Although there are average cultural differences in temperament, this belief involves another profound confusion of race and culture. Even if temperament is partly determined by genetic factors, there is no scientific basis for considering it part of a supposed complex of racial traits.

The fifth basic belief in racist ideology is that racial mixing lowers biological quality. It is not surprising that people consider miscegenation dangerous when they also believe that physical, mental, and behavioral traits are all tied to racial heredity, and when they make the value judgment that their own culture is far superior to others. The mixing of what are presumed to be superior stocks with "inferior" and detested stocks allegedly leads to blood poisoning and other physical deterioration, to mental inferiority, and to immorality and cultural degeneracy (Snyder, 1962:23–24). Despite evidence to the contrary, many white Southerners have believed that mulattoes cannot reproduce among themselves after the third generation and that they are troublesome by nature while unmixed blacks just naturally "know their place." It has also been widely believed that a light mulatto parent, even one who looks white, can have a very black child. Actually, if one parent is fully white, it is extremely unlikely that a child will be any darker than the darker parent (Day, 1932:106–27; Hooton, 1948) This and other beliefs about miscegenation, not all logically consistent with each other, have flourished in the traditional racial ideology in the South. The traditional Germanic view, held in North Europe and Great Britain, has been that racially mixed children are flawed.

There is no scientific proof that miscegenation produces either lower or higher overall biological quality than that of the parent stocks. Racially mixed persons are often socially marginal, not fully accepted members of either parent group. They have often experienced discrimination, but in some societies they have received social benefits (see Chapter 5). Although skin color may have adaptive advantages or disadvantages in given physical environments, there is no evidence that color is associated in any way with overall biological quality. Society's value judgments about genetic quality should not be confused with scientific judgments. High civilizations sometimes emerged when many peoples met and amalgamated—as in the Near East and Middle East and in Central America—as a result of the stimulating effects of cultural contact and communication. Miscegenation may have major social and cultural consequences, then, but these should not be attributed to genetic effects (Berry, 1965:280–85).

Aristotle praised the institution of slavery, saying that people with poor reasoning power cannot be happy with freedom and that their menial labor frees those with superior minds to pursue higher goals. These views of Aristotle were often cited to justify slavery in the American South (Campbell, 1974:286–300). The Roman writer Tacitus attributed the advanced culture of the Teutonic Germans to their racial superiority and racial purity. This view was resurrected in mid-nineteenth-century France by Joseph-Arthur de Gobineau, who wrote of the cultural superiority of the Aryan (or Nordic) race and warned against the degenerative effects of racial mixing (1853–55). From de Gobineau's views stemmed the claims of Teutonism, Celticism, and Anglo-Saxonism (Newman, 1973:255–57). Thomas Carlyle promoted the claims of Anglo-Saxon superiority, and Rudyard Kipling provided rhyme, meter, and the stirring concept of the "white man's burden." These views loomed large in justifications of colonialism, the slave trade, and later the control of immigration.

The German composer Richard Wagner cited de Gobineau to support his views about the heroic superiority of the Aryans and the extreme cultural inferiority of the Jewish "race." Wagner's English son-in-law and biographer, Houston Stewart Chamberlain, characterized the Aryans as culture-builders and sustainers and the Jews as destroyers (Chamberlain, 1899). Adolf Hitler was heavily influenced by the views of Wagner and Chamberlain, and he inspired a vast literature on "racial purity." Aryan racism was legalized in the Nuremberg Laws of 1935, which denied citizenship to all who were not of "German or kindred blood" and stated that anyone who had one (full) Jewish grandparent was legally a Jew. Jews were forbidden by law to marry Christians, and in 1939 they were excluded from the nation's economic, political, and other institutions. In the end, these racist beliefs were used to justify the extermination of at least six million Jews, four million Poles, other Slavs, Gypsies, homosexuals, the mentally ill or deficient, Jehovah's Witnesses, and other "inferior" people. Discriminatory treatment can be rationalized by other sets of beliefs, but racist beliefs have the potential for bringing out and rationalizing the most bestial extremes in intergroup relations.

Early in the twentieth century in the United States, proponents of the American Nordic Movement issued strong warnings against the "mongrelization of the races." Publication of their ideas strengthened the Jim Crow system of segregation and crystallized the opposition to immigration from Southern and Eastern Europe. Grant (1916) wrote that blacks cannot be civilized by schools and churches and that they should be totally separated in colonies of manual laborers. He warned against the alleged unscrupulousness of the Polish Jew, the inferiority of Italians and immigrants from other nations of Southern and Eastern Europe, and the horrors of an ethnic melting pot. He and others led the rejection of the melting pot ideal in favor of the forced assimilation of Anglo-American ways and of the segregation of blacks.

Grant contended that the one-drop rule should apply to all "inferior races," not only to blacks (see Chapter 1), and Stoddard (1920) maintained that the quality of the onetime largely Nordic population was being drastically lowered by mixture with "inferior races." These beliefs were incorporated into segregation statutes and immigration controls, laws that proved very difficult to change. Pro-Nazi groups in the United States encouraged racist beliefs from the early 1930s on, lending support to such organizations as the Ku Klux Klan and the White Citizens Council, as well as to less extremist opponents of change in race relations.

THE JUDGE BRADY PARADOX

This discussion of race and beliefs about race helps explain the paradox posed by Judge Brady's warning about the impending tragedy of miscegenation, noted at the opening of this chapter. How could Judge Brady and large numbers of other people so passionately espouse beliefs that condemn racial mixing as if it had never happened, when all around them was overwhelming evidence to the contrary? The answer requires some knowledge of the Jim Crow system of racial segregation, especially its supporting beliefs and social control mechanisms. Judge Brady's rhetoric was actually an expression of strong determination to resist the fall of the Jim Crow laws of the Southern states, counties, and municipalities, the legal backbone of the system of segregation that prevailed for more than half a century in the American South. Under the influence of this system, support for the one-drop rule finally became uniform in the United States as a whole, not just in the South, among both whites and blacks.

The practices and beliefs of the Jim Crow system are examined in detail in Chapter 4, along with segregation in the North and recent developments in the entire United States. Miscegenation and beliefs about the process of miscegenation must be placed in relevant contexts before, during, and after the Jim Crow era if we are to understand the rise, testing, and operation of the one-drop rule. Chapter 3 focuses on the different contexts of the two and a half centuries of miscegenation in the United States during slavery, the emergence of the one-drop rule, and the conflict over this rule and a competing rule. But here we must note briefly the settings of the black-white miscegenation that occurred before slavery in America began.

MISCEGENATION IN AFRICA AND EUROPE

Some black-white miscegenation had been occurring in Africa for many centuries before the European settlement of the North American continent began. Portuguese, Dutch, Italian, Spanish, and other European explorers, traders, conquerors, and colonizers had produced racially mixed offspring, especially in African coastal areas. Phoenicians, Greeks, Romans, Arabs, and Norse had plied the same coasts long before. Hamitic-speaking caucasoids from North Africa had mixed with Bantu-speaking and other black tribes in East Central and Central Africa a thousand years ago, and much earlier. Arabs (Mediterranean caucasoids) had spread Islam from the Sudan to Nigeria and on west from there, mixing especially with the Senegalese and taking slaves (Reuter, 1970:24–25). In Morocco the Arabs intermarried with the native Berbers, who were caucasoid except that many of the latter had mixed with black peoples in the lower Sahara. Thus the population of Morocco, the Moors, came to include many mulattoes. Moreover, some of the first slaves in the American colonies were brought from the West Indies, where a considerable amount of racial mixing had taken place among Europeans, African black slaves, and West Indians. Thus, some of the slaves were already racially mixed, whether in Africa or elsewhere, before they had any sexual contact with Europeans in the American colonies.

An unknown amount of white-black miscegenation had also taken place in Europe in ancient times and later. At least small numbers of black Africans were taken to Europe, usually as slaves or indentured servants, and absorbed by the white populations. As a result of the several centuries of occupation of much of Spain and Portugal by Arabs and Moors, until their expulsion (along with the Jews) in 1492, considerable numbers of mulattoes were among the Moors that were absorbed by European populations, especially in Portugal. The Germanic peoples of Northern

Europe, apparently including the Angles and Saxons, tended to reject the legitimacy of mixed offspring. However, had a strict one-drop rule been operating, the descendants of the mixed people would have been defined as blacks. Thus the European settlers in the American colonies were not all pure whites, and the slaves they brought were not all pure African blacks. The process of miscegenation had begun long before, much of it limited and slow, but would be greatly accelerated.

RACE VS. BELIEFS ABOUT RACE

As blacks in the United States were becoming a racially mixed people, they were also forging a new cultural style and a new sense of identity out of their American experiences and remnants of their African past and thus becoming a new people both physically and culturally. It is essential to keep the racial and cultural processes separate in our thinking, although they have taken place together in the same social situations. Races are groupings of human beings based on average differences in biological characteristics, while cultures are group patterns of behavior and beliefs. Racial traits are transmitted from generation to generation by the genes, while culture is transmitted in the process of socialization, by social communication. Blacks in the United States are a group with visibly distinctive racial traits, but they also are an ethnic group with a sense of identity and a shared lifestyle.

Using the physical anthropologist Alfred Kroeber's classification system of the caucasoid, negroid, and mongoloid races, the population defined as black in the United States has remained predominantly negroid, but with a large infusion of caucasoid and a significant amount of American Indian mongoloid ancestry. More precisely, at least 20 percent of the genes of the black population are estimated to have come from European ancestors, with estimates varying considerably for different regions of the United States. Probably about 1 percent of the genes of the white population are from African ancestors, and there are millions of white Americans who have at least small amounts of black genetic heritage. From 75 to well over 90 percent of all American blacks apparently have some white ancestry, and up to 25 percent have Indian background. Not surprisingly, the black population, as defined by the one-drop rule, includes people whose racial characteristics run the full range from Kroeber's negroid to caucasoid to American Indian mongoloid types.

The black population in the United States is a socially constructed category backed by law, not a grouping established by physical anthropologists or biologists. Both the definition and the treatment of the group are based on publicly held beliefs about race and racial mixing, not on scientific conclusions. The beliefs are crucial. A particular version of the set of beliefs known as racism has played a central role in American race relations, in the development of the one-drop rule, in immigration policy, and in anti-Semitism. Although these beliefs confuse genetic processes with cultural processes and are generally rejected by scientists as false, they have been widely held.

The key beliefs in racism are that some races are physically and mentally superior to others, that racial differences cause cultural and temperamental differences, and that racial mixing causes the biological and cultural degeneration of the "superior races." These beliefs have been used to justify slavery, and the last one has been particularly important in resisting the end of the Jim Crow system in the South. While less widely supported than in the past, the "superior race" ideology continues to be openly propounded by pro-Nazi and other groups, such as the Ku Klux Klan. Group discrimination can be based on other sets of beliefs, but the record is clear that racist beliefs are capable of arousing and providing justifications for many of the most brutal extremes in ethnic relations.

Some knowledge of the physical anthropology of race makes it possible to understand better the complexities of miscegenation in the United States and the operation and significance of the one-drop rule. Keep in mind that miscegenation does not require marriage and that most black-white sexual contacts in the United States have been illicit. It is also important to remember that genes are being mixed in mulatto-mulatto and mulatto-African black unions, since mulattoes transmit genes from both white and black populations. Also, the number of "negroid genes" received by an individual is not necessarily proportional to the amount of African ancestry. Some general appreciation of the role of beliefs about race and miscegenation helps us understand certain patterns of belief and practice during slavery and its aftermath, during Jim Crow times, and in the present. We now turn to miscegenation during slavery and the rise of two competing rules for determining who is black in the United States.

THREE

CONFLICTING RULES

How did it happen that some of the slaves on the plantations of the founding fathers appeared to be white? Was it the universal practice during slavery to define the lightest mulattoes as black? A look at miscegenation and the rules for determining who is black in the various periods and geographic areas of slavery in the United States, and during the Reconstruction era after emancipation will help answer those questions. The one-drop rule appeared early and eventually became the dominant rule, but for a long time it had a vigorous competitor, a rule that defined mulattoes not as blacks but as a racially mixed group between blacks and whites. Attention must be given to the different patterns of white control and the associated beliefs, to the different circumstances of miscegenation, to the issues surrounding mulattoes and the status of freedpersons, and to the shift in the sense of identity held by mulattoes. The one-drop rule did not become uniformly accepted until during the 1920s (see Chapter 4), but before that there had been more than two and a half centuries of miscegenation, most occurring during slavery.

In this chapter and the next, I rely on Joel Williamson's *New People* (1980), especially his lengthy first chapter, more than any other single source, but detailed citations of this excellent work are avoided. Those who read Williamson's book will note that, although he stresses the nation's public definition of black, he prefers a different definition for his analysis. He limits his own use of the term "black" to unmixed African blacks; he defines "mulattoes" in the usual way, as persons with any mixture of black and white ancestry; and he uses the term "Negro" to mean any group that includes both blacks and mulattoes. While there is some logic in limiting the term "black" to unmixed African blacks, it is not defined that way now by the American public or by legislators and judges. The terms Negro, mulatto, colored, black, and African American have all come to mean persons with any African black ancestry, no matter how little, and "black" has been the usual term since the early 1970s (see Chapter 1). Our public usage of "black," and the one used in the present book, reflects the one-drop rule. The terms black, African American, Negro, and colored all include both unmixed African blacks and "mulattoes." Racially mixed blacks are designated "mulattoes" in this book, regardless of the degree of white-black mixture, and blacks who are not racially mixed are called African blacks or unmixed blacks.

Williamson emphasizes that the one-drop rule is unique to the United States, and also that it is paradoxical to have millions of people whose origins are more European than African defined by the general public, by law, and by themselves as black. The paradox is especially striking with regard to racially mixed people who appear white. He suggests that racial mixing in other societies has usually produced a third group loosely allied with the dominant race and asks why this pattern was broken in the United States (Williamson, 1980:2). Actually there are at least five other distinct patterns (see Chapter 5). However, Williamson has posed and provided convincing answers to the key questions: Why indeed have racially mixed persons of all shades in the United States been lumped with unmixed blacks into a single category called Negro—and later black or African American—and why have mulattoes in general come to accept and insist on that identity?

EARLY MISCEGENATION IN THE UPPER SOUTH: THE RULE EMERGES

Miscegenation occurred in the early colonial experience wherever there were slaves and free blacks. The first extensive mixing was in the seventeenth century in the Chesapeake area of the colonies of Maryland and Virginia, between white indentured servants and slave and free blacks (Williamson, 1980:6–14). White males and females were both involved in the mixing, and both whites and blacks, males and females alike, were punished by whipping or public humiliation when interracial sexual contacts were detected. Strong public condemnation failed to prevent illicit contacts from becoming widespread, however, and in some cases intermarriage occurred. Most of the white parents of the first mulattoes born in the United States, then, were from the underclass. Whether they had been imprisoned for debt, crime, or prostitution, had been kidnapped and sold, or had freely contracted for their passage, they all had been transported to the colonies to work off their indenture (Reuter, 1970:126–28). Although many of the resulting mulattoes were free, especially those born to white mothers, they were generally despised and treated as blacks. The genetic mixing of mulattoes with unmixed blacks, and with other mulattoes, also proceeded.

From the beginning, the one-drop rule for mulattoes seemed natural to the elites of the upper South, since the whites involved in the racial mixing were an underclass of indentured servants. However, the English rule had been that a child had the class status of its father, so for half a century or so the social position of the mulattoes was uncertain. Then, in 1662, the colony of Virginia passed its first laws to discourage miscegenation, proclaiming that any sexual intercourse between a white and a black was twice as evil as fornication between two whites. Mulattoes born to slave mothers were relegated to slave status. Until 1681 the mixed child of a white woman was free, but thereafter the mother had to pay a fine of five years of servitude, and the child was sold as an indentured servant until the age of thirty. The white parent, male or female, was to be banished from the colony within three months of the mixed child's birth. In 1705 the penalty for the white parent was changed to six months in jail. The mulatto children already existing in Virginia before these punitive statutes were passed remained a problem, and the status of their descendants was uncertain for two centuries.

Although there were legal uncertainties, by the early eighteenth century the one-drop rule had become the social definition of who is black in the upper South. After 1691, legal steps were taken to make manumission (the freeing of a slave) more difficult in Virginia. Included was the requirement that freed slaves had to leave the colony so that they would not become a public burden when they became too old or too ill to work. Maryland, Pennsylvania, and other colonies from New Hampshire to the Carolinas followed Virginia's lead during the first quarter of the eighteenth century, passing anti-miscegenation laws and otherwise limiting the rights of mulattoes. Apparently, the primary motive for adopting these laws was to prevent sexual liaisons and marriages between white indentured women and black male slaves, yet both white and black women continued to be involved in miscegenation. By the 1750s the legal status of mulattoes in the Chesapeake area was still uncertain, although the whites clearly thought of them as Negroes. During the era of the American Revolution the amount of manumission increased considerably in the area, enlarging and darkening the free mulatto population, which in turn resulted in renewed determination on the part of whites to maintain a firm color line.

In 1785 Virginia drew a genetic line, legally defining a Negro as a person with a black parent or grandparent, a definition generally adopted at that time in the upper South (Berlin, 1975:49, 97–99). This allowed mulattoes to be legally white if their black ancestry was any amount less than one-fourth, such as three-sixteenths or seven thirty-seconds—but those fractions were much too liberal in the eyes of most whites. Being legally white conferred certain privileges, such as freedom from whipping by the police for petty offenses. Intolerance for these lighter mulattoes, who were legally white but socially black, became very strong. The pressure grew to make the legal definition correspond to what had become the customary social definition of a Negro as a person with any degree of black ancestry, and the legislatures and courts began to move in that direction.

SOUTH CAROLINA AND LOUISIANA: A DIFFERENT RULE

South of North Carolina, mulattoes appeared later and in smaller numbers than in the upper South. Most of the white parents were men of some means, although occasionally a white woman was involved, in contrast to the underclass white men and women involved farther north. Usually the fathers acknowledged their mixed offspring, most of whom were slaves, since plantation economics discouraged manumission. The small numbers of mulattoes who were freed outnumbered unmixed blacks in the free Negro communities by three to one. Mulatto clans emerged to become the elites of the freedperson communities, especially around New Orleans and Charleston, South Carolina, and whites looked to their mulatto kin for help in controlling the large numbers of black slaves. When the settlement of South Carolina began in 1670, most of the area's first slaves and early white settlers came from Barbados, where the pattern of free mulatto dominance over unmixed blacks was well established. Thus, instead of being defined as blacks by a one-drop rule, free mulattoes became a third class, between blacks and whites.

Rapid importation of slaves continued in South Carolina until, by 1708, blacks outnumbered whites. Sexual contacts between whites and slaves were tolerated until the number of white women in the colony increased significantly. Then, in 1717, punishments were adopted for both white males and females involved in interracial pregnancies. Unprecedented, controversial restrictions of mulattoes followed. Free Negroes lost the right to vote in 1721, and in 1740 newly manumitted Negroes had to leave the colony. But the restrictions generally were not severe, and free mulattoes received fairly good treatment until the 1850s. It was then that interracial marriage was first seriously questioned in South Carolina, and the state's first anti-miscegenation statute was passed in 1865. Not even the failed insurrection plot of 1822, led by freedman Denmark Vesey, turned the whites against their traditional allies, the free mulattoes. In fact, a state legislative commission investigated the plot and pointed out the advantages of having a mulatto group as a buffer between whites and unmixed blacks.

South Carolina's refusal to apply a one-drop rule to the free mulattoes, at least until the 1850s, became explicit in the courts. In the case of a mulatto with an invisible but known one-sixteenth black ancestry, a Judge Harper declared the person to be white on the basis that acceptance by whites is more relevant than the proportions of white and black "blood." As late as 1835 the same judge made a similar ruling in the case of a person who apparently had some visible negroid traits, rejecting the criterion of racial visibility and embracing the test of reputation and acceptance in the white community. He commented that a slave cannot be white but that a free mulatto can, thus rejecting the one-drop rule (Catterall, 1926–37, 2:269). Until the 1840s in South Carolina, then, both known and visible mulattoes could become white by behavior and reputation and could marry into white families. Mulatto slaves at this time also received preferential treatment in South Carolina, becoming house servants and artisans. Mulattoes thus ranged in status all the way from favored slaves to free Negro elites and those who passed or were legally declared white. In other states in the antebellum South, there were also occasional court cases in which some persons with one-fourth or less "Negro blood" were declared legally white. The United States had not yet lined up solidly behind the one-drop rule.

The status of mulattoes in lower Louisiana evolved from the French Catholic culture, at first by way of Santo Domingo and later by way of Haiti after the mulatto revolutionaries there ejected the French in the 1790s. Some of the free mulattoes rose to elite status in the Louisiana sugar economy, and then with cotton. Some, such as the Metoyer family, became wealthy, cultivated the arts of education, bought freedom from slavery for their own relatives, and themselves owned slaves. The mulatto elites avoided identification and marriage with both blacks and whites, following the Haitian pattern, carefully arranging marriages with other mulattoes. The southern Louisiana mulattoes in general developed and preserved the status of an in-between third group that was neither black nor white, thus avoiding the imposition of the one-drop rule until the 1850s. The Louisiana Civil Code of 1808 prohibited "free people of color" from marrying even blacks, in addition to whites, which was official recognition of a three-layered system of racial classification rather than a black-white dichotomy (Dominguez, 1986:23–26).

The Creoles of Louisiana, American-born whites of French or Spanish origin, employed terms of reference for different degrees of racial mixture. The term "Creole" itself came to be used by freedpersons to refer to free mulattoes with some French or Spanish ancestry—thus, "Creoles of Color" or "Black Creoles." The meaning of the Creole identity varied and became a point of contention, especially in the mid-nineteenth century, when the tripartite scheme of racial classification came under intense pressure to change to a twofold scheme (Dominguez, 1986:12–16, 32, 94–151). Mulatto, meaning hybrid, comes from Spanish. A person who was seven-eighths African black was called a "mango" or a "sacatra." Someone three-quarters African was a "sambo" or a "griffe." "Quadroon" and "octoroon" became widely used for one-fourth and one-eighth African. The term "mustee," derived from the Spanish word *mestizo* (mixed European and Indian ancestry), meant an octoroon, often one who was part Indian, but in some places this term seemed to mean any mixture of black and Indian. A person one-sixteenth African was called a "meamelouc," and someone who was one sixty-fourth black a "sang-mele." The French Creoles had still other terms, and the Spanish had a total of sixty-four. In view of the broad spectrum of ancestral fractions, such terms were usually just approximations.

Keeping mulatto concubines became a luxury of many white men in Southern cities during slavery, and nowhere was this more institutionalized than in Charleston and New Orleans. It also became frequent among wealthy men in Virginia, whose mulatto mistresses usually remained slaves. Sally Hemings, alleged mistress of Thomas Jefferson, was not freed until two years after his death (McHenry, 1980:35–38; Williamson, 1980:44–48). Jefferson's descendants and some of his biographers have insisted that the father of Sally Hemings's mixed children was one of Jefferson's nephews (Editors of Newsweek Books, 1974:336). Prospective concubines as well as prostitutes were sold as "fancy girls" in the internal slave markets, and New Orleans and Frankfort, Kentucky, became the largest markets for pretty quadroons and octoroons (Bennett, 1962:256). The respectable New Orleans *plaçage* system featured elaborate "quadroon balls" for meeting and courting prospective free mulatto mistresses and for meeting the parents and discussing details of agreements for housing and child care. Some arrangements lasted only months or a few years, while others became permanent.

In New Orleans, as in Charleston, both mulatto servants and concubines were brought in from the plantations, and lighter and lighter mulattoes appeared in each successive generation. As in South Carolina, the free mulattoes enjoyed more privileges than unmixed blacks, but fewer than those enjoyed by whites. Homer Plessy and Mrs. Susie Phipps, plaintiffs in two widely publicized lawsuits (see Chapter 1), were both descendants of some of these "free people of color." There was considerable passing as white, and, although legally forbidden in Louisiana, some intermarriage (Blassingame, 1973:17–21). Most interracial sexual contacts were between white men and nonwhite women, but some involved white women. Miscegenation was both widespread and tolerated, as lower Louisiana accepted the in-between status of mulattoes and rejected the one-drop rule.

MISCEGENATION ON BLACK BELT PLANTATIONS

The spread of plantation slavery after 1720 throughout the lower South, and eventually west and north, brought large numbers of unmixed black slaves into the cotton- and rice-growing areas. White-black miscegenation was slow for a time, due to the initially low ratio of whites to nonwhites. The freeing of mulattoes in these new slave areas was a one-by-one process, and the exception rather than the rule, in contrast to the wholesale manumission that had occurred in the Chesapeake area. The large numbers of mulattoes produced in the early settlements in the upper South provided the main base of the nation's racially mixed population, and many of these mulattoes were sold as slaves to owners in the lower South. As this mixed population grew and became diffused, increasing steps were taken to restrict the rights of free mulattoes and to limit further mixing with whites. However, a very large number of white genes were already present in the Negro population, both slave and free. Also, as we shall now see, miscegenation involving whites never ceased, and on the plantations it even increased.

Ownership of the female slave on the plantations generally came to include owning her sex life. Large numbers of white boys were socialized to associate physical and emotional pleasure with the black women who nursed and raised them, and then to deny any deep feelings for them (Blassingame, 1972:81–89). From other white males they learned to see black girls and women as legitimate objects of sexual desire. Rapes occurred, and many slave women were forced to submit regularly to white males or suffer harsh consequences. Frederick Douglass recounted the vicious beatings of his aunt by their slavemaster, who was probably also Douglass's father. His aunt paid a heavy price for rejecting her owner's sexual advances and remaining true to the slave man she loved (Martin, 1984:3–4).

However, slave girls often courted a sexual relationship with the master, or another male in the family, as a way of gaining distinction among the slaves, avoiding field work, and obtaining special jobs and other favored treatment for their mixed children (Reuter, 1970:129). This direct competition with white women was a dangerous game. Although the white fathers rarely acknowledged the paternity of their mixed offspring, they often did look out for them. Many of the sexual contacts between the races at this time took still other forms, such as prostitution, adventure, concubinage, and sometimes love. In rare instances, where free Negroes were concerned, there was even marriage (Bennett, 1962:243–68). Yet there is little doubt that at the height of the plantation era much of the miscegenation was marked by exploitation of slave females by white males. Generally, in spite of the physical intimacy, white dominance was maintained by the master-slave etiquette. Sexual contacts between white women and black men were not tolerated, because a mixed child in a white household violated and threatened the whole slave system. A mixed child in the slave quarters was not only no threat to the system but also a valuable economic asset, another slave.

The vast majority of mulatto slaves on the plantations must have been permitted to find mates among other mulattoes or among unmixed Africans. Thus, large numbers of white genes were diffused into the slave population, and the percentage of unmixed blacks declined. Social distinctions, based on whether one was a house servant or a field hand and on the amount of "white blood," developed among the slaves, particularly if the whites concerned were aristocrats. A family prominent today in black society in Washington, D.C., traces its lineage back to George Washington through one of his mistresses. After being freed from slavery, the social status of a mulatto also depended on the length of time he or she had been free (Ottley, 1943:168).

The "genteel tradition" among mulattoes began in the "big house" on the plantation. The slave servants learned white manners, habits, beliefs, and the master's English rather than the pidgin dialect of the field hands. Sons of house servants often were apprenticed to skilled artisans and in rare instances were then freed or allowed to purchase their freedom. House servants and skilled artisans attended the white church but sat in a segregated section, while field slaves attended their own churches and developed the black spiritual tradition (Frazier, 1957). When house servants and craftsmen were freed, whether before or after the Civil War, they transplanted the genteel tradition to the cities, where they joined the mulatto elites, perpetuating plantation-white ways and the value of lightness as marks of high status in the Negro community. Blue-vein societies, and other organizations that excluded all but the very light mulattoes who could meet certain physical standards of lightness, became crucial in keeping the gates to upper-class status in the urban Negro communities. Black male preference for light-colored mulatto women who met caucasian standards of beauty continued long after the end of slavery, although serious questioning of this priority began in the 1850s.

On the slave plantations there were strong social forces among whites to define all racially mixed persons as blacks. When the French Count de Volney visited Thomas Jefferson at Monticello in 1795, he was startled to see children who appeared to be white but were defined and treated as black slaves. Although the sons and daughters of owners often received preferential treatment, they were still slaves, and freeing them was costly and rare. But manumission did occur, for such reasons as kinship, affection, or faithful service. In general, miscegenation was successfully managed by maintaining the master-slave etiquette. Violating the etiquette by treating mulattoes more like whites than blacks, and especially as members of the white family, could result in condemnation, ostracism, and even violence against the offending whites or their property. Thus, although there were some strains, exceptions, and ambiguities, the one-drop rule generally prevailed on the Black Belt plantations, in contrast to the general rejection of that rule in lower Louisiana and the Charleston area.

The 1850 census showed mulattoes to be 11.2 percent of the population classed as Negro. This was based on visibility only, and thus was a gross undercount of all Negroes with some white ancestry. Two-thirds of the mulattoes counted were in the upper South, and more than half of them were free. Of the smaller number of mulattoes counted in the lower South, including the Black Belt, less than one-tenth were free. Georgia's mulattoes were mostly slaves, as were most of those west and northwest of there, except for lower Louisiana. The majority of the mulattoes in both New Orleans and Charleston were free in 1850—exceptions to the general mold in the lower South. The pattern in the newest slave states of Missouri, Kentucky, and Tennessee was like that in the Black Belt: nine-tenths of those counted as mulattoes were slaves. In this sense, white men were increasingly enslaving their own children and grandchildren. Frederick Douglass expressed his confused feelings about having a white father "who would enslave his own blood" (Martin, 1984:3–4). By mid-century, then, the proportion of mulattoes in slavery was both very high and rising in areas and states settled after 1720, while farther north, in the area where mulattoes were more numerous, the majority were free. The 1860 census showed that this trend toward the "whitening" of slavery continued during the 1850s, owing to the low rate of manumission of mulattoes, and more to mulatto-unmixed black and mulatto-mulatto unions than to unions involving whites.

During the 1850s the South came under heavy pressure to defend its institutions against criticisms from the North and from other countries. This included answering questions about the apparent inconsistencies in the slave system, such as the enslavement of the predominantly white persons, the double standard of sexual morality in miscegenation, institutionalized concubinage, and the differences in the status of mulattoes in different areas of the South. Fear that slavery might be prohibited also promoted fear of slave revolts and of free blacks. Tolerance of special treatment for mulattoes on the plantation declined, and further legal restrictions on manumission were imposed. Serious strains appeared in the alliance between mulattoes and whites in Charleston and lower Louisiana, and the status of mulattoes began to decline in free Negro communities as well. Thus the exceptions to the one-drop rule, particularly the buffer status of the mulatto elites in some situations and areas, began to be eroded by the forces leading up to the War Between the States.

Southern white hostility toward free mulattoes grew after 1850. In Virginia the discrepancy between the social and legal definitions of "black" erupted into bitter controversy, and the law that anyone less than one-fourth African was entitled to be white came under attack. A Charlottesville editor argued that endless mixture with whites cannot make a white person out of a Negro, thus lending his support to the one-drop rule (Berlin, 1975:365–66). Fear of insurrection and of the abolition of slavery turned whites against mulattoes even in South Carolina and Louisiana. There, as elsewhere in the South, vigilante groups were formed to watch free Negro communities and to punish whites who continued sexual liaisons with mulatto mistresses. This encouraged some Southern white women to speak out against mulatto concubinage. There was agitation to have only two classes of people rather than three and to expel non-property-holding mulattoes from South Carolina, Louisiana, and other states. The freeing of mulatto slaves became increasingly unpopular and legally restricted. In the 1860s the vigilante activity spawned the Ku Klux Klan.

Support for the rule that mulattoes were not blacks but an in-between group rapidly diminished during the 1850s, even in the Charleston and New Orleans areas. The Louisiana "Creoles of Color" began their long struggle to retain the advantages of an in-between status that was neither black nor white (Dominguez, 1986:134–41). Public opinion became more and more polarized, and all persons had to be classed as either white or black. The one-drop rule received more solid support than ever throughout the South, for the simple reason that it helped defend slavery. Public ideologists contended that God created blacks to be slaves, but the explicit argument that mulattoes were naturally slaves too was avoided. However, the contention that racially mixed persons are against nature and would die out because of their unsuitability to the American climate constituted an implicit embracing of the one-drop rule. All beliefs were shaped by the need to defend the institution of slavery, and thus all blacks came to be seen as natural slaves and all persons with any amount of black ancestry as blacks (Williamson, 1980:73–75).

As whites in the lower South guardedly rejected the lighter mulattoes whom they had previously half-accepted, the latter sought alliances where they could find them. Despite the traditional distrust of mulatto elites in the free Negro communities, all Negroes began to be more allied in pursuit of their common causes. In this realignment of race relations, whites gained the one-drop rule but lost their alliance with the free mulattoes and the advantages of having a buffer group between themselves and unmixed blacks. This realignment started a basic shift in mulattoes' sense of identity, especially lighter mulattoes, who began to see themselves as Negroes rather than as a marginal group of "almost whites." This shift in self-identity was accelerated early in the Civil War, and dramatically so in Louisiana. In 1861 mulattoes formed a Negro regiment to defend Louisiana but were disarmed by white officers and became alienated from the white South. In 1862 the same regiment defected and joined the Northern army. Receiving much bad treatment from whites in the Northern forces, this regiment and other mulattoes came more and more to trust blacks rather than any whites, North or South.

RECONSTRUCTION AND THE ONE-DROP RULE

The Civil War ended in 1865, and the Reconstruction decade began with the passage of the Thirteenth Amendment to the U.S. Constitution, which freed the slaves. The North attempted to oversee the reconstruction of the South on a foundation of racial equality in place of slavery. But the Negroes had helped the North win the war, so a great many Southern whites considered them to be treacherous and disloyal—they had become enemies. The racist ideas that were spread included many about mulattoes, who were lumped more and more decisively with blacks in general. Whites and all Negroes were now competitors for jobs, land, and political power. Job competition with mulattoes was especially feared because of their experience in the skilled crafts.

These postwar developments hastened the alliance between mulattoes and unmixed blacks that had begun in the 1850s. Mulatto elite leaders began to speak for Negroes as a whole and to lead the development of new American black institutions and a black culture. The lower South, especially South Carolina, Florida, and Louisiana, had the highest percentage of black legislators and other public officials during the Reconstruction period, and most of them were mulattoes. Many mulattoes migrated from the North and upper South to the lower South to help in the reconstruction as teachers, relief administrators, or missionaries.

Southern whites widely feared that the newly freed black males would take advantage of the postwar shortage of white males and that miscegenation involving white women would be rampant. By 1867 this idea became an obsession with the Ku Klux Klan. Some whites advanced the view that they had lost the war because God was punishing them for miscegenation. Black Republican political participation, at the polls and in the legislatures, led temporarily to abolishing the South's statutes against racial intermarriage, the so-called anti-miscegenation laws—for example, Mississippi and Louisiana dropped their laws in 1870, South Carolina in 1872 (after having such a law for only seven years), and Arkansas in 1874. It was claimed at this time that every county in South Carolina had up to three or four mixed marriages involving white women, but the rate was always quite low.

Edward B. Reuter and others have concluded that sexual contacts between whites and blacks increased after the war, but contrary evidence and reasoning are more persuasive. In fact, sexual contacts not only seem to have decreased considerably during the war and its aftermath, but also probably reached a low point during Reconstruction. While some Southern white women did take black lovers, and a very few married them, these instances stand out as exceptions. The race groups became more segregated as the slave plantations were replaced by small farms, so that daily contacts between whites and blacks were less frequent. There was less opportunity and also less inclination for interracial sexual contacts (Williamson, 1980:88–91). All this took place in the context of vast devastation, social upheaval, resentment against the North, and economic distress, as Southern whites strove to replace slavery with a new system of cheap labor.

The economic development programs of the Reconstruction, including efforts to get blacks and landless whites settled on land of their own, largely failed. Rebuilding the South required a large amount of unskilled labor but also a great deal of construction work involving expertise. It was generally the mulatto slaves who were skilled in carpentry, masonry, cabinetmaking, painting, and maintenance of buildings and machinery, and mulatto slave women had been the dressmakers, gardeners, food preservers, and skilled cooks, as well as nursemaids and house servants. New industrial job opportunities began to emerge, and white Southern workers feared the competition of former slaves in industry as well as in the skilled crafts. Slaves had also been prohibited from learning to read, and there was fear that blacks would become literate and take over clerical jobs in business and government. Most whites in the South wanted blacks to be restricted to field work and other manual labor.

Eight Southern states adopted Black Codes, designed primarily to prohibit blacks from holding a large number of certain skilled and industrial jobs and to provide special penalties for black debtors and vagrants. These codes were quickly declared unconstitutional by the U.S. Supreme Court, and Congress responded by passing the Fourteenth and Fifteenth Amendments to the Constitution. The Fourteenth Amendment, ratified in 1868, provided that all citizens were entitled to equal protection and due process of law. The Fifteenth Amendment, ratified in 1870, ensured equal voting rights for all citizens regardless of "race, color, or previous condition of servitude"—all citizens except women, that is, since the attempt to add the word "sex" to the amendment failed. The clear aim of the Thirteenth, Fourteenth, and Fifteenth Amendments was to ensure that the freed slaves had equal rights under the law. In 1867 Congress passed the Reconstruction Acts, providing for the temporary military rule of the South, which continued until 1875. During the Reconstruction years, many blacks served in state legislatures in the South, and twenty served in the U.S. Congress. It is little wonder that, during these strained years when Southern whites and blacks were competitors and enemies, white sexual contacts with blacks apparently were at a minimum.

Although blacks could no longer be owned as property objects, the demand was great for their hard physical labor at low cost, and the vast majority of them became tenant farmers under sharecropping agreements with white owners. The black women and girls helped in the fields, and the women were also in demand for household skills at low pay. Black children received little schooling in their separate and unequal schools, so that good field hands would not be "spoiled." The white landowners and new industrialists opposed white labor demands for segregation laws during the Reconstruction era, favoring instead paternalistic goodwill toward the blacks. In return, the white owners expected the sharecroppers, who had been used to slave quarters, to be content with inferior housing and public facilities (Woodward, 1957). Only toward the end of the nineteenth century did the white Southern elites join the white working class in urging legislators to enact state and local segregation laws, and then the tide was overpowering (Wilson, 1976:440–46).

Despite growing anti-mulatto sentiment among whites during the Reconstruction, antebellum attitudes and practices did not die all at once, especially in the lower South. Although the general disposition was clearly to move away from miscegenation and to embrace the one-drop rule, there was also much sentiment in favor of dealing equitably with the results of the previous practices. In New Orleans, for example, the census of 1880 showed 205 mixed marriages (which had been legalized by the Reconstruction government), 29 of which involved white women. Of the 205 whites involved in these marriages, 107 were foreign-born. All the couples tended to be older people. Thus, many of these marriages were antebellum, and many of the whites had been new in the community.

Well after the Reconstruction in South Carolina, as late as 1895, there was political conflict between proponents of an unqualified one-drop rule and those who favored exceptions for descendants of antebellum mulattoes. In the state constitutional convention of 1895 it was proposed that the state again outlaw interracial marriages, and a legislative committee attempted to define a Negro, suggesting at first that anyone with one-eighth or more black ancestry was a Negro. Some legislators objected to this, proposing instead the one-drop rule, to which a George Tillman took strong exception. Tillman maintained that a one-drop rule would prevent marriage among many white families in South Carolina, since so many of them had black ancestry. He argued further that these families had produced men who had served creditably in the Confederate army and that it would be unjust and disgraceful to discredit them by declaring all their descendants to be black. This reasoning carried the day, and a Negro was defined as a person with one-eighth African black ancestry. Judge Harper's old reasoning about white conduct and acceptance thus prevailed one more time over a strict one-drop rule. This result was reached only a year before the separate-but-equal precedent case of *Plessy v. Ferguson* in Louisiana, in which the U.S. Supreme Court declared Plessy (who had one-eighth African ancestry) to be black and embraced the one-drop rule (see Chapter 1).

An interesting part of the above debate involved a mulatto congressman named Robert Smalls, who put forth a proposal that whites who cohabited with Negroes be barred from public office and that their children be given property rights and the privilege of bearing the name of their father. Although Smalls's proposal was defeated, this open reminder of concubinage and other miscegenation in antebellum days caused much embarrassment and delay. This bold conduct by a mulatto in the South Carolina legislature came at a time when hostility toward miscegenation and mulattoes was reaching a peak and when segregation laws were being passed to keep the races apart, to get blacks out of politics, and in general to get the blacks all back in "their place." This Restoration effort will be looked at further in Chapter 4.

THE STATUS OF FREE MULATTOES, NORTH AND SOUTH

The status of freed slaves before the Civil War greatly influenced the subsequent spread and national acceptance of the one-drop rule. Although the first free Negroes had full rights and privileges of citizenship, we have seen that the upper South began early to impose legal restrictions on them. The limits placed on the freedom of the mulattoes in the Charleston and lower Louisiana areas were relatively mild compared with those throughout the plantation Black Belt. If freed slaves were caught without the periodically renewable certificate of their freedom, they could be arrested and sold at a public slave auction. They were always under suspicion of stealing, indolence, or plotting slave insurrections. They were denied education, the right to vote, public assembly, equal treatment in the courts, freedom of movement, and freedom to pursue many kinds of work. Although there were rare success stories, most freedpersons remained poor and insecure. Some slaves refused the offer of freedom, preferring slavery to the uncertainties, poverty, and severe legal restrictions. Many of these restrictions were extended to the newly emancipated blacks in 1865.

The status of freed blacks in the North before the Civil War was little better than in the South, and in some respects worse. The 1857 Supreme Court decision in the Dred Scott case denied citizenship to blacks and said that escaped slaves could be pursued into free states, arrested, and returned to slavery. Free blacks in general were then suspected of being escapees and were often asked to show the certificate of freedom. Typically in the North, blacks had been barred from hotels, theaters, and other places of entertainment and from skilled crafts and professional schools. They had been segregated on trains and in churches, limited to menial jobs, and taxed but not allowed to vote, serve on a jury, be a witness, or serve in the peacetime military forces (Reuter, 1970:110–12). Two Northern states had prohibited intermarriage, one had prevented blacks from owning real estate or signing contracts, and five had not allowed blacks to testify in court (Litwach, 1961). Job competition produced tensions, and blacks were subjected to white race riots in several Northern cities in the 1820s, 1830s, and 1840s. Freedpersons in the North were generally poor, and their legal status was uncertain, varied, and changing. Thus, well before 1865, the entire nation had many precedents for systematic discrimination against "free" blacks, and the one-drop rule was in widespread use in the North and most of the South.

THE EMERGENCE AND SPREAD OF THE ONE-DROP RULE

In this chapter we followed the process of black-white miscegenation in the United States after its beginnings in Africa and Europe through over two centuries of varied experience with slavery and through the Reconstruction era. In each place and period, miscegenation has been related to the pattern of white domination and the associated beliefs, and to the ways of defining who is black. To underline the emergence of the one-drop rule, let us review the main themes. The first large-scale black-white mixing in the United States took place in the Chesapeake area between white indentured servants and both slave blacks and free blacks. Most of the whites involved were from the underclass, and the mixed children were generally treated as blacks, although in Virginia many were legally white by virtue of the (then) one-fourth rule. Miscegenation in the lower South was on a small scale during the early colonial period and generally involved illicit unions between white males and black females, either slave or free. At this time, especially in the Charleston and New Orleans areas, mulattoes had an uncertain, in-between status, in contrast to that of unmixed blacks. Southern Louisiana and South Carolina became major exceptions to the one-drop rule, as miscegenation came to be accepted and free mulattoes developed an alliance with whites.

Later, during the height of the plantation era, sexual contacts between whites and blacks were frequent and typically involved white male exploitation of black females, often under threats of violence or other punishment. Sometimes the contacts involved adventure, love, prostitution, or concubinage, and often they were initiated by the slave girls or slave women to gain special favors for themselves or their mixed children. Preferential treatment in the "big house" initiated the "genteel tradition," which was transferred by the limited amount of manumission to the free Negro communities. In general, the master-slave etiquette made it possible for white males to have interracial sexual contacts but to remain in total control of the slaves. Intimacy between white women and black men was not tolerated, because a mixed child in a white family threatened the slave system, but another mulatto in the slave quarters was an economic asset, not a threat.

The temptation to think of miscegenation only in terms of intermarriage must be avoided, since most black-white sexual contacts in the United States have not had the benefit of legal sanction, either during slavery or since. One must also avoid the temptation to think of miscegenation as involving only white-nonwhite sexual contacts. Long before slavery ended, miscegenation had been occurring in mulatto–African black and mulatto-mulatto unions, and often American Indian ancestry was involved as well. Genes from white and black populations were mixed in these matings, since mulattoes transmit white genes as well as black, and this is so whether one individual is mainly African black and the other mainly white, or the two have more nearly equal ratios. Thus, by the end of slavery, the visible traits of the population defined by the one-drop rule as American blacks showed a very wide and continuous variation from unmixed black to white. In fact, as early as the time of the American Revolution there were plantation slaves who appeared to be completely white, as many of the founding fathers enslaved their own mixed children and grandchildren.

Although strong forces motivated Black Belt plantation whites to define a racially mixed child as a black slave, many white owners and other white kin of the mixed child were inclined to grant special treatment when they could do so with impunity. The chief competition to the one-drop rule remained in the Charleston and New Orleans areas. At the height of the plantation era, most of the mulattoes remained slaves, mixing with the African blacks and thus "whitening" the slave population. In the 1850s the strong fears of abolition and slave insurrections resulted in growing hostility toward miscegenation, mulattoes, concubinage, passing, manumission, and of the implicit rule granting free mulattoes a special, in-between status in the lower South. The discrepancy between the social and legal definitions of black in Virginia became a bitter public issue. Thus the South came together in strong support of the one-drop rule in order to defend slavery, although some issues and exceptions to the rule continued for decades.

The growing rejection by whites of the tie with mulattoes produced a shift in the sense of identity of free mulattoes, who began to seek alliances with Negroes in general. The Civil War greatly accelerated the alienation of mulattoes from whites and caused Southern whites to see all Negroes as enemies. During the Reconstruction, after the war ended in 1865, mulattoes emerged as leaders of blacks in the South, and especially as teachers, relief administrators, missionaries, and legislators. Thus mulattoes, having no real choice, were themselves increasingly accepting the one-drop rule.

Black-white sexual contacts apparently declined after 1850, reaching a low point during the Reconstruction years, despite the temporary abolition of the anti-miscegenation laws. Opportunities for intimate contact were reduced when the slave plantations were replaced by the paternalistic sharecropping system, and both white and black inclination for close contacts had declined. Despite the shortage of white males, only a few white women took black lovers or husbands, but that was enough to fan the fear that racial mixing involving white females would run rampant. Poor white males, who feared black competition in skilled trades and in industry, joined the Ku Klux Klan and other vigilante groups to protect "white womanhood." Some intimate contacts between white males and black females continued, but in the midst of all the chaos and change there was far more mulatto-mulatto and mulatto-unmixed black miscegenation than that involving whites. And, despite some court cases and statutes that limited the definition of black persons to those with one-fourth, one-eighth, or some other definite fraction of black ancestry, support for the one-drop rule was strong in the decades following the Civil War. The rule was supported in the North as well as in the South, and by both whites and blacks, including mulattoes.

F O U R

THE RULE BECOMES FIRM

During Reconstruction, the name that came to symbolize the later system of segregation, which became known as the Jim Crow system, was alive and well. Jim Crow—a blackface singing-dancing-comedy characterization portraying black males as childlike, irresponsible, inefficient, lazy, ridiculous in speech, pleasure-seeking, and happy—had become a widespread stereotype of blacks during the last decades before emancipation, and Southern whites wanted the behavior of blacks to continue to fit that image. This stereotype had prevailed over two competing ones: Nat the rebellious, cunning runaway, and Jack, sullen, resentful, and shrewd. The Nat image came from the revolt led by Nat Turner in Virginia in 1831, in which about fifty-five whites and more than one hundred slaves were killed. After the Civil War, whites wanted the black sharecroppers to be happy and harmless, like Jim Crow.

Eventually the Jim Crow picture of the black man became part of the clowning Sambo stereotype, the "good nigger," which also incorporated the beloved images of Uncle Tom and the loyal, devoted, story-loving

Uncle Remus (Blassingame, 1972: chap. 5). The term "Sambo" came from the New Orleans area and originally just meant a person who was three-fourths black. The Sambo image was to become familiar to a generation of movie fans from the 1920s through the 1940s, the most classic portrayal being that of Stepinfetchit, while black women were presented as confident and strong. This stereotype of the ridiculous black male played an important role in whites' sexual exploitation of black women and in the set of beliefs used to justify it. In the early 1940s the NAACP and the 1940 Republican presidential candidate, Wendell Willkie, appealed to film producers to present blacks as ordinary human beings. The producers repeatedly replied that they could not risk offending the censorship boards in the Southern states (White, 1948:202–3).

CREATION OF THE JIM CROW SYSTEM

In 1875 the military occupation of the South ended, and Southern efforts to undo the Reconstruction and to restore blacks to a very low status were intensified. Thus, the term "Restoration" is used to describe the efforts that created the system of legal segregation known as Jim Crow. The Congress tried to prevent such a development by passing the Civil Rights Act of 1875, which provided that states must not deny equal access to public facilities for all citizens, regardless of race or prior slave status. However, in 1883 the U.S. Supreme Court nullified this act, holding that it was unconstitutional with respect to "personal acts of discrimination." This interpretation meant that state laws requiring segregated schools and other facilities were constitutional and did not deny civil rights because they regulated only close personal contacts.

That 1883 decision opened the gates, and from the late 1880s to 1910 the Southern legislatures passed a flood of segregation statutes. These laws prohibited racial intermarriage, required separate seating in trains, buses, theaters, libraries, and stores, and required separate schools, rest rooms, drinking fountains, parks, swimming pools, and other public facilities. Building on the 1883 decision, the federal courts upheld these state statutes. In 1896 the U.S. Supreme Court established the constitutional doctrine of "separate but equal" in the precedent-setting case of *Plessy v. Ferguson* when it ruled that Louisiana's requirement that seating on trains in interstate commerce be separated by race was constitutional if the accommodations were equal (see Chapter 1). The separate-but-equal doctrine legalized segregation laws for well over half a century, but facilities did not become equal.

Early in the twentieth century, when the Restoration was pushing the status and hopes of blacks lower and lower, Booker T. Washington promoted vocational schools as a means of gradual economic improvement for blacks. Large industries were rapidly expanding, and his schools were both industrial and agricultural. Although he established the excellent Tuskegee Institute for technological research and teacher training, Washington's vocational schools had little other effect, except to channel some rural blacks into restaurant work and other menial service jobs. Some began to move to the cities, often in the North, but most blacks continued as sharecroppers. World War I produced considerable black migration to cities in the North, and in the 1920s the blocking of immigration from Southern and Eastern Europe opened up housing space in the inner cities for blacks and Hispanics. During World War II and the 1950s, large numbers of blacks migrated to cities in the North. Booker T. Washington's prediction that change would be very gradual proved correct. Half a century would pass before the federal courts began declaring the segregation laws unconstitutional.

The castelike Jim Crow system was firmly entrenched by 1910; the restoration of Southern blacks to an inferior legal status was complete. Although the pattern was most rigid in the states of the Deep South, with some variations it prevailed throughout the entire South. The system was enforced both by law and by extralegal force and threats of force, which amounted to the use of terrorism to keep blacks "in their place." The ultimate threat of lynching is best known and was carried out more often in the early years of Jim Crow than later, when the system was more entrenched. Figures kept by the Tuskegee Institute and the *Chicago Tribune* show that 1,111 blacks were lynched during the last decade of the nineteenth century and that the reported numbers for the first five decades of the twentieth century were 791, 563, 281, 120, and 32, respectively. The most common alleged offenses of black men who were lynched were rape or attempted rape of a white woman, killing a white person, or robbery or other theft from whites. However, the real reasons were often that the black person had "insulted" a white or whites, or did not "know his place," or had attempted to vote—and sometimes these reasons were openly acknowledged (Vander Zanden, 1972:162–63).

More common than lynching were other terroristic methods, such as threats of and actual job-firings, loss of credit, loss of sharecropping contracts, destruction of property, beatings, whippings, and torture by cigarette burns or other means. Perceived challenges to white dominance in the Jim Crow system, however subtle, were usually behind the terroristic threats and actions. For example, it was deemed "insulting" and not "knowing one's place" for a black man to tell a white man to stop seeking sexual favors from the black's wife or daughter. This could lead to loss of the black man's job, or the job of his wife or someone else in the family, or to even more drastic actions. Coercive sexual relations with black women symbolized white male dominance and black male powerlessness.

This terrorism was most marked in small, rural communities, where the vast majority of the blacks in the Jim Crow South still lived. The enforcers were usually poor whites, often joined in their extralegal activities by law-enforcement officers. The Ku Klux Klan, dedicated to protecting "the purity of white womanhood," became a major force in the extralegal support of the norms (rules) of the system. One interpretation is that Southern elites fostered, or at least tolerated, conflict between working-class whites and blacks in order to keep unions out and wages low (Roebuck and Hickson, 1982: chaps. 2, 3), but the vigilantes needed little encouragement. Later in this chapter we look more closely at the operation of social controls in the Jim Crow system and show how they strongly reinforced the one-drop rule. But first we must note some other developments during the creation of the system and the responses among mulattoes and the black community at large.

THE ONE-DROP RULE UNDER JIM CROW

During the Restoration, the animus against miscegenation and mulattoes in the South became very strong, reaching a peak by 1907. As in the 1850s, this hostility was expressed in heightened concern about the numbers of mulattoes, about who was and was not a Negro, and about passing as white. Census figures showed that mulattoes increased from 11.2 percent of the black population in 1850 to 20.9 percent in 1910—no doubt an undercount both times, since both were based only on visible white ancestry. The 1890 census showed a count of 70,000 octoroons—

again no doubt a gross undercount because a great many such persons are not visibly black. The increased number of mulattoes was actually due mainly to mulatto-African black unions, although some white-black liaisons continued in the South, mainly coercive ones involving white men and black women.

As the segregation laws were being passed in the years before and after the turn of the twentieth century, vigilante committees and anti-miscegenation leagues were formed in Mississippi, Louisiana, and elsewhere in the South. Stereotyped beliefs about mulattoes flourished as never before, and the analogy to the mule received much attention. White guilt about the large number of mulattoes was probably an important factor in this preoccupation, and the inclination to think of mulattoes as a temporary phenomenon was strong. Yet many of the same male protectors of white womanhood helped mold the Jim Crow practice of sexual exploitation of black females by white males, thus contributing to miscegenation while they were fighting to keep the races pure. This ideological tour de force was accomplished by defining mixed children born to black women as black, as had been done on the slave plantations, thus reinforcing the one-drop rule.

The passing of the post-Reconstruction statutes on racial intermarriage put pressure on the state legislatures to define "Negro," although at that time Louisiana failed to come up with an explicit definition. The courts in Louisiana usually defined "persons of color" to mean those who were visibly black, and they continued to classify many mixed persons as white. The fourteen remaining Southern states considered a definition essential, and seven of them adopted the one-drop rule by defining a Negro as someone with any black ancestry. Virginia finally abandoned its one-fourth rule in 1910 and settled for one-sixteenth, assuming that lesser amounts could not be detected. Not until 1930 did Virginia adopt the one-drop rule explicitly, saying that "any Negro blood at all" makes a person black. Seven states resorted to the one-eighth rule early in the century, thus allowing some persons to be classed as white who appeared to be partly black or who had at least been known as blacks. These latter laws made some exceptions possible, but the legislators knew well that the one-drop rule would generally prevail in case of any serious question (Mangum, 1940:238–48).

The Southern states that adopted the one-drop rule found, however, that it did not resolve all the mulatto problems. Centuries of miscegenation had produced large numbers of mixed persons who appeared white and who could pass when they wanted to, either permanently or for temporary convenience. And a great many Southern whites became extremely anxious—perhaps paranoid is not too strong a term—about the specter of "invisible blackness." Thousands and thousands of Southern whites were not sure they were racially pure—as many of them surely were not, a frequent theme in William Faulkner's novels. At a time of increasing polarization into black and white categories, it became more tragic than ever not to be sure of one's own racial identity, a fate that both sides of the color line shared. Concern about people passing as white became so great that even behaving like blacks or willingly associating with them were often treated as more important than any proof of actual black ancestry. Then, not even one drop of "black blood" was needed to define a person as a "white nigger"—and race became entirely a social category with no necessity for any biological basis (Williamson, 1980:98–108).

Brick by brick the Jim Crow system became a powerful instrument of oppression, denying Southern blacks the American dream of upward mobility through education and effort, until by 1910 the pattern was well established. As both extralegal practices and governmental machinery were developed to enforce the hundreds of segregation laws, the motivation to pass as white grew, and some black families gave their blessing to their own members who could do so. Passing as white probably reached an all-time peak between 1880 and 1925. Walter White, who personally passed only for the limited and dangerous task of investigating lynchings in the South, estimated the number who passed annually during the peak years at about 12,000. Although the estimates of some alarmists were much higher, subsequent research indicated that White's figure was probably high. Estimates based on the 1940 census indicated that, by then, the annual number passing as white did not exceed between 2,500 and 2,750 a year (Burma, 1946:18–22), and possibly no more than 2,000 to 2,500 (Eckard, 1947:498).

Most passing as white was done in order to get a better job, and some who passed as white on the job lived as black at home. Some lived in the North as white part of the year and as black in the South the rest of the time. More men passed than women. Some not-so-light mulattoes passed by taking Latin names and moving to an appropriate locale. Many found that passing was easy but that the emotional costs were high, and some therefore returned to the black community. Even during these peak years, the vast majority who could have passed permanently did not do so, owing to the pain of family separation, condemnation by most blacks, their fear of whites, and the loss of the security of the black community.

Toward the end of the nineteenth century, southern white elites abandoned their paternalistic concern for blacks and joined working-class whites in getting the segregation laws passed. This not only provided overwhelming political support for building the Jim Crow system, but also accelerated the alienation of mulattoes from whites. Mulattoes in general became more hostile toward their white ancestors than proud of them. In strong terms they condemned white males for exploiting mulatto women and then failing to assume responsibility for their mixed children. They heaped scorn on the mulatto elites for placing such a high value on their lightness, and in their turn the mulatto elites became bitterly opposed to further mixing with whites.

In the Jim Crow era, blacks widely shared the belief that black-white sexual contacts occurred mainly between the irresponsible underclass of both groups. Even the black scholar Carter Woodson wrote that it was the weaker members of both race groups, biologically and morally, who engaged in miscegenation (Woodson, 1918:339). The popular belief spread among blacks that this alleged weakness produced a certain light or "high" yellow color—thus the epithet "yellow niggers." And because white urban vicelords, and owners of theaters and nightclubs, preferred light mulatto girls as prostitutes, chorus girls, and singers, lighter mulattoes came to be associated with sin and degradation. Entertainer Lena Horne learned (see Chapters 1 and 7) that "high yaller" people came under suspicion everywhere in the black community unless they could demonstrate respectable parentage. Many blacks, especially mulatto elites, became as anxious about lightness as whites were about blackness (Williamson, 1980:117).

In 1918 the Census Bureau estimated that at least three-fourths of all blacks in the United States were racially mixed, and it predicted that pure blacks would disappear. We must attribute the rapid decline in the proportion of unmixed blacks in the prior decades primarily to mulatto-African black miscegenation, not to the more limited number of white-black sexual unions. After the 1920 census, no further attempt was made to count the number of visible mulattoes, partly because there were so many of them, but also because so many persons with some black ancestry appeared white. The Census Bureau became preoccupied instead with counting foreign-born whites and sought other ways to count the black population, in a way that implemented the one-drop rule. What the nation wanted was a count of all persons with any black ancestry.

Blacks and whites had been increasingly segregated since the 1850s, and miscegenation within the black population had lightened its color and moved it toward homogeneity. This emergence of what many then called a "brown" people was accompanied by the increasing alliance of mulattoes with other blacks. Hastened by the oppressiveness of the Jim Crow system, this alliance was led by such mulatto leaders as W.E.B. Du Bois, William Monroe Trotter, James Weldon Johnson, A. Philip Randolph, and Walter White, as they struggled against Jim Crow segregation and all discrimination against blacks. In the racially polarized nation of the early 1920s, old alignments were gone as mulattoes allied themselves totally with the black community, demanding their rights as blacks. Despite a lingering preference for lightness, mulattoes had come to insist that all persons with any black ancestry are black, even if they appear white. By 1915, white America, including the New Orleans and Charleston areas, had accepted the one-drop rule completely, and at least by 1925 mulattoes and blacks in general were convinced that no alternative definition was possible. Finally, the nation had become firmly committed to the one-drop rule—North and South, whites and blacks, even the mulatto elites (Williamson, 1980:199), except for the more traditional Creoles of Color.

EFFECTS OF THE BLACK RENAISSANCE OF THE 1920s

The development of a new American black culture was both symbolized and led by the "Black Renaissance" of the 1920s, which had both national and worldwide influence and helped give blacks a sense of identity and group pride. The identity had African roots, but it was also American. Often the theme was that because whites would not let blacks in, blacks had to build a satisfying way of life of their own. This renaissance implied a rejection of both physical amalgamation with whites and the total assimilation of white culture, and the creation instead of a new culture that was neither African nor white, but drawn from both. Black writers and composers began publishing as blacks, expressing black themes, and, in the crowded New York neighborhood that was Harlem, whites also began to see black culture.

The Black Renaissance (also known as the Harlem Renaissance) was led by mulatto poets, novelists, musicians, dancers, and other artists who, in expressing black ideas and feelings, had implicitly adopted the one-drop rule. They had turned away from the long-standing effort of mulatto elites to achieve in the white world, had faced toward their African origins, and had begun to celebrate the new unity with their brown brothers and sisters. Jean Toomer, a product of the mulatto elite tradition, discovered his black roots in rural Georgia. In *Cane* (1923) he wrote about both white ways and black ways, and he portrayed black as beautiful. Mulatto elite societies still existed, including the persistent and exclusive Bon Ton Society of Washington, D.C., but they took heavy criticism from the Black Renaissance because of their white orientation. The Renaissance leaders exalted all colors in the black community, and Claude McKay—himself an unmixed black from Jamaica—censured the all-light chorus lines.

Another Jamaican in Harlem, Marcus Garvey, carried the "Black is beautiful" theme to its logical extreme, contending that only pure African blackness is beautiful. As one of the 80 percent of Jamaicans who were unmixed black, Garvey had been discriminated against at home by the socially dominant mulattoes. The leaders of the Black Renaissance, stung by Garvey's contention that mulattoes are not really blacks, successfully attacked his view. After all, by Garvey's reasoning, most American blacks were not black. Garvey also failed to realize his separatist goal of establishing an African homeland for American blacks, but he forcefully condemned white racism and promoted black pride. He made effective use of impressive uniforms and parades, ceremonies, rituals, and public rewards and got much attention from white crowds and the New York news media. Although he ran into legal difficulties over alleged mail fraud when selling stock in his steamship company, and was deported in 1927, Garvey's movement helped large numbers of newly arrived urban black migrants experience a sense of identity and black pride (Cronon, 1955:172–76, 222). He failed, however, to eliminate the one-drop rule.

The term "Brown America" gained currency in the 1930s and 1940s and was symbolized by the great affection the black community expressed for the "Brown Bomber," Joe Louis, the world champion heavyweight boxer. The slow growth of the black middle class, which would be greatly accelerated during and after World War II, brought education and upward mobility to the fore in the black community. But although light color still helped blacks get a good job, succeed, and achieve respectability and higher status, most mulattoes continued to reject close association with whites, assimilation, passing, and amalgamation. A 1932 study of 2,500 mulattoes showed that many quadroons and persons with three-eighths African ancestry could pass as white and that the octoroons in the sample simply appeared white (Day, 1932:9–11). However, most of those who could "pass" apparently were not doing so.

The "browning" of the population defined as black had reduced the proportion who were either unmixed black or very light, as both types mated primarily with other blacks rather than whites, yet the full range of physical types from unmixed blacks to white-appearing remained. A study by Charles Johnson showed that the skin color preferred by rural Southern black children was light brown and that too white or too black or too "yellow" were all undesirable (Johnson, 1941:258–66). In a study of upward mobility among New Orleans blacks from the 1930s to the 1950s researchers found that lighter color generally facilitated achievement and that, for this reason, middle-class blacks in the 1950s indicated a preference for adopting children of light color (Rohrer and Edmonson, 1960:76, 92–94). Class background was becoming more important in shaping the destiny of a black child, but color still played a large role.

THE RULE AND MYRDAL'S RANK ORDER OF DISCRIMINATIONS

When Gunnar Myrdal and his associates made their study at the beginning of World War II, the Jim Crow system of segregation had changed little from the classic pattern that was entrenched by early in the twentieth century. Myrdal found that Southern white attitudes supported segregation in some areas of life more strongly than in others. The more intimate the contact between blacks and whites, the stronger the whites' feelings that segregation must be maintained. Social distance researchers have also demonstrated that whites have been less willing to accept blacks or other minorities in the more intimate relationships (Bogardus, 1968:149–52). The following "rank order of discriminations" was reported, ranging from most intimate to least intimate (Myrdal, 1944:60–61):

1. Intermarriage and sexual contacts with white women
2. Personal relations (greeting, talking, eating, dating, dancing, swimming, and other matters governed by the racial etiquette)
3. Public facilities (segregated schools, churches, trains, parks, etc.)
4. Political participation (voting and holding public office)
5. Legal treatment (in courts and by the police)
6. Economic activities (jobs, credit, housing, getting land, public assistance, etc.)

Most of the Jim Crow laws required segregated public facilities (rank 3), but there were anti-miscegenation laws (rank 1) and laws to supplement the customary extralegal controls for maintaining segregation in the other ranks. For example, there were poll taxes, literacy tests, and other laws designed to prevent blacks from voting (rank 4). In addition, discriminatory modes of enforcing laws in general, such as police procedures and jury selection, helped maintain segregation. For protecting ranks 2 and 1 there was the "racial etiquette," which will be discussed in detail later. The etiquette, and indeed the entire system, was ultimately backed by extralegal terrorism.

Evidence for this rank order of discriminations has been reported by other researchers in the South and by some in the North as well. However, according to some data from Texas, North Carolina, and the state of Washington, economic activities rank third rather than sixth (Williams and Wienir, 1967:448–54). It seems plausible that the rank order may vary from one region or community to another and that the degree of local economic competition between the race groups affects the rank of economic activities. Also, housing is included in the economic category, and residential location affects personal contacts and can become an intense issue.

Myrdal also reported that the rank order of the black community's resistance to segregation and discrimination was just the reverse of the whites' rank order of discriminations—that is, blacks resisted discrimination most in the economic area and next in legal treatment, and what they wanted least was sexual contact and intermarriage with white women. Another study in the South and one in Ohio found the same. Myrdal optimistically suggested that orderly changes might occur, since blacks wanted changes most in the areas that whites were least anxious about. But instead, when the movement to end the system gained strength, change was strongly resisted in all six aspects of life, not just in the more intimate areas. Desegregation of the schools and other public facilities (rank 3) was bitterly contested, as were the moves toward political, legal, and economic equality.

Yet the hallmark of the Jim Crow system was the zealous guarding of "white womanhood" (rank 1), and while they were joking that a white boy doesn't become a man until he has had sexual relations with a black girl, the guardians of this concept kept the white woman on a pedestal. Why was it considered tragic—in fact, unthinkable—for a white woman to have a racially mixed child, but not at all unthinkable for a black woman to have one? Although in both cases mingling of genes occurs, miscegenation was taboo only for white women. The answer rests on two premises: that the strong community expectation is for the child to stay with its mother and that the neighbors and the census taker will readily define the child as a black if the mother is black. But if the mother of a racially mixed child were white, her family, the white community, and the whole system would be threatened. The supposed inferiority of the mixed child, according to the racist ideology, posed no threat so long as the white population remained "pure." However, if a white woman or girl were to keep a mixed child, the alleged racial superiority of whites and the entire system of white domination would be in jeopardy. The only options were (1) secretly to spirit the child away and have it grow up elsewhere, (2) secretly to give the child to a black family, (3) to move the white family away from the community, or (4) to have the white family join the black community. Unthinkable as these drastic options were, they occasionally had to be used.

Here we see why the Jim Crow system required the continuation and strengthening of the one-drop rule for defining who is black, and why there was such complete opposition to the fall of the entire system. Judge Brady (see Chapter 2) knew well that large numbers of white males had willingly participated in producing a racially mixed people in the South. While enthroning white women, they had followed a double standard with respect to interracial sexual contacts. What the judge meant was that mixed children would not be allowed to live in white homes. Custom, beliefs, and the law all followed the one-drop rule, defining all mixed persons as blacks (Myrdal, 1944:60–67). This definition of who is black was crucial to maintaining the social system of white domination in which widespread miscegenation, not racial purity, prevailed. White womanhood was the highly emotional symbol, but the system protected white economic, political, legal, educational, and other institutional advantages for whites, not just the sexual and racial purity of white women. The poor white enforcers received few economic benefits, but at least they could act out their social superiority to blacks and exploit black women sexually.

From 1930 to 1943, Southern white women who were tired of the use of the slogan of white womanhood to justify the system were represented well by the Association of Southern Women for the Prevention of Lynching. Although the lynchings had been on the decline for some time, this group was credited with reducing them almost to zero. Some of the women were from leading black families, but most were rural, white women from established families and churches, and most of their husbands were respected local or state leaders. They presented themselves as "church women."

These influential women challenged the belief that lynchings helped protect Southern white womanhood, and they demanded that women of both races be protected. Based on information and logic, they used reasoned persuasion (Laue and McCorkle, 1965:80–90). They met with law enforcement officials and other agencies of government and called for the protection of black men from white violence. They published facts about lynchings and their consequences for the South and sponsored studies, lectures, discussions, and petitions. Later, during the civil rights movement of the 1950s and 1960s, they opposed segregation in public facilities, even in the churches. Violating a deep-seated taboo, the black and white women in the Association ate together (Smith, 1949:128–30). Their tactics were adopted during the 1960s by Southern women's groups known by such acronyms as HOPE, OASIS, SOS, COPE, and STOP in response to the violent backlash against the desegregation of the public schools, in order to keep the schools open.

Another aspect of the Jim Crow system—the so-called racial etiquette—is also closely related to sexual contact, intermarriage, and the one-drop rule. The norms of the system required segregation in the second rank order of discriminations, close personal relationships, insofar as possible. This is the area generally known as social segregation, often euphemistically referred to as "just choosing one's own friends." Some close daily contacts were inevitable in the play of small children, in domestic work, at other places of work, in discussing rental and work arrangements, in stores, and on the streets, but when such contacts occurred, the interaction had to follow a strict pattern of interracial etiquette. The white person had to be clearly in charge at all times, and the black person clearly subordinate, so that each kept his or her place. It was a master-servant etiquette, in which blacks had to act out their inferior social position, much the same way slaves had done. The black had to be deferential in tone and body language, as portrayed by the actors who played the Sambo stereotype, and never bring up a delicate topic or contradict the white. Even small white children, as little Shirley Temple so heroically demonstrated in her 1930s films, had to be totally in charge of black children and patronizing to black men. Older white children were forbidden to play with black children.

The racial etiquette was complex, and the penalties for not learning and following it well could be severe. There were countless lessons to be learned by black and white children alike. The courtesies expected of blacks were not reciprocated by whites. The black went to the white's back door and knocked; the white went to the black's front door and didn't need to knock. The sidewalk was for whites, not blacks. The white man had to be called "Mister," but he called the black man "Boy," "Uncle," or by his first name. To whites, black women had only first names. White males could stare and make lewd remarks and passes at black women, but it was dangerously taboo for black men to behave in the same way toward white women.

If any suggestion of lack of proper deference arose, the etiquette required the black to clown and act stupid, like Stepinfetchit, in order to defuse the tension and show that there had been no intention to get out of the black person's place. For a black to be inept at this, or deliberately to challenge the racial etiquette even slightly, could lead to warnings and even threats and violence. For example, at or near Camp Robinson in Arkansas in 1946, two black soldiers from the North were killed because they had unwittingly failed to show proper deference to whites (White, 1948:341). Punitive actions often followed when a black male was alleged to have leered, winked, or whistled at a white female or to have made remarks about her. The racial etiquette thus helped to control sexual contacts (rank 1) as well as close contacts of a more casual nature (rank 2).

The racial etiquette restricted the form, content, and contexts of interracial conversations, thus reinforcing stereotypes of blacks. Whites typically felt that they knew "their" blacks well, since they saw and interacted with them often. However, much of what they observed was prescribed, stereotyped role-playing. A "good nigger" (Sambo) was one who observed the etiquette carefully and stayed out of trouble. Black people dropped the mask and stopped clowning when among themselves, just as India's untouchables have done, and often laughed at how easily white folks could be fooled. That this etiquette was so strongly demanded and uniformly observed indicates that there was a high degree of white consensus, as well as compulsory accommodation to the total system by blacks and whites alike. Whites had to conform or face gossip, ridicule, and ostracism. Open offenders were called "white niggers" or "communists" and ran the risk of economic sanctions, threats, or violence. Outward conformity to the etiquette by blacks camouflaged their widespread inner resentment of the prescribed role-playing performances and of the whole system.

Economic changes in the Jim Crow South were evidently not greatly threatening to whites unless they resulted in visibly direct or very keen competition between the races. However, threats of significant change in any of the four lower ranks in the whites' rank order of discriminations often prompted charges that blacks were seeking to attack white womanhood. Moves to desegregate the schools and other public facilities often elicited the question "Would you want your daughter to marry one?" Violence and threats of violence were often related to Southern black attempts to vote and to testify in court or serve on juries, and to direct racial competition for jobs or welfare benefits. White threats and actions in such situations usually were rationalized as necessary to protect white womanhood—showing how the different areas of institutionalized discrimination were connected. Clearly, the racial etiquette served not only to protect ranks 1 and 2, but as a major means of maintaining the entire system (Rose and Rose, 1948:154–65). Thus, to blacks, Stepinfetchit was not funny.

The rigorous controls of the Jim Crow system limited miscegenation involving whites almost exclusively to illicit liaisons between white males and black females. As in slave times, a great many white males were raised by black women, then forced to deny their feelings for them, and finally expected to seek sexual favors from black females. Most of the sexual contacts were no doubt coercive and exploitive, and sometimes they involved rape. However, as during slavery, it sometimes took other forms, such as concubinage, prostitution, adventure, or love (Bennett, 1962:250–56). Racial intermarriage was impossible without moving to a state that allowed it, and on the rare occasions on which this happened, white women were as likely to be involved as black women. Some observers believe that illicit contacts declined after the early years of the twentieth century. The overall amount of miscegenation involving whites was probably much lower than it had been during slavery, especially before 1850, and possibly as low as during the Reconstruction period. Even so, many white males were involved in racial mixing. The large number of genes from European peoples already in the black population by 1850 continued to mix with genes from African blacks in African-mulatto and mulatto-mulatto unions.

SEXUAL NORMS AND THE RULE: JIM CROW VS. APARTHEID

The contrast between the sexual norms of Jim Crow and those of the Apartheid system of the Republic of South Africa is striking and informative. In the latter, sexual contact across the white-nonwhite line is taboo, and until 1985 it was punished as a felony under the 1950 Immorality Act, an amendment to the 1948 Apartheid laws. Violations, by whites as well as nonwhites, women as well as men, were uniformly and severely punished (Hunt and Walker, 1974: chap. 6). Repeal of the Immorality Act is one of several actions the government has taken in recent years in response to protests and strong criticism expressed around the world, although the Apartheid system generally has remained firmly in place. Now the punishments for sexual transgressions across the color line are again extralegal only, but probably still quite effective, including ostracism, economic sanctions, and threats of violence. There is no double standard as there was in the Jim Crow system, no exalting of white womanhood. Under the Apartheid system, whites have tried to prevent *all* further miscegenation in South Africa, not just that which involves white women and nonwhite men, believing that their dominant political and economic position depends on keeping the white group "racially pure."

Yet there has actually been a large amount of miscegenation in South Africa, producing a so-called "Coloured" population that numbered well over two million by 1980, or approximately 10 percent of the nation's population (Banton, 1983:234). The Coloureds are a largely Westernized,

Christian group that is valued by whites as a buffer between the large black population and the much smaller white one. Much of the black-white mixing occurred during the early days of the Dutch settlement, beginning in the mid-seventeenth century. The Boer (Dutch farmer) settlers mixed with the Khoi-Khoin tribes (called Hottentots by the Dutch) in what became the Cape Province, and later with slaves from Madagascar, Mozambique, and Indonesia. At least 87 percent of the Coloured population of the Republic of South Africa today is still in Cape Province.

Later the Dutch became convinced that further white-black mixing was against their interests and began to take measures to prevent it. It is estimated that from 10 to 25 percent or more of all Cape Province whites today have some black lineage, by now very diluted. The limited amount of white-nonwhite sexual contact since the eighteenth century has involved British, German, French Huguenot, and other European settlers, as well as the Boers, who now prefer to be called Afrikaner. For more than two centuries the Coloureds have been mainly an inbreeding population, although they have also mixed with the native black peoples and to some extent with the Asians, who are mostly from India.

The South African Coloureds are defined as a "mixed blood" group, and only unmixed blacks are socially and legally defined as blacks. Clearly a one-drop rule is not used. The Coloureds are defined to include not just mulattoes resulting from the mixing of European and African black peoples, but all descendants of matings across the lines of what are called "the four race groups"—whites, Coloureds, Asians, and African blacks. Everyone carries several identification papers that indicate his or her race group, as officially determined by a race classification board. (In 1986 only the "pass card" laws, concerning the travel of blacks outside their native reservations, were dropped, not the racial identification papers.) Coloureds, as officially defined, result from black-Asian and white-Asian mixing as well as from black-white and black-Coloured. The black-Asian mixtures are actually mulattoes, of course, but the white-Asian mixtures (or Eurasians) have no African black ancestry. Many Coloureds have all three ancestries—European, African black, and Asian—and the Coloured group has an extremely wide range of racial characteristics, just as the American population defined as black has. Coloureds, Asians, and blacks are all defined as nonwhite, and whites do not tolerate any intergroup sexual contact or marriage between themselves and any nonwhites. There has long been great concern about the fact that many of the lighter

Coloureds can pass as white, as many have. Under the Apartheid system the concern has been especially great, yet some passing continues to occur, in spite of the need for official reclassification (Watson, 1970:17–18). This complex system is dealt with further in Chapter 5.

EFFECTS OF THE FALL OF JIM CROW

The U.S. Supreme Court's decision in the case of *Brown v. Board of Education* (1954) prompted Representative Williams's and Judge Brady's strong warnings against the dangers of miscegenation (see Chapter 2). The theme of protecting white womanhood was sounded again and again in the next fifteen years in a vain effort to save the Jim Crow system. In the Brown case, the Court decided unanimously that state laws requiring racially separate public schools were unconstitutional, thus overruling the spirit of the 1896 Plessy case and signaling the end of the separate-but-equal doctrine (Greenberg, 1959:208–74). The South, especially the Deep South, went all out to prevent the *Brown* decision from being applied to the countless other state laws requiring segregated public facilities. Explanatory comments (*dicta*) in the *Brown* decision indicated that the Court intended to do just what the South feared. Both the methods and the result in the case were labeled "unconstitutional" by the bitter opponents, and the justices were called communists. The whole Jim Crow system, not just racially segregated schools, was indeed at stake, just as slavery and states' rights had been at stake a century earlier.

In a flood of subsequent cases, the *Brown* decision was quickly extended by analogy to cover parks, golf courses, bathing beaches, public transportation, restaurants, theaters, and other public facilities, as well as housing. The Brown case became a key precedent, as the Court consistently held in other cases that legislation based on racial classifications is discriminatory and therefore unconstitutional (Bland, 1973: chap. 4). The legal strategy of the NAACP was to encourage sit-ins and other violations of the segregation laws in order to precipitate arrests and take test cases to court. In 1967 the Supreme Court ruled that state statutes prohibiting interracial marriage are discriminatory and unconstitutional (Bland, 1973: chap. 4). (Twenty-two states, including many Northern states, still had anti-miscegenation laws in the early 1960s.) The Brown case triggered the downfall of the legal support for the entire Jim Crow system, just as Judge Brady had feared. In the latter 1950s and the 1960s, Southern reaction to the judicial extensions of the Brown case was often especially strong when it had to do with public parks and swimming pools, many of which were closed for a time rather than have them racially integrated. Playgrounds and swimming pools involve close personal relations (rank 2) and thus infringe on white womanhood (rank 1).

These court decisions took place in the context of the civil rights movement—the bus boycotts, protest marches, sit-ins, freedom rides, and the unceasing and visible efforts of black leaders, all symbolized by the leadership of the Rev. Dr. Martin Luther King, Jr. The decisions also reflected the passage of the Civil Rights Acts of 1964 (the comprehensive law), 1965 (voting rights), and 1968 (housing discrimination) and other legislation and executive orders against segregation and discrimination. During these years there was also heavy white backlash against the civil rights developments, often accompanied by warnings that wholesale miscegenation would ensue if the schools were integrated. Acts of violent repression by white police and vigilantes were shown on television news programs night after night. There were the murders of Malcolm X, Martin Luther King, Jr., Robert Kennedy, Medgar Evers, voting rights workers, and others. These events exacerbated the frustrations felt in the Northern ghettos over economic and housing conditions and caused some of the protest marches to turn into urban black riots that included burning and other violence to white-owned property. All these developments fostered awareness of black unity, black pride, and black power.

School desegregation proceeded slowly and spottily—and not at all in the six Deep South states (Louisiana, Mississippi, Alabama, Georgia, Florida, and South Carolina) until the Supreme Court's unanimous decision in a Mississippi case in 1969, *Alexander v. Holmes County Board of Education* (396 U.S. 19). The Court had remained unanimous on a large number of cases, on all areas of the segregation laws, despite constant delays and other legal tactics. In this case the Court ruled that further delays would be unconstitutional and that school boards had to put forth realistic plans for desegregation immediately (Davis, 1978:233–41).

School desegregation then came rapidly to the entire South, and during the 1970s the region experienced great changes in race relations. Not only were schools and all other public facilities desegregated, but even lunchrooms, athletic teams, dressing rooms, and cheerleading squads were racially integrated, and white Southerners began cheering for black athletes. Gallup polls during the 1960s and 1970s showed that increasing percentages of Southern parents were willing to accept racially integrated schools. In 1963, for example, 78 percent of the sample of Southern white parents said they would object to having half the students in the school be black, while in 1978 only 28 percent objected. For Northern white parents the corresponding figures for the same years were 33 percent and 23 percent. As early as 1972–73 the public schools of the South were actually a bit more racially integrated than those in the North, but it must be noted that since the early 1970s in the South there has been much resegregation of white children in private academies.

Although the Jim Crow system was legally dead, vestiges have remained, and Southern whites have taken steps to retain as much political power as possible. For example, efforts to register white voters and get them to the polls have produced very high turnouts, 100 percent in a large number of counties, far outdoing the endeavors to get out the black vote. Since 1965, however, a great many more blacks have been voting, and some black candidates have achieved political office in places where the black vote is very large. But for the most part Southern whites have retained political control. During the 1960s and 1970s, attitudes of prejudice against blacks, including approval of racist beliefs and traditional stereotypes, declined substantially in the South, but with an important qualification. Although whites became increasingly willing to accept black persons in public and semipublic situations, the vast majority remained unaccepting in closer relationships, such as dating (Muir and McGlamery, 1984:967–72). It is not surprising, then, that the great changes attending the racial integration of public facilities in the South have apparently not brought about much increase in black-white sexual contacts involving white women. Despite Judge Brady's fears, miscegenation in the South seems to have been affected very little by the fall of the Jim Crow system and other successes of the civil rights movement.

DE FACTO SEGREGATION AND MISCEGENATION

While de jure (by law) segregation prevailed during the decades of the Jim Crow South, there was systematic de facto (in fact, or actual) segregation and discrimination in the rest of the nation. Although it was built into Northern institutions, de facto segregation was less uniform and rigid than Jim Crow and generally not backed by law, except for the anti-miscegenation laws in some states. Until World War II, Northern blacks were, by custom, excluded almost completely from all but the most menial jobs, and until the end of the 1950s Northern blacks were widely excluded from white restaurants, hotels, barbershops, theaters, and other facilities, and typically not welcome in smaller communities at all. White public opinion and informal social controls were strong, and there were even Ku Klux Klan lynchings in the Midwest during the 1920s. *The Birth of a Nation,* a highly influential film in the 1920s, presented the Klan as having saved the South and warned the nation against black political participation. A violent anti-black riot in Springfield, Illinois, in 1908 precipitated the establishment of the NAACP in 1909, with the goals of protecting blacks from white violence and achieving racial equality. Black rural-urban migration northward resulted in major riots in many cities during and after World War I, including East St. Louis, Chicago, and Washington, D.C., and during World War II in such cities as Detroit, Los Angeles, Newark (New Jersey), and Seattle.

As blacks moved North, they and other nonwhite migrants increasingly occupied the crowded low-rent slums being vacated in the inner cities by the Southern and Eastern European immigrants. These white ethnics were only partly replaced by other Europeans, because movement from those countries was virtually ended by the Immigration Acts of 1921 and 1924. Thus the immigration quota laws made room in the inner cities for large numbers of black and Hispanic migrants, and some American Indians. But because of their racial visibility and racial discrimination in housing, the nonwhite "new urban ethnics," especially blacks, could not easily move out of the slums when their economic status began to improve. Residential segregation grew rapidly, producing de facto segregation in the schools, parks, shops, and other facilities, so that the nonwhite areas of the inner cities became ghettos.

This de facto segregation has meant limited contact of any kind between blacks and whites, which makes informal, small-group contacts especially infrequent. This, in turn, has meant little white-black miscegenation, because that requires opportunity. Even when there is opportunity, there are strong feelings of social distance with respect to intimate relationships. Although some intermarriages have occurred, involving white women more often than black, the volume has been quite small. In general, intermarriage is strongly opposed by both white and black families. Intermarried partners run the risk of estrangement from one or both families, or of constant strains and only partial acceptance.

Most racially intermarried, urban couples have few children. Child-rearing and community acceptance of the child pose complex and painful problems, the child being socially marginal. There are also severe difficulties in obtaining a job, a place to live, credit and other services, and acceptance by relatives, friends, churches, other associations, and the general public. The difficulties of interracial marriages are even greater than those of marriages that cross religious and ethnic lines. Some racial intermarriages survive these trials and grow strong, while others disintegrate (Berry, 1965:291–95).

The ending of the anti-miscegenation laws in the 1960s, and other changes, have not increased the amount of intermarriage very much. The 1960 census showed that about 12 out of 1,000 marriages in the United States were black-white unions, many of them involving war brides from abroad after World War II. By 1970 the rate of black-white marriages had increased by approximately 63 percent in a decade, due entirely to more unions between white women and black men, while those between black women and white men declined a little (Williamson, 1980:189). In the state of Illinois, according to a census sample estimate provided by the Census and Data Users Services of Illinois State University, the number of black-white marriages almost doubled from 1960 to 1980, with most of the increase coming in the 1970s. Only about half of these interracial unions in Illinois in 1960 were estimated to involve black husbands, while that figure grew to about 70 percent by 1980. These are large percentage increases, yet the intermarriage rate in Illinois remains low. For the nation as a whole in 1980, only 1.3 percent of American-born black women in their first marriage had a white husband (Lieberson and Waters, 1988:171–77). Unless there are substantial further increases in the black-white marriage rate in the United States, such unions will continue to constitute no more than between 1 and 2 percent of all marriages.

In contrast to the Jim Crow South, interracial sexual experience in the North has been less coercive and exploitive of black females, has more often been for adventure or affection, has involved a higher proportion of black males, and has more often included marriage. However, most of the sexual contacts have taken place outside of marriage and, especially until the 1960s, many of them have involved white or black prostitutes.

We must bear in mind that the overall volume of white-black sexual contact and miscegenation in the North has been quite small, primarily because of de facto segregation but also because of white unwillingness to accept blacks in close relationships. Black opposition to informal and intimate contacts with whites also seems to have grown since the 1960s. When sexual contacts do occur, the increased use of contraception has limited the likelihood of births. Most of the miscegenation in the North has taken place *within* the black population, as defined by the one-drop rule, since a great many of the blacks who moved North took with them large numbers of genes from the Southern white population.

MISCEGENATION SINCE THE 1960s

The unanimity of the Supreme Court on desegregation and other civil rights questions was broken by the mid-1970s, over the complex issues of mandatory school busing and affirmative action procedures as remedies for racial discrimination. De facto segregation in the North then proved strongly resistant to change, and buses carrying black schoolchildren were attacked in Boston and other cities. By 1980, some 63 percent of all black students in the nation were still in "racially unbalanced" (more than half nonwhite) schools, and the public schools of the South were considerably more integrated than those in any other region of the country. Housing segregation continued as nonwhite populations expanded, whites moved further out, and large areas were resegregated—and thus the "black belts" grew. Although many major cities and even some suburbs became predominantly nonwhite, the federal government backed away from action to combat housing discrimination. In the 1980s, federal administrative decisions and many judicial decisions indicated determined opposition to measures that were designed to reduce racial segregation, and also to affirmative action remedies, especially annual quotas. The Ronald Reagan administration was strongly opposed even to long-range numerical goals for hiring, promotions, and school admissions, despite general support for such goals by the courts, state and local agencies of government, and employers in business and industry.

Ongoing housing segregation on a huge scale in the cities means continued limiting of contacts between blacks and whites, although major desegregation probably would produce only a small increase in intimate contacts. The black children and white children who attend integrated schools tend to accept racial stereotypes less than they used to, but they generally go home to segregated residential areas and have little social contact with each other. Much the same is true for college and university students, for adults in integrated workplaces, and in the military services. Even so, since the 1960s there apparently has been some overall increase in black-white personal relationships, and there is more choice about interracial contacts in campus, work, and public situations. Since the 1960s the amount of interracial dating and marriage is up from the very low levels of earlier decades, but the rates are still low. Most of the increases are apparently in the middle class. There is evidence that white attitudes of prejudice against blacks have declined somewhat nationwide, yet for most whites there are still strong deterrents to close interracial contacts.

For blacks, the growth of black pride has apparently become an important deterrent to sexual contacts and marriage with whites. In the 1960s the white backlash against the civil rights movement greatly strengthened the unity within the black community. After 1965, the Soul Movement, with its emphasis on black pride and black political power, revived the affirmation of blackness that had characterized the Black Renaissance of the 1920s. Although the 1960s Black Muslim goal of totally separate institutional development was generally rejected, the black community embraced the Muslim emphasis on black pride, black beauty, black achievement, black history, and use of the term "black" rather than "Negro." The term "Brown Americans," a popular expression of group unity in the 1930s and 1940s, gave way in the late 1960s to "Black Americans" and "Afro-Americans."

In the 1960s, growing black pride brought the lighter mulattoes into an even closer alliance with blacks in general than the Black Renaissance of the 1920s had produced. At the same time, the intense focus on blackness often put lighter persons on the defensive. Previously, having respectable parents had generally nullified the stigma of being "high yellow." In the 1960s, lighter persons in general often felt they had to prove their loyalty to the black community, and some complained of discrimination from other blacks (Williamson, 1980:190). What a change from the historical advantages of lightness! Lighter color, and having freedperson ancestors before the Civil War, have long been associated with higher education, the professions, good taste, old family connections, and prestige in the black community (Edwards, 1958:112–15). One hundred years after the Civil War, the black upper-upper class in the United States could still trace its origins to the antebellum mulatto elites through three generations. A study of *Who's Who Among Black Americans* in 1978 showed that the majority of those listed had ancestors who were freed from slavery before the Civil War and that a disproportionate number of these freedpersons had been light mulattoes (Mullins and Sites, 1984:679–80).

By the mid-1970s the devaluation of the prestige of light color had influenced marital choice and the class structure of the black community significantly. Lightness had become less valuable as a criterion for moving up from the lower-upper class to the aristocratic upper-upper class. Being light seemed often to retard rather than facilitate upward mobility, at various levels in the black class structure (Blackwell, 1975:73–94). Many lighter persons reacted by displaying "Afro" hairstyles and other symbols of blackness, a response that put young Creoles of Color in Louisiana in conflict with their more traditional elders (Dominguez, 1986:172–76, 181). Although lightness seems to have been under attack less since the mid-1970s, its prestige value appears unlikely to regain its historical level.

A study of black junior high and senior high school students in the Detroit area showed strong endorsement of the "Black is beautiful" slogan but a preference for "light brown" skin color and a negative valuation of both "black" and "light" color (Anderson and Cromwell, 1977:80–81). Other studies in the 1970s produced similar results (Goering, 1972:231–41; Holzman, 1973:92–101). These color preferences agree with those reported three decades earlier in Johnson's study of black children in the rural South (1941:258–66). In the 1970s, black men apparently no longer preferred as mates women lighter than themselves, and light males seeking high-status mates often were losing out to darker men and experiencing a lowered sense of self-esteem (Udry et al., 1976:722–23). Light women were reported to be weighing the advantages to their children of "marrying darker" and to be worrying about their color and other physical features (Glasco, 1974:33).

Growing black unity on civil rights goals during the latter 1960s was accompanied by wide disagreement about the means of achieving those rights, as frustration mounted over the often violent white backlash against nonviolent protests. The concept of black power came to have many different meanings, including political participation (voting rights, election of black officials, and more government appointments), rejection of the help of whites in the struggle, rejection of racial integration as a means of achieving equality, support for violence in self-defense against whites, or support for violence against white property. For a time, a small but vocal minority of black leaders proposed racial violence, guerrilla warfare, and revolution (Blackwell, 1975:206–8, 291–95). The assassination of the Rev. Dr. Martin Luther King, Jr., and Senator Robert F. Kennedy in 1968 contributed to the radicalization of black power, although the rhetoric was usually much more revolutionary than the protest actions. The strong language, the sometimes violent urban and campus protests, and some armed battles between the police and the Black Panthers convinced many whites that black power was an ominous political threat. Repressive actions, both on campuses and on the streets, were often very harsh.

Although the key leaders of black nationalism and separatism became powerful symbols of group pride and determination, most American blacks continued to favor significant reforms, not revolution. This was not clear to whites for some time, however, and the fear of black power had a chilling effect on close contacts between whites and blacks, just as white backlash had for years a chilling effect on blacks. Most blacks embraced black unity and pride and called for major reforms in practice as well as in law, but most also agreed with Dr. King that totally separate economic and political institutions for blacks could not work (King, 1967:32–66). By the 1970s, black power had become chiefly a pluralistic concept—that is, most blacks were demanding equal treatment, mutual respect of all ethnic groups and cultures, the right to voluntary integration into dominant community institutions as much or as little as desired, and retention of their own group identity, not total assimilation (Killian, 1975:161–75). The central themes of the Black Renaissance of the 1920s were revived and extended, and strong support was expressed for building a black culture on both African and American foundations.

It is now much more clear why the judicial and legislative successes of the civil rights movement, even the ending of the anti-miscegenation laws, resulted in only modest increases in black-white sexual contacts and intermarriage. More legal equality, and greater racial tolerance and freedom of choice, have been largely offset by strong deterrents to informal and intimate interracial contacts, in the black community as well as the white community. The emergence and articulation of a pluralistic view that emphasizes pride in the black identity has discouraged blacks from seeking close contacts with whites. The general response of whites to black power and black pride has evidently been to continue to maintain considerable social distance between themselves and blacks, as indicated by determined opposition to housing integration. There has probably been some increase in white-black miscegenation since the 1950s, but the amount remains small. Mixing of genes from white and African (and Indian) populations continues to occur mainly within the confines of the population defined by the one-drop rule as black.

DEVELOPMENT OF THE ONE-DROP RULE IN THE TWENTIETH CENTURY

The one-drop rule for determining who is black was clarified and solidified during the first decades of the twentieth century, and it has withstood the momentous changes in race relations since mid-century. Before we move on, we need to review what happened to the rule at several key points in the century. The Jim Crow system of segregation in the South, built during the years just before and after the turn of the century, was based on the legal doctrine of separate but equal public facilities. Southern white elites abandoned their paternalistic alliance with black sharecroppers and helped working-class whites get the segregation laws passed. By 1910 the system was thoroughly established, with potent legal and extralegal controls for keeping blacks "in their place," which was the lowest it had been since slavery. In legislative efforts to define a Negro in order to enforce the anti-miscegenation statutes, many states adopted the one-drop rule explicitly, while others moved in that direction. Before World War I it was clear that in questionable cases the one-drop rule would generally prevail in social practice and in the courts, and in the North as well as the South. By 1915 whites in the United States had completely accepted the one-drop rule.

Hostility toward mulattoes and miscegenation was very strong during the years when the segregation laws were being passed, and a great many Southern whites became extremely worried that their own families might have some "invisible black blood." Embittered mulattoes, largely alienated from the white community since the 1850s, increasingly allied themselves with blacks and began to lead the twentieth-century struggle for equality. Mulattoes became scornful of lightness and opposed to further mixing with whites. However, the Jim Crow system became so oppressive that many who could do so passed as white in order to escape the racial barriers to individual opportunities. Passing reached its peak from 1880 to 1925 or so, yet the costs were so great that most of those who could pass did not. As urban black migration increased, mulattoes led the Black Renaissance of the 1920s, which was symbolized by such slogans as "Black is beautiful" and "Brown America." This movement embraced the black identity and the development of a black culture with both African and American roots. By 1925 the black community had fully accepted the one-drop rule, as even the lightest mulattoes allied themselves more and more firmly with blacks.

In the Jim Crow system, sexual contacts between blacks and whites were limited to certain kinds of situations, and the one-drop rule was strongly reinforced. Miscegenation involving whites was restricted almost entirely to illicit matings between white males and black females and characteristically involved coercion and exploitation of black women. Sometimes the contacts took other forms, even love, but intermarriage required leaving the state and was extremely rare. The total amount of miscegenation involving whites was evidently much less than during slavery, and perhaps as low as during Reconstruction. Mulatto-mulatto and mulatto-African black mixing continued, of course, and accounted for most of the miscegenation. The highly repressive system was symbolized by the Jim Crow stereotype and eventually the Sambo image, the "good nigger" who made no trouble. The system lasted for well over half a century and was the main target of the civil rights movement of the 1950s and 1960s.

Southern white determination to maintain the Jim Crow system was symbolized by the firmly held belief that the sexual and racial purity of white womanhood had to be protected. Most of the segregation laws pertained to public facilities, including schools, although there were also anti-miscegenation laws and statutes to help maintain segregation in political, legal, and economic areas. The racial etiquette was the chief means of maintaining white dominance in personal contacts that were unavoidable, and this master-servant ritual had to be acted out carefully lest the black person be accused of "getting" out of his or her subordinate "place." Especially for violations of the etiquette, but also for challenges to other aspects of the system, blacks were warned, threatened, and finally subjected to extralegal violence. The segregation laws and the racial etiquette were backed by terroristic methods employed by poor whites, including the ultimate weapon of lynching.

While white womanhood was being protected so determinedly, and strong rhetoric used to condemn racial mixing, many white males were engaging in sexual activity with black females. Unlike the Apartheid system in the Republic of South Africa, where white males have been severely punished for crossing the sexual color line, the norms of Jim Crow gave interracial sexual license to the white male and thus did not prevent miscegenation. Genes derived from African and European populations are mixed whether the mother of a mixed child is white or black, of course. The child is expected to stay with its mother, and a mixed child in a white family would "mongrelize" the white population and threaten the entire Jim Crow system. If the child stayed with the black mother there was no threat to "white racial purity," or to the system of white domination. Thus the one-drop rule and the symbol of white womanhood were crucial to the maintenance of the system.

While the legalized system of Jim Crow held sway in the South, there was systematic de facto segregation of blacks in the North involving many public facilities and discrimination in jobs and housing. Although generally not backed by laws, except for some anti-miscegenation statutes, the force of public opinion was strong, supported by threats and sometimes by violence. The Ku Klux Klan exerted its influence across the nation in the 1920s. De facto segregation and attitudes of social distance made opportunities for intimate contact between blacks and whites very limited. Although in the North interracial sexual contacts were less coercive of black women than in the South, and more often involved black males, intermarriage was almost as rare in the North. Births often were prevented in interracial liaisons. Overall, as the black populations of Northern cities grew, the amount of black-white miscegenation remained quite small.

The rallying cry about white womanhood did not save the Jim Crow system from its downfall during the 1950s and 1960s. The precedent of the *Brown v. Board of Education* decision was extended from public schools to make state segregation laws in all public facilities, as well as the anti-miscegenation laws, unconstitutional. In the 1969 Mississippi case, the U.S. Supreme Court finally rejected all further delays in school integration, and from that time desegregation proceeded so fast that by 1972 the Southern schools were more integrated than those in the North. Then came the crises over affirmative action and over mandatory busing in the North, and the sharp slowdown in the federal enforcement of civil rights laws in the 1980s. Increasingly segregated urban housing has thwarted efforts to integrate the public schools and other facilities. Both de facto segregation in the cities and mutual unwillingness to accept close interracial relationships have limited informal contacts between whites and blacks, North and South.

White backlash actions against the civil rights movement, first in the South and then the North, caused deep frustration among blacks in spite of major legal successes. The result was greater black unity. In the late 1960s, black pride and black power were often expressed in such strong rhetoric that many whites feared an armed revolution. Early in the 1970s it became clear that most American blacks supported major reforms to achieve equal treatment in racially integrated institutions, not revolution. Blacks also generally rejected total assimilation as well as total separation, favoring a strong black identity and pride in Afro-American culture. Light skin color lost its remaining value as a means to upward mobility in the black class structure and even became a liability, at least for a time.

The repeal of the anti-miscegenation laws, and other civil rights gains, have not produced a large increase in extramarital liaisons or intermarriage since the 1960s, although there have been some increases. Black pride has operated as a deterrent to interracial sexual contacts, and cultural affinity, black mistrust of the white community, and opposition by both black and white families prevent all but a relatively small number of couples from entering mixed marriages. Intermarried couples have relatively few children, and the extramarital sexual contacts result in few children too. The net result is that black-white miscegenation has not risen much since the low levels reached during the Reconstruction and Jim Crow eras. Most of the genetic mixing continues to occur within the black population as defined by the one-drop rule.

While the ancestry of American blacks is still predominantly black African, at least one-fifth of it is derived from white populations and a significant portion from American Indians. Nevertheless, this increasingly homogenized, "browning" ethnic group has a wide and continuous range of racial traits, and some members who appear to be biologically white because they are indeed mostly so. Although the "Black is beautiful" slogan was used often in the latter 1960s and early 1970s to encourage pride in black identity, studies since the 1960s have shown that light-brown skin color is preferred over either "light" or "black." The one-drop rule is now as fully accepted in the black community as a whole as it is in the white community (see Chapter 6).

FIVE

OTHER PLACES, OTHER DEFINITIONS

Populations that differ in racial traits have been coming into contact and engaging in miscegenation for a very long time, both before and during recorded history. How has the group identity of the racially mixed offspring and their descendants been determined? Has there always been a one-drop rule, and is it perhaps a universal social rule? What group identity was assigned to the mixed progeny when ancient Egyptians or other Hamitic-speaking white peoples first mixed with black tribes along the Upper Nile, when blond Phoenicians mingled with various black peoples along the African coasts, when mongoloid and caucasoid peoples mixed in Siberia and Central Asia, or when the groups met that produced the racially mixed peoples we now know as the Malaysians, the Filipinos, the Polynesians, or even the Australian aborigines? For countless such prehistoric meetings this question can probably never be answered by archeological evidence, but information is available about many historical encounters around the globe, especially those of recent centuries. A consideration of some of this comparative historical evidence is illuminating and provides the kind of perspective needed for a fuller understanding of the one-drop rule in the United States.

Societal rules for determining what group racially mixed persons belong to reflect and clarify the position these people are to occupy in the community. Using the one-drop rule to define persons with any black ancestry as blacks clearly assigns them to the social status occupied by blacks. People in the United States have become so accustomed to this rule that it rarely occurs to anyone that there might be any other way of defining black persons and assigning them to a status group. However, another rule competed with the one-drop rule during slavery. This other rule classed mulattoes as an in-between group and not as blacks, but it lost out when the continuation of slavery was threatened and the race groups became strongly polarized during and after the Civil War (see Chapter 3).

By the 1960s, using cross-cultural comparisons, some sociologists had identified four different statuses occupied by racial hybrid groups (Berry, 1965:191–95). We can now say that there are at least seven statuses, each embodying its own definition of racial identity. Although racially mixed populations are treated by people in their societies as mixed rather than as members of either parent group in all the types except the sixth (the one-drop rule), their social status varies greatly from one type to another. Racially mixed progeny may have (1) a lower status than either parent group, (2) a higher status than either parent group, (3) an in-between, marginal status, (4) a highly variable status, depending more on social class than on color, (5) a variable status independent of racial traits, (6) the same position as the lower-status group, and (7) the status of an assimilating minority. These seven statuses are discussed in the order listed here. In this chapter we look at each of these seven statuses closely.

RACIAL HYBRID STATUS LOWER THAN BOTH PARENT GROUPS

When people with racially mixed ancestry are not accepted on equal terms by either of the parent groups (unmixed original race groups), their status in society is lower than that of either parent group. They are therefore defined as a totally different and lowly people. For example, mulattoes among the Ganda peoples of Uganda, East Africa, are regarded with condescension and contempt by the Ganda and are not accepted by white society either. For a time there was consideration of a plan to solve the problem by removing all the mulattoes to an island in Lake Victoria, where they could be completely isolated (Berry, 1965:192). There is a similar bottom-of-the-ladder status position for the Métis in Canada, the Anglo-Indians in India, Korean-Americans in Korea, and Vietnamese-Americans in Vietnam.

For a considerable time the Métis occupied a middle-minority position, a variant of the third type discussed below, then suffered a drastic drop in status. This population was begun in the seventeenth century by unions, sometimes involving marriage, between French and Scottish trappers and Indian women in the Canadian wilderness. The children were at first called Métis if they spoke French, or "half-breeds" if they spoke English, but gradually all racial hybrids were known as Métis. They developed a strong identity and came to be looked on as a completely separate people, neither Indian nor white, centered at the Red River Settlement at what is now Winnipeg, Manitoba. They felt superior to the Indian tribes, and tended to marry each other, or sometimes whites. They dominated the buffalo hunt and did other work no one else did, including being interpreters between white trappers and the Indians and transporting supplies by canoe or in a distinctive cart for the Hudson's Bay Company. They wore a colorful sash and danced the Red River jig, symbolizing a strong group identity.

The coming of the railroad and white settlement in the latter half of the nineteenth century ended the need to freight goods by canoe or cart and brought an end to fur-trapping and the buffalo hunt. Instead of a gradual eroding of the in-between status of the Métis, however, catastrophe fell after the Canadian government acquired the Hudson Bay territory and began settling it. In 1870 Louis Riel led the Red River Settlement in a rebellion, demanding and getting French Catholic schools and other rights, but he made the mistake of executing a white Protestant settler who opposed him. British troops were sent to punish Riel, and he fled to the United States. In 1884 Riel led a much bloodier Métis rebellion in Saskatchewan and was tried and hanged. The Métis then dispersed throughout the Canadian West, despised by whites and Indians alike.

Under Canadian law, Indian identity and rights were defined strictly, so that Métis could never become legal Indians, yet some managed to become accepted on the reservations. Those who were sufficiently educated and looked white enough passed into the white population. Most of the remainder have lived as outcasts in poor, isolated areas or moved to towns and cities to become an urban underclass. There may be as many as 750,000 Métis now in Canada, more than the number of full Indians. In the 1980s, organizations such as the government-sponsored Manitoba Métis Federation have had only limited success in reviving a sense of pride in the Métis identity. For the most part the Métis remain a broken, desperately poor people with little hope and extremely high rates of unemployment, welfare dependency, crime, school dropout, and alcoholism.

Under the long British occupation of India, the mixed Anglo-Indian people went from a relatively protected, middle-minority status to a declining and precarious position. Then, after India's independence, the status of the Eurasians dropped still more drastically (Gist and Dean, 1973). At first, in the latter seventeenth century, the colonial administration favored intermarriage, and mixed persons were protected and given advantages over the Indians. Many became clerks or officials in the colonial administration, dealing with Indians on behalf of the British. Useful as intermediaries, some Anglo-Indians even married into the British nobility. However, miscegenation came into disfavor with the British when their control was consolidated and the means of transportation home improved. The decline in status left the Eurasians a helpless minority, avoided both by Indians and by the British. They wore English clothes and tried to identify themselves with the Europeans, but that made the Indians even more contemptuous of them. In the traditional Hindu caste system there is no place for people of "mixed blood," and the Indians considered these hybrid people a threat (Ballhatchet, 1980). The position of the Eurasians became still more precarious as Indian nationalism grew, and many of them fled to Australia or England (Berry, 1965:275–76). When national independence finally came in 1947, however, most stayed in India, where nearly a quarter of a million Eurasians remain a despised outgroup. Caste has been legally abolished, but the traditions still have considerable force.

We must note that this Anglo-Indian experience is an instance of mixing of different subraces of the caucasoid race, as defined by physical anthropologists earlier in the twentieth century, not a mixing of two major race groups. The South Asians have been classified by Kroeber (1948:14), among others, as Hindu caucasoids (see Chapter 2). However, the British people have considered all dark-skinned "native peoples" to be nonwhite, and therefore to belong to other races. In intergroup behavior, race is what people believe it to be, and the bottom-of-the-ladder status outcome for the Eurasians has been the same as that assigned in many instances where two major racial groups have been involved.

During the Korean War, thousands of Korean-American children were born to Korean women, some fathered by white servicemen and some by blacks. The numbers were greater than they might have been because Korea had already lost two million of its own men to war when American military forces began arriving in 1950. Most of the women would not have a child without some sort of promise of marriage, knowing the extreme difficulties mixed children face in Korea, where there is a traditional prejudice against marrying someone from a different class or region of the country, but particularly someone of another racial or ethnic group. Moreover, most of the mothers were from the lowest social class and were destitute under wartime conditions. Some marriages did occur, and some of the wives and children were brought to the United States sooner or later, but not in most cases. Some of the fathers never took any responsibility for their children, some intended to but were killed or seriously wounded, some went home and made efforts to obtain their children but often gave up, and some who went home made promises and were never heard from again. American armed forces have been in Korea since the 1950s.

Citizenship in the Republic of Korea is based on the father's, so that the mixed children have been defined not as Koreans but as Americans. Unless the father can be found and a valid marriage proven, the child has no proof of American citizenship. Children of American males are not granted American citizenship if born out of wedlock outside the United States. Thus the great majority of the children have had no country and have been denied the rights of Korean citizens. The U.S. government has refused to take responsibility for finding the fathers of these children, even if the Korean mother or child can give a name and home town. The children have felt the sting of epithets that are even more powerful than "bastard," such as *trigge*, meaning polluted, *eyenokko*, meaning round eyes, or "Yank." These terms symbolize the terrible war and South Korea's political powerlessness. Some Korean families have refused to accept the mixed children, calling them monsters, a cross between a human and an animal. There have even been reports that some mixed children were put to death.

Mixed children can be adopted in the Republic of Korea if their families have registered them with the government as orphans. This means the mother must give up the child, the family having certified that it has no parents. This enables the child to have citizenship in Korea, in the United States, or wherever it is adopted. Children over the age of fourteen cannot be adopted, so that older orphans who want to get to the United States must try for student visas or go through the long and difficult process of immigration. The Korean mother who acknowledges and keeps her mixed child has no hope of getting either herself or the child to the United States unless the father takes responsibility for it and succeeds.

During the war in Vietnam, around 80,000 mixed children fathered by white and black military personnel from the United States were born to Vietnamese women. These children are virtual outcasts in their own society, where they are called the "dust of life" and treated with contempt. There, as in Korea, the child's identity and citizenship rights derive from the father. The American approach to this problem has contrasted sharply with that of the French, who withdrew from Vietnam after they were defeated in 1954. The French took 25,000 mixed children with them when they left, and the French government provided for those who stayed behind with their Vietnamese mothers. They offered French citizenship to all at the age of eighteen.

There has recently been some change in American policy toward the Amerasian children of the wars in Korea and Vietnam. In 1982 the U.S. Congress began supporting preferential treatment in immigration for the mixed children, if Americans offer to adopt the younger ones and sponsor the older ones. The Vietnamese government, having previously refused to acknowledge that the Amerasians were abandoned or despised, has indicated its willingness to allow emigration if the American fathers offer to take the children. Although the process is quite restricted, it can succeed. A considerable number of Korean orphans have been adopted in the United States in recent years, but the status of most of the mixed children of the Korean and Vietnam wars, and their descendants, seems destined to remain that of lowly outcasts. The same is true of most mixed children fathered by American troops stationed in Korea since the 1950s.

Earlier we noted that very light mulattoes in the United States have at times experienced marked drops in status in the black community, especially during the very first years of the twentieth century, in the 1920s, and again in the late 1960s. Also, at least from early Jim Crow times to the present, "high yallers" have been put on the defensive and those who cannot prove respectable family connections have been derogated in the black community. At its strongest, this condition of minimal acceptance, of barely being tolerated, borders on rejection by the black community. At the same time, however, blacks in general insist that the very light blacks be loyal to the black community, thus actually affirming rather than rejecting the one-drop rule. And even the lowest status in the black community does not involve loss of family, friends, or citizenship. However, treatment that comes at all close to that of the outcast Eurasian and Amerasian children or the Métis in Canada is very threatening to the people who receive it. Having a lower status than either parent group is the worst possible outcome for a racial hybrid group, which is thereby defined as a separate and debased people.

STATUS HIGHER THAN EITHER PARENT GROUP

The exact opposite of the status outcome above has been unusual, yet sometimes racially mixed people have achieved a status that is higher than that of either parent group. In that case, the racial hybrid group is defined as a separate and socially superior people. Both the examples discussed here required a successful political revolution. The first was led by a remarkable slave named Toussaint L'Ouverture, who succeeded in ending slavery in the wealthy French colony on Saint Domingue (Hispaniola), later called Haiti. By 1789 some 30,000 whites were exercising extremely harsh control over about half a million black slaves, and there were about 24,000 free blacks and mulattoes with in-between status. Slaves were deliberately worked to death in a few years and then replaced, and many slaves committed suicide as a symbolic form of migration back to Africa. Inspired by the French Revolution of 1789, the slaves began their largest and most successful rebellion in 1791. Although an army sent by Napoleon captured L'Ouverture, other leaders carried on and achieved independence from France in 1804.

After the Haitian revolution the mulattoes emerged as the economically and politically dominant elites, although their control was fiercely contested by the elites of the far larger black group. Mulattoes retained their ascendancy through more than a century and a half of often tumultuous Haitian history before they lost political power, and in the 1960s they began determined efforts to regain it from the Duvalier regime. Since then they have regained control of the government and lost it again, and the volatile struggle for political power goes on. The Haitian mulattoes monopolized wealth and power as long as possible, requiring of themselves elite standards of education, aesthetic taste, and use of leisure time. They have maintained tight kinship ties among mulatto families, preventing intermarriage with both whites and African blacks. They look down on unmixed blacks and despise the small white population. Lebanese, Syrians, and other whites have been involved in middle minority commercial activities in Haiti for about a century, operating in the face of considerable difficulties, including not being allowed to own land (Nicholls, 1981:427).

After Spain conquered Mexico under Hernando Cortés, the Spanish ruled for three centuries before a revolution succeeded in 1821. During the long period of conquest and colonization, there was massive miscegenation between the Spanish and the Indian populations, and some that involved African blacks. At first the term "Mestizo" meant half-Spanish and half-Indian, and it was often used to mean "illegitimate" or "bastard." Eventually it came to refer to the entire mixed population regardless of the degree of mixture. The terms of reference listed in Table 1 show how finely tuned the Spanish concern for racial ancestry became during the eighteenth century in Mexico and in all the Spanish possessions in the Western Hemisphere. The term *lobo*, for example, means half-Indian, one thirty-second African black, and the rest (30 sixty-fourths) white ancestry. The largest genetic contribution to the Mestizo population today came from the Indian peoples, then the Spanish and other Europeans, with small infusions from blacks and East Asian and South Asian groups.

During the long Spanish rule, the Mestizos occupied a middle status position while the Indians were on the bottom of the ethnic status ladder. The Spanish colonial policy was strongly assimilationist, requiring Indians to learn the Spanish language and culture and give up their own tongues and customs. Indian groups that would not comply could barely survive, much less prosper. The lighter Mestizos were given preference by the Spanish, and there developed a structure of status levels that was based on skin color and the degree of Spanish ancestry. The belief that Europeans were biologically and culturally superior to Indians became widespread, and Mestizos took pride in Hispanic ancestry and tried to deny their Indian backgrounds (Stoddard, 1973:59–60).

TABLE 1 Ranked Racial Categories Denoting Ancestry in New Spain During the Eighteenth Century

Parents		
Male	Female	Offspring
1. Spaniard	Indian	Mestizo
2. Mestizo	Spanish	Castizo
3. Spaniard	Castizo	Spaniard
4. Negro	Spanish	Mulatto
5. Spaniard	Mulatto	Morisco
6. Spaniard	Morisco	Albino
7. Spaniard	Albino	Torna atrás
8. Indian	Torna atrás	Lobo
9. Lobo	Indian	Zambaigo
10. Zambaigo	Indian	Cambujo
11. Cambujo	Mulatto	Albarazado
12. Albarazado	Mulatto	Barcino
13. Barcino	Mulatto	Coyote
14. Indian	Coyote	Chamiso
15. Mestizo	Chamiso	Coyote Mestizo
16. Coyote Mestizo	Mulatto	Ahi te estás

SOURCE: Magnus Mörner, *Race Mixture in the History of Latin America* (Boston: Little, Brown, 1967), p. 58, table 4.1. Reprinted by permission.

The Mestizos became the rulers when Spanish control was overthrown, and except for the years 1864–67, when an Austrian archduke reigned as Maximilian I with the backing of French troops, they have continued to govern Mexico ever since. Some Spanish and other whites in Mexico have retained considerable wealth and influence, but political power remains chiefly in Mestizo hands. The Indian peoples have remained on the bottom of the ladder. Early in the twentieth century the old racial beliefs and customs were still strong. Not until the 1930s did the Mexican government abandon the policy of forced assimilationism and begin to support the preservation of Indian languages and culture (Stoddard, 1973:78–79).

The Mestizos are by far the largest group in Mexico today. Within this group the mingling of genes from the parent populations continues, and new unions with other population groups occur. Next in size come the unmixed Indians, and then the much smaller category of unmixed white Gringos (foreigners), composed of Spanish, Italians, other Europeans, and Americans. The numbers of unmixed blacks, darker mulattoes, East Asians, and South Asians are small, and prejudice against very dark skin is strong (Stoddard, 1973:80–84). The overwhelming size of the Mestizo group would appear to be a major factor in its dominance, yet in Haiti the mulatto elites managed to maintain control for a long time with relatively small numbers.

IN-BETWEEN STATUS: SOUTH AFRICA AND OTHERS

The third type of position racially mixed populations can occupy is between that of the two parent groups. Such a racial hybrid group is defined as being derived from, but marginal to, both parent groups and intermediate in status. Often there is a firmer tie with one parent group than the other, but sometimes groups in the middle position develop a strong separate identity. We have already noted two groups that slipped downward from this in-between position—the Métis of Canada and the Anglo-Indians of India—to fall below both parent groups in status. We have also seen that the Mestizos of Mexico and the mulattoes of Haiti moved up from the in-between status to a dominant position over both parent groups. The middle position is volatile and uncertain, although changes in status are not always so great as in the above cases. All racial and ethnic groups may experience ups and downs in status as conditions vary, but those in between are particularly vulnerable to changes.

Many if not most racial hybrid groups with an in-between status are to some degree what economists call "middleman minorities" and what is here called simply "middle minorities." This means that they meet special occupational needs that the dominant community is unable or unwilling to fill, as did the Métis. A given group may or may not have previous experience with the particular work involved, or any other competitive advantage, but it must at least have the motivation to move into the status gap. Middle minorities in this sense need not be racial hybrid groups, of course. One example of middle minorities that are not racially mixed is the Asian Indians in Kenya, who were transported there by the British as indentured servants to build the railroads. The Indians remained to assume the middle-minority functions of collecting crops for export and distributing European trade goods, services that were valued by both the British colonists and the Kenyan peoples, who preferred not to deal with each other. The Indians were excluded from many kinds of employment, and their landowning and political participation were restricted. They were paid less than half of what the British were paid for the same work, but much more than the Africans. Kenyan independence in 1963 brought more severe restrictions and hardships on the Indians than on the British, and many of the former left the country in distress.

Asian Indians, Chinese, Lebanese, Syrians, Armenians, and other peoples have occupied middle-minority positions in many different countries, although before leaving home most of these people had been farmers. In the past, both Christian groups and Jews have often been the moneylenders, tax collectors, and traders in Islamic societies. Often the occupational specialties have involved work that is very onerous (such as running hand laundries or disposing of garbage), highly stigmatized (such as junk-dealing or tax-collecting), or involves long hours and high risk (such as family restaurants, Mom and Pop stores, or the clothing business). At first the motion picture industry in the United States involved both high risk and the stigma of burlesque theater. So, until it became more respectable and highly profitable, the film industry was largely left to the new Jewish immigrants from Eastern Europe. Although mostly from rural settlements, some of these immigrants had had experience in Yiddish theater (Davis, 1978:120). Such stigmatized or risky occupational gaps have often been filled by racially mixed groups, who already have a stigma.

Political and economic changes, especially when they eliminate the group's special occupations, can have drastic consequences for the middle minority. Many members of middle groups have managed to achieve considerable success in business, government service, or the professions, in spite of much exclusion and other discrimination by the dominant community. Their comparative success is resented by lower-status groups and often feared by the dominant groups. Very often middle minorities have been stereotyped as overly ambitious, greedy, cunning, and clannish. When crises come, the dominant group rarely protects the middle minority from the animosity of lower-status groups. As a safe target for hostility, the middle minority serves as a buffer between the groups above and below it. In Europe, Jews perfomed this buffer role for many centuries. Although valued for its occupational functions and buffer role, especially by the dominant community, the middle minority is politically powerless (Blalock, 1967:79–84).

Because of the special problems with identity and group acceptance, the vulnerability of the middle-minority status is especially great when it is occupied by a racially mixed group. This may make it easier to understand the bitter fate of such groups as the Métis in Canada and the Anglo-Indians, both of whom had considered themselves superior to the native parent group and then lost the special occupations and mediating functions. To parent groups it has often seemed right initially that their racially mixed offspring should occupy an in-between status. When special occupations and go-between functions are added, the middle-minority position can become valued and relatively stabilized, sometimes for long periods of time. However, the latent fragility of this status quickly becomes apparent when major crises and changes occur, and the problems are then exacerbated by the racial marginality of the group.

The Republic of South Africa has had two buffer groups between the dominant whites and the native blacks: the Coloureds and the Asians. In 1980 blacks made up 70.9 percent of the total population of more than 26.5 million people, whites 16.4 percent, Coloureds 9.7 percent, and Asians 3.0 percent. It will be helpful to note the nature of the white and black populations. The first language of three-fifths of the whites is Afrikaans, spoken mainly by Dutch descendants, while two-fifths of the whites speak primarily English. British control of South Africa was very firm after the second Boer War (1899–1902), and in 1910 they established the Union as a parliamentary democracy. The Afrikaner disapproved of what they considered the liberal racial policies of the British. When the Afrikaner won the 1948 elections and began running the government, they immediately established the Apartheid system. In 1961 the British Dominion status was rejected and the Republic was established. The Afrikaner see themselves as pragmatists rather than racists, and as the destined rulers of South Africa. The English, while favoring more moderate racial policies, have generally supported Apartheid.

Some 2,000 years ago the Bantu-speaking tribes began their slow migration southward from the Great Lakes region of Central Africa. Centuries ahead of the main thrust were the Xhosa peoples, including the Khoi-Khoin (Hottentots, to the Dutch) and the San (Bushmen), who were in Cape Province when the Dutch arrived in 1652. Although they nearly annihilated the San, the Dutch interbred with the Khoi-Khoin, beginning what is now defined as the "Coloured" population. Actually the Khoi-Khoin and the San were relatively light-skinned, or brown, having apparently mixed centuries earlier with Hamitic-speaking white peoples in Central Africa. Some of the early Coloureds in Cape Province migrated north to avoid further contact with the Dutch and became known as Basters (Bastards), and today some 12,000 of them live in Namibia, where they retain Dutch customs and exploit tribal labor.

Although the Zulus and other Bantu tribes arrived in what are now the other provinces of the Republic of South Africa about the same time the Dutch arrived at the Cape, there was no contact between them until the Boers (Dutch farmers) migrated to the east and later to the northeast. The Bantu tribes were never enslaved, but they were defeated in battle, beginning in 1779 with the Kaffir Wars. Tribal power was broken with the Battle of Blood River in 1838, in which 40,000 Zulus were killed by cannon and other firearms while no whites died, convincing the Boers that God had given them the Velt (inland plateau) to rule.

Since 1948, the ultimate goal of Apartheid has been to restrict all blacks who are not employed in the Republic to the native reservations called Bantustans or Homelands, which comprise less than 14 percent of the country's land although blacks make up more than 70 percent of the population. Whites occupy the best farm and pasture lands, and the mines, while the Bantustans are discontinuous wastelands with few resources, no industrial cities, and no seaports. The tribal peoples are now dependent on a money income, yet there is almost no work on the reservations. Most black men who work in the cities must leave their families behind, visiting them only once or twice a year. A great many black women domestic workers in the cities must leave their children on the reservations and live in single-sex dormitories, seeing their children only three weeks a year. Those who have husbands and a rented home in the urban black ghettos must leave their children unattended from dawn to dusk. In these and other ways the Apartheid system splits black families apart.

The Apartheid strategy is to represent the Homelands to the world as if they were politically independent and to use the cheap native labor in the industrial cities and the mines and on the white farms. Three of the Bantustans (Transkei, Bophutatswana, and Venda) were granted nominal independence in the 1970s, although they were not recognized as nation-states in the rest of the world, and Ciskei received independence in 1981. These Homelands remain politically and economically dependent on the Republic of South Africa, in which they have no vote. Although Botswana, Swaziland, and landlocked Lesotho (in the Orange Free State) have had political independence since the 1960s, they too are economically and politically dependent on the Republic.

The Homelands policy is the so-called macro-segregation part of the Apartheid system, the part that pertains only to blacks and not to the Coloureds and the Asians. Meso-segregation consists of the Group Areas Act provisions for residential separation of the "four race groups" in urban areas, while micro-segregation is composed of the so-called petty Apartheid requirements for racially separate facilities in public areas (Van den Berghe, 1971:37), such as trains, buses, and beaches. By early 1990 most if not all of the petty Apartheid laws had been rescinded, yet much de facto segregation of public facilities remains. Although the "pass card" laws were repealed in 1986, several documents indicating one's official racial classification must still be carried. During 1990, President F. W. de Klerk promised political participation to blacks, although not on a "one man, one vote" basis, and also supported reforms to move toward ending the Apartheid system. Such reforms are strongly opposed by the most conservative whites and are likely to be gradual and piecemeal, despite the determined movement for comprehensive and immediate change.

In 1980 the Coloureds numbered more than 2.5 million, and the Asians more than 750,000. In Cape Province, where the Coloured group originated in the mid-seventeenth century, the Coloureds outnumber the Asians by almost 100 to 1. At least 87 percent of all the Coloureds in the Republic in 1980 were living in Cape Province. Many are descendants of slaves brought in from Mozambique and Madagascar. In Natal Province the situation is reversed: the Asians outnumber the Coloureds by more than 13 to 1. About 80 percent of the Asians in the Republic live in Natal. In the northernmost province of Transvaal, where Johannesburg and Pretoria are located, there are nearly twice as many Coloureds as Asians. The Orange Free State province has a modest Coloured population but has never admitted any Asians (Banton, 1983:234). Both the Asians and the Coloureds are now mainly urban, the Asians more so, and on the whole the Asians have a higher educational and economic status.

Although our main concern here is the Coloureds, we need to take brief note of the Asians, who have had more distinctively middle-minority occupations. The Asian group is composed mainly of Indians, first brought in 1860 by the British as indentured servants to work in the sugar cane fields of Natal. Those who stayed after indenture could send their children to school. They became moneylenders to black farmers and white farmers, and became grain dealers, and later began to succeed in other businesses. The Asians could vote until 1896, at which time the British passed restrictions designed to reduce the business competition of the Indians. From 1894 to 1913, Gandhi waged his campaign for Indian rights in South Africa, especially against the pass laws. In 1913 immigration from India was restricted, and with the passage of the Apartheid laws in 1948, the Indians suffered major setbacks in status. Although they may own land and build houses, their residence is restricted to their own segregated areas. Their educational and economic statuses have risen, and in 1961 they were recognized as citizens—but without the right to vote. The Indians remain politically powerless, having received only token representation in a segregated parliament as a result of the limited constitutional changes of 1984. They are highly vulnerable in the ongoing crisis over the Apartheid system and have suffered some violent attacks by resentful blacks. In 1949 about 150 Indians were killed and 1,000 were injured in Zulu outbursts, and many smaller attacks have occurred since.

The Coloureds have been valued as a buffer group by the whites, especially in Cape Province, where they outnumber the whites by almost two to one. Coloureds are officially defined as any "mixed blood" persons (see Chapter 4) and therefore include children and descendants resulting from black-Asian and white-Asian unions, not just those from black-white and black-Coloured unions. The bulk of the Coloureds are mulattoes, with racial traits ranging from black to white, and thus correspond to the vast majority of the population defined as black in the United States. Most of the remainder of the Coloureds are Eurasians and Afro-Indians. Malays, who are Sunni Muslims and who were brought as slaves and have been on the Cape Peninsula for more than three hundred years, have been classified as Coloureds rather than Asians. Even other Sunni Muslims who live among the Malays, including some Chinese, Arabs, and European Muslims, are also classed as Coloureds. The racial classification system is thus affected by the religion of the people being classified.

South African whites often explain who Coloureds are by saying that they are not black and not Asian. This underscores the rejection of the one-drop rule and also suggests that there is less social distance between whites and Coloureds than between whites and blacks. Not only are the Coloureds largely Westernized, mostly Christian, and 70 percent urban, but 80 percent of them speak Afrikaans as their first language. White-black and white-Coloured sexual contacts were frequent for a century or more after the Boers first settled in Cape Province, and then firm steps were taken to limit interracial liaisons and intermarriage. Whites and blacks, males and females—all were then punished for crossing the sexual color line. By that time the Coloureds identified little with their tribal relatives and were already Europeanized. While some miscegenation involving whites continued, the Coloureds have been chiefly an inbreeding population for more than two centuries, with some infusions from blacks and Asians. Having learned European values, the Coloureds came to identify their welfare with the white people and their regimes, and many who could do so passed as white in order to gain more opportunities. As they moved in increasing numbers from farms to towns and cities, most of the Coloured men became industrial workers or other laborers, while the women became concentrated in textiles and clothing manufacture.

In 1910 the Coloureds attained the right to vote in the newly established Union of South Africa, but they lost this right in a highly controversial action in 1956. Prime Minister J. G. Strijdom had to pack the Parliament and the Supreme Court in order to disenfranchise the Coloureds, since many whites felt strongly about it. The Asians had lost the right to vote in 1896, and the blacks had never had it. The franchise is only one of the status losses the Coloureds have experienced as a result of the coming of the Apartheid system in 1948. They have been subject to the Group Areas Act for urban townships, and large numbers had to move in order to comply with the multiple residential segregation of the "four race groups." Commuting to work on overcrowded trains and buses typically has involved as much time and discomfort for Coloureds as for blacks. And housing, schools, parks, and other facilities for Coloureds have been better than those for blacks but poorer than those for whites. Coloureds have been subject to the so-called petty Apartheid laws, liberalized in recent years and largely abolished in 1990, which have required the race groups to use four-way segregated public facilities such as restaurants, theaters, toilets, beaches, trains, and taxis.

A major motive of the National Party in passing the Immorality Act and other Apartheid measures, including those requiring race classification documents, was to prevent Coloureds from secretly passing as white. The criteria for formal racial reclassification were difficult to meet, and an amendment in 1967 made the tests still tighter. Under Apartheid the motivation for Coloureds to "pass" has been stronger than ever: to gain better opportunities for upward mobility, to avoid humiliation and inconvenience, to avoid harsh criminal prosecution as nonwhites, or to facilitate intermarriage with whites. Many Coloureds sympathize with those who pass, while others resent the loss to their own community of the most educated and skilled members. The Coloured elites consider those who make the status leap over them to white status to be upstarts and traitors. Although passing requires official reclassification to a different racial category, it is still occurring to a considerable degree, especially in urban neighborhoods that have the poorer whites and the "better class" of Coloureds. Passing is facilitated by the infinite gradations of racial traits among the Coloureds, as it also is in the United States, so that many mixed persons appear white (Watson, 1970:10–24). However, far from being secret, as in the United States, the process is open and legalized in the Republic of South Africa.

The bureaucracy employed to classify South Africans by race groups is large, cumbersome, and inconsistent. Different members of a family may be designated differently, and some individuals and couples have had their classifications changed more than once. Persons may request reclassification and may appeal local board decisions to a Population Registration Board and the nation's Supreme Court. The bureaucracy reflects local public opinion, and whites often find it helpful to cooperate with those who want to pass. For instance, school principals in all-white schools can keep up their enrollments by getting some Coloured children reclassified as whites, but if principals push too hard they run the risk of having the school itself reclassified as Coloured (Watson, 1970:50). Neighbors and work associates must go along if an attempt to pass is to succeed, and this cooperation is often forthcoming. Aspiring "pass-whites" must not only look white but also prove that they are accepted as such in both informal and more institutional situations. Appropriate class behavior must be demonstrated, such as having the right occupation, income, social club, and church, so that it is clear the person "acts white." Despite the bureaucratic hurdles and the strong determination of the government to prevent passing, it occurs because it is often in the interest of both the Coloured person and influential local whites (Watson, 1970: chap. 4). Such reclassification could not occur if there were a one-drop rule.

Stung by their considerable loss of status and severe treatment by whites under Apartheid, Coloureds have identified increasingly with the nonwhite groups and less and less with the white community. They are still treated better than blacks are, and increased education has enabled many to move into the middle class. However, Coloureds aspire to achieve according to white values, and their schools, job opportunities, housing, community facilities, political participation, and freedom of movement are all restricted and inferior to those of whites. Not only have they been experiencing relative deprivation in comparison with whites, but since 1948 they have suffered marked setbacks, after having experienced gains and rising expectations. These are the frustrating conditions under which minority groups are most likely to organize and support protest actions, as blacks in the United States did in the 1950s and 1960s. Moreover, the more sudden and drastic the setbacks, after hopes have risen, the more likely the protests are to turn violent (Davies, 1971:133–37; Wilson, 1973:132–36). From the 1950s on, much of the protest against Apartheid has been by Coloureds against their segregated and unequal schools, the punishing complexities of crowded and segregated transportation, high bus fares, and other conditions. In the current crisis the Coloured leaders are inclining more and more toward alignment with black labor, black churches, and other black protest organizations. Growing alienation of Coloureds from whites has increased the number and intensity of the protests.

The National Party believes that maintaining both the Asians and the Coloureds as buffer groups bolsters continued white control and that the number of Coloureds must be limited by preventing further miscegenation. We have seen that the Immorality Act was designed to prevent all white-nonwhite sexual contacts, not just those involving white women. Although the act has been repealed, informal controls effectively prevent white-nonwhite liaisons. Apartheid has made it necessary to distinguish racially mixed persons sharply from the other groups. The implied rule, that racial hybrids shall have a separate identity with an in-between status, is a clear rejection of the one-drop rule.

Both Apartheid and Jim Crow were designed to keep power in white hands. Passing as white has occurred in both systems, but in significantly different ways, because the different social structures have required different rules for defining who is black. The longtime exception in the Charleston and New Orleans areas, allowing free mulattoes an in-between status, had to give way to the one-drop rule. Both under Jim Crow and under Apartheid, the repressive imposition of white control has shifted the allegiance of mulattoes away from whites and toward blacks. If this trend continues in South Africa, the Coloureds will be less and less effective as a buffer group, and white control will be more difficult to maintain.

HIGHLY VARIABLE CLASS STATUS: LATIN AMERICA

On a network television talk show in New York in 1982, a woman singer from Jamaica said in her clipped British accent, "I like to do black songs sometimes. I am half black, you know." How startling this must have sounded to American listeners, black and white alike, so accustomed to defining as black a person with any black ancestry at all. Could she really mean that she is not a black and acknowledges only some black heritage? That is, of course, what she meant. North Americans do not easily grasp the meaning of this fourth type of position of racially mixed people, a variable status that depends more on social class than on color or other racial traits. This type is found in Latin America and on the islands in the Caribbean Sea, as well as in Europe.

We must note the significant variations of this fourth type as well as the common features. The same person defined as black in the United States may be considered "coloured" in Jamaica or Martinique and white in Puerto Rico or the Dominican Republic (Hoetink, 1967:xii). We have already noted that the Mestizos are dominant in Mexico and that there are relatively few blacks and mulattoes. Otherwise, we may say that the upper class in lowland Latin America is called white but that it also includes many light mulattoes and Mestizos. Except in the French, British, and Dutch Caribbean islands, the upper class continues to absorb light mulattoes with visible negroid traits and Mestizos, by marriage. In general, the middle class is composed mostly of mulattoes, and many Mestizos in some countries, but also of small numbers of whites and unmixed blacks. The middle class is a long ladder with many rungs, not a rigid, single status. The lower class includes most of the unmixed blacks and Indians, along with some mulattoes, Mestizos, and a few whites. Despite the plethora of terms for the innumerable gradations of racial mixture, the color designation applied to a family or person depends more on the place on the class ladder than on racial traits. Race influences class placement, but it is only one factor and it may be overcome. These broad statements are best understood within particular national contexts. The discussion here is concerned mainly with Brazil, Colombia, Puerto Rico, and the two subtypes of status in the Caribbean islands, both of which have counterparts in Europe.

Unmixed Indians in Latin America who adopt the modified European lifestyles tend to be identified as Mestizos, so that whether one is considered an Indian or a Mestizo is a matter more of culture than of racial ancestry. Unmixed Africans, however, are generally considered to be blacks irrespective of their cultural styles. The racially mixed people, the "people of color," are accorded much more favorable treatment than the unmixed Africans. In fact, the class placement of and terms of racial classification for individual mulattoes and Mestizos depend heavily on lifestyle, especially on economic and educational achievement. One explanation is that unmixed blacks differ racially more from Latin American whites than either Indians or mulattoes do, and that social distance is directly correlated with the degree of the perceived physical differences. Whatever the reasons, Latin Americans can accept light mulattoes and Mestizos as whites, referring to any visible traces of African traits in such euphemistic terms as "brunette" or "a little mulatto." The Spanish term *morena* connotes an ideal type of beauty and may refer either to brunette Iberians or to mulattoes or other racially mixed types. *Morena* means Moorish and is sometimes defined as the darkest a person can be and still be considered white (Solaún and Kronus, 1973:3–9, 56). In Brazil it appears to be possible but very difficult to overcome the stigma of being an unmixed black, while in the rest of Latin America it seems to be impossible.

During the early colonial period in lowland Brazil there was heavy mixing between the Portuguese and the Indians, producing a Mestizo group with a status between the white masters and the Indian slave caste. The Portuguese brought in well over three million African slave workers during the seventeenth and eighteenth centuries alone, resulting in massive miscegenation and another in-between group. Manumission was very frequent, and the freed Mestizos and mulattoes were given special treatment, often educated, and valued as buffer groups. Several social strata emerged between slaves and masters, the mixed groups eventually outnumbering both African blacks and whites. Unmixed blacks were also often manumitted, further complicating the picture, and in 1888 all slaves were freed. Many blacks intermarried with Mestizos, a frequent phenomenon also in Peru and elsewhere in Latin America. Being African black continued to be associated with the bottom rank. As some whites slipped downward in status, new immigrants from Europe and elsewhere came and often prospered, so that the older caste system was replaced by a complex class structure.

Brazil's emerging class system had a large and very poor lower class, a rapidly growing middle class, and limited upward mobility across rigidly drawn class lines. Class placement of a family or person came to depend on several criteria, including income, occupation, education, family position, and racial appearance, the latter being more important in some communities and regions than in others. Being light has tended to facilitate a higher placement within the middle and lower classes, yet race can be outweighed by other factors. A fairly dark mulatto who is prosperous and educated may even be called white, but an unmixed black can never be. Light mulattoes have been admitted to marriage in the upper class, even when they have obvious African (or Indian) traits. Darker color, however, has meant almost certain exclusion, especially from the upper-upper stratum. Otherwise, the preference for lighter color throughout the class structure is mild and has little effect on behavior. The correlation between color and class is not high, and there is no rigid racial caste line (Wagley, 1963:143–58).

Racial classification in Brazil is informal and reflects the policy and practice of amalgamation rather than systematic segregation and concern for racial purity. The implied rule is that a person is classified into one of many possible types on the basis of physical appearance and class standing, not by ancestry. The designation of one's racial identity need not be the same as that of the parents, and siblings are often classified differently from one another. There are many alternatives from which to choose, depending on variations in hair color, hair texture, eye color, and skin color. The same Brazilian may be referred to by many different Portuguese terms of racial classification, and there is even disagreement about the meaning of the terms of reference. In a study in a fishing village in the state of Bahia, in which one hundred Brazilians were asked to classify seven portraits, forty different terms for racial types were used (Harris, 1964:57–58). Moreover, as people climb the class ladder by educational and economic success, their racial designations often change. No secrecy or change of residence is needed to "pass" to another racial identity, and it is a common aspect of upward mobility. The expression "money whitens" indicates that class can have more weight than physical traits in determining racial classification. Brazilian census estimates for racial categories thus provide better information on the class structure than on racial composition, and comparisons with the number of persons counted as black in the United States are very misleading.

There are no Brazilian groups whose identities are based exclusively on racial criteria. *Preto* (black or very dark) and *branco* (white) are not definite social groups with an assigned status. There are *preto* stereotypes, anti-*preto* attitudes, and a belief in *preto* inferiority, and whiteness is generally preferred to blackness. However, *preto* identity is rebuttable by educational and economic achievement, and a person is not just black, mulatto, white, or any other specific racial designation. It is position on the class ladder, not race, that determines who gets into the club, and each class includes a wide spectrum of racial types. It is class discrimination rather than racial discrimination that is pervasive, sharp, and persistent, even involving class-segregated public facilities and a class-based master-servant etiquette. Being poor and having restricted opportunities is made only a little worse by being dark-skinned. For Brazilians, poor or rich, classes exist, but definite race groups do not (Harris, 1964:59–61).

Probably one reason the Portuguese in Brazil embraced amalgamation and rejected the one-drop rule was the scarcity of European women, which led to widespread unions with Indian women and later with black slave women. It is often suggested that the Portuguese and the Spanish brought with them greater color tolerance than did the British and other Northwest Europeans, due to five hundred years of contact with the Moors. The Portuguese tradition of concubinage, along with the strong traditional attachment of parents to their offspring, may also have contributed. If the one-drop (or hypo-descent) rule had been adopted, the children of these racially mixed marriages would have been assigned to a lower status than that of their European fathers. The Roman Catholic church has also been more tolerant of miscegenation, at least after the natives are converted, than have the Protestant denominations (Berry, 1965:137–38).

However, it has also been argued that initially the major reason for rejecting a one-drop rule was that Brazilian whites needed the freed mulattoes and Mestizos to perform some specific middle-minority economic functions and to be a buffer between the large slave population and the smaller European group. By contrast, Southern whites in the United States greatly outnumbered their slaves, and they also had a large group of poor whites (indentured servants at first) to act as a buffer group. Both during and after slavery in North America, the wealthier whites exploited and controlled the poor whites and encouraged anti-black attitudes and actions to keep blacks under control. Thus, North America had a built-in white middle minority, while Brazil needed free mulattoes and Mestizos to fill that role. The contrasting ratios of whites to nonwhites resulted from the fact that Portugal and Spain feared depopulation and thus restricted migration to their colonies, while England encouraged emigration to remove surplus small farmers and even unloaded large numbers of criminals and the poor on its colonies (Harris, 1964: chap. 7). In the United States the one-drop rule was adopted in order to maintain white domination (see Chapters 3 and 4). In Brazil the middle-minority position of mulattoes gave way to a highly variable status, in a society where amalgamation continues to be embraced and where class overshadows race.

Researchers in Cartagena, Colombia, in the early 1970s observed both mulattoes and whites in all three major social classes and no unmixed blacks in the upper class. Lightness was preferred, and blackness was inversely related to class standing, and there were acts of discrimination as well as attitudes of prejudice against unmixed blacks. However, group tensions and conflicts were based on class differences, not race. The lack of race conflict was attributed to the availability to mulattoes of upward mobility and to the distribution of racially mixed persons throughout the class structure. Mulatto experience in Latin America generally was likened to that of European ethnic groups in the United States, for whom acculturation and upward mobility have overcome prejudice and discrimination, resulting in eventual acceptance and intermarriage into the dominant community. In Cartagena the terms of reference to racial identities were being used differently in different situations, were often used euphemistically, and referred to personal physical traits instead of racial categories. Racial identity was found to be flexible, ambiguous, dependent on dress and context, and negotiated rather than being rigidly assigned (Solaún and Kronus, 1973:33–35 and chaps. 5, 6, 7).

In Puerto Rico, miscegenation of whites, native Indians, and African blacks has produced the entire range of skin color and other racial features. Unmixed Africans and the darkest mulattoes are disproportionately concentrated at the bottom of the class ladder, and black skin color is the least preferred. Some color discrimination has been alleged in job hirings and promotions and in interpersonal relations, but color does not appear to affect access to education, and Puerto Ricans generally insist that color is not of major importance in their lives (Tumin and Feldman, 1969:204–14). The terms for racial identities indicate gradations of color and have varied meanings, including *branco* (white), *negra* (African black), *mulata* (mulatto), and *trigueño* (wheat-colored, olive-skinned, brunette, attractively dark). *Trigueño* connotes a status almost equal to that of *branco*, and even some unmixed whites (as well as blacks) prefer to be identified by this favorable term (Tumin, 1969: chap. 11). *Trigueño* may be used to indicate a nonwhite person when one wants to avoid saying *prieta* (very dark, swarthy) or *negra*, terms generally considered offensive. *Grifa* (someone with frizzy hair but light skin and caucasian facial features) and *jabá* (someone with light skin but African facial features or frizzy hair) are often used interchangeably (Jorge, 1979:134–35). Throughout the Caribbean, such terms of reference have uncertain meanings, and individuals are allowed some choice and room to negotiate for a racial identity (Dominguez, 1986:273–77).

A substantial proportion of racially mixed Puerto Ricans who are successful and educated are considered white, including many who might otherwise be described by such terms as *trigueña, mulata, jabá,* or *grifa.* As elsewhere in Latin America and the Caribbean, class position can outweigh physical traits in the designation of racial identity. About 10 percent of the Puerto Ricans who have migrated to the United States are unmixed blacks, and half or more of the remainder have some African ancestry. Thus, some three-fifths of the migrants are perceived in the United States as being black, while in Puerto Rico most of these were known either as whites or by one of the many color designations other than black. It is a shock to the majority of the migrants—and not just to those mulattoes who were previously known as whites—to be called black in the United States, which recognizes no racial categories between black and white. Some migrants who are not too African in appearance manage to become known as Hispanic whites by emphasizing their Spanish language and heritage, but some fail in this attempt. Puerto Ricans in New York City are listed as white unless they are quite dark and have African features. During World War II all Puerto Ricans in the U.S. Army were in segregated camps, even in Puerto Rico, and the U.S. Navy refused to accept any Puerto Ricans (Marden and Meyer, 1973:340).

When Puerto Ricans designated by the terms *negra* and *prieta* migrate to the mainland, they are not surprised at being treated as blacks, but in the immigrant community their families put heavy pressure on their young to "whiten" the family by marrying a light mulatto or a white. This means avoiding contact with the majority of American blacks, who have great difficulty understanding this prejudice. Within the barrio the *negra* and *prieta* types are Puerto Ricans, but outside they are perceived simply as blacks. The families hope that "whitening" will help their progeny climb the class ladder and eventually have descendants light enough to pass as white by stressing their Spanish heritage (Jorge, 1979:135–41). In

Puerto Rico the many gradations of racial identity are less important than class position. Those who migrate to the United States, whatever their physical traits, face the difficult transition to life in a racially polarized society with a one-drop rule.

Plantation slavery was experienced throughout the West Indies, both on the Iberian (Spanish and Portuguese) islands and on those colonized by Northwest Europeans (the British, French, and Dutch). Miscegenation of Indians, whites, and African blacks has been extensive on all the islands, although on some islands the Indians were decimated by disease and economic exploitation. Everywhere concern about color variations occupies much time and energy, in relation to anxieties about position on the class ladder. Perhaps one-third of all the islanders are mulattoes (Lowenthal, 1969: chap. 16), with the high percentages generally on the Iberian islands and the low ones on the islands in the Northwestern European mode. About 73 percent of the people in the Spanish-speaking Dominican Republic are considered mulatto, and 11 percent unmixed black. On the western end of the same island of Hispaniola, in French-colonized Haiti, mulattoes are well outnumbered by the unmixed blacks. Jamaica and Barbados estimate from 15 to 16 percent mulatto and more than 75 percent unmixed black. The British colonials brought in indentured workers from India, especially on Trinidad and Tobago, where the population on both islands is now 40 percent East Indian and many people are mixed African and Asian.

TWO VARIANTS IN THE CARIBBEAN

All the Caribbean islands were long dominated by whites, and many still are, at least economically, with unmixed blacks largely at the bottom and mulattoes ("coloureds") comprising the bulk of the multilayered middle class. Earlier we noted the exception of Haiti, where the mulattoes assumed control after the French were overthrown in 1804. Light color has everywhere facilitated upward mobility, as we have seen in Puerto Rico, yet wealth and education are more important. Sexual contacts between whites and African blacks have generally been illicit, since whites have not married unmixed blacks. The main difference between the two West Indian patterns is that the Iberian whites have continuously married lighter mulattoes who have visible African traits, while the Northwest Europeans have married only those who appear white (Hoetink, 1967:39–41).

One suggested explanation for the difference in the two West Indian patterns is that the human physical image idealized by the Iberians is somewhat darker than that of the Northwest Europeans. Both groups reject the image of the unmixed black. Further, it is suggested, the ideal image the Iberians brought with them allowed for the inclusion of light mulatto features, due to the lengthy Moorish occupation of Spain and Portugal. Thus they could accept light mulattoes with visible African features in close personal relationships, including marriage, while the Northwest Europeans generally could not. Perhaps also the Roman Catholic church fostered a warmer relationship between masters on the one hand and slaves and their offspring on the other. The explanation includes the view that the intimacy of sexual contact with mulattoes is acceptable to the Iberians but not to the Northwest Europeans (Hoetink, 1967: parts 2 and 3), but this is belied by the frequency of illicit sexual contacts between both of the European groups and blacks and mulattoes. What the Northwest Europeans have not accepted is close social relationships and intermarriage with mulattoes whose appearance indicates some black ancestry, but without widespread illicit miscegenation there would have been no mixed groups on those islands. The same point applies in the United States, where illicit interracial sexual contacts have never been lacking.

Even though both the Northwest Europeans in the Caribbean and whites in the United States generally reject marriage with mulattoes who have discernible negroid traits, the former do not have a one-drop rule that defines anyone who has any African ancestry as a black. The British, French, and Dutch in the West Indies have been concerned enough about African ancestry, or at least about color, to exclude persons with any visible negroid characteristics from their families. However, in colonial times they accepted as legally white all persons with one-sixteenth known African ancestry, and by special legislation they sometimes accepted those whose known fractions were one-eighth black, one-fourth, or even more. Even the British in the Caribbean have readily married persons with known black ancestry as long as they appear to be white. Being white has been a matter of appearance, not of ancestry, so there is no anxiety about "invisible blackness." Nowhere in the Caribbean or Latin America is there a one-drop rule that defines mulattoes of all descriptions, including those who look white, as blacks.

Another approach to explaining the difference in the two West Indian patterns emphasizes differences in the plantation slave systems. This approach may also explain why the color line was drawn so differently in the British West Indies and in the United States, both of which were under the influence of British culture. Only the British West Indies are discussed here, although the French and Dutch patterns are largely similar to those of the British. We should note that colonial treatment of the "free people of color" in the British West Indies was similar in important ways to the pattern that prevailed in South Carolina and Louisiana until the mid-nineteenth century. Concubinage was openly practiced by the West Indian British colonials, and most white males had a black or brown mistress. Usually the fathers acknowledged their children and freed them from slavery. Most of the children were educated, some in England, and were willed substantial amounts of property. Being free, educated, and having some economic means, the free "coloured" people had a very different status from that of the African slaves, and they identified with their European ancestry and culture.

Despite their favored status, the free "coloureds" in the British West Indies were not accepted as whites as long as they had any visible African traits. They could not cross the castelike line into white clubs and families, so they had to develop their own separate social activities, many of which were subject to legal restrictions. On colonial Jamaica, Trinidad, and the other British islands, free "coloureds" were legally prevented from voting, holding public office, holding military officers' commissions, marrying whites, or inheriting property worth more than certain amounts from a white person. Even so, the free "coloureds" had a special status between slaves and whites which was superior to the position of the freed unmixed blacks. Moreover, those free "coloureds" who appeared white could be accepted as fully white regardless of known black ancestry (Horowitz, 1973:510–13). The one-drop rule is not inherent in British culture, then, or in that of Northwest Europe generally, despite the traditional Germanic view that racial hybrids are flawed. In fact, the implied rule in Great Britain and Northern Europe is like the Northwest European variant in the Caribbean.

In both West Indian patterns the three general categories of color stratification emerged: white, coloured, and (unmixed) black. The British borrowed from the Spanish the complex set of terms that refer to the gradations of color in the "whitening" process, and wealth and education helped "coloureds" to climb up the long ladder within the middle class, outcompeting and passing some of the poor, uneducated whites. On Barbados the poorest and least educated whites have continued to be an underclass group, the so-called Redlegs, economically exploited as much as the blacks by the colonial system (Simmons, 1976:13–22). Upward mobility became more restricted for "coloureds" on the British islands than on the Iberian islands, and color became more difficult to overcome by achievements. We have already noted the legal limitations placed on free "mulattoes" by the British, including the forbidding of marriage with whites. Even so, the West Indian British placed the "coloureds" in a restricted middle position rather than force them to accept the status of unmixed blacks (Horowitz, 1973:515–20).

In the British colonial West Indies, the free "coloureds" tended to become urban and marginal to plantation life. Rather than filling middle-minority economic gaps in the plantation economy, they came to play a key role in preventing and controlling slave uprisings, which had a long history in the Caribbean. Large numbers of slaves were imported to boost the production of sugar and other crops, until they far outnumbered whites on the British and other Northwest European islands. In Jamaica, after the mid-eighteenth century, slaves outnumbered whites by ten to one. Adequate military assistance was unavailable from Great Britain, unmixed black troops were considered unreliable, and there were too few American Indians for the task. A major motive for manumitting mulattoes was to use them as soldiers to combat rebellions, and they were given strong incentives to remain loyal to the whites and to adopt British culture (Horowitz, 1973:530–38).

All Jamaican "coloureds" were freed and given full rights in 1830, after which they challenged the slave system and other white policies; yet they worked within the political system rather than rebelling (Heuman, 1981). The free "coloureds" became Europeanized allies of the British West Indians and achieved a middle status that was to remain distinctly separate from that of unmixed blacks after slavery was ended. Under British colonial restrictions the position of free "coloureds" was not very different from the middle-minority, buffer status of Coloureds in South Africa. Now, however, their position is more similar to the variable status of their counterparts on the Iberian islands in the Caribbean, although with somewhat less flexibility and upward mobility.

Just as the Northwest European variant in the Caribbean seems to reflect the implied rule for assigning social status to racially mixed persons in Northern Europe, the Iberian variant mirrors what seems to be the general rule in Southern Europe and in the Near and Middle East. Although European societies have valued lightness over blackness for two millennia or more, they have absorbed at least small numbers of African blacks, more in Portugal then elsewhere. Southern Europeans have been more accepting of amalgamation and open to intermarriage with mulattoes who have visible negroid traits. North Europeans, although less tolerant of physical differences and more prone to hold racist beliefs, have accepted intermarriage with persons of known African black ancestry if they appear white and have the desired class attributes. Until recent decades the main contact Europeans had with nonwhite peoples was in colonial situations, where the status outcomes varied considerably with local conditions. Perhaps studies will show that the mixed progeny of the sizable groups of nonwhites now in Northern Europe are becoming middle minorities (status type 3) or assimilating minorities (type 7) rather than the Northwest European variant of type 4. At any rate, neither Northern nor Southern Europe has had a one-drop rule.

EQUALITY FOR THE RACIALLY MIXED IN HAWAII

The status of racially mixed people in the Hawaiian Islands and in Latin America is similar in that their class placement can range from very low to very high, depending on economic and educational achievement. The key difference is that color and other racial traits do not affect the class position of racially mixed persons in Hawaii as they do in Latin America and the Caribbean. There is no color ladder with a preferred hue at the top, and no great preoccupation with color. Hawaii was admitted as the fiftieth state in 1959, and since then the nation's one-drop rule has presumably been the law there, if not since 1900 when the islands became a territory of the United States. However, Hawaii has a long tradition of treating the racially mixed in a very different way, and the one-drop rule does not fit. This tradition represents a fifth type of status of racially mixed people.

The original Hawaiian settlers came from the Marquesas Islands about 1,500 years ago, followed by a migration from Tahiti (Howard, 1980:449). They were Polynesians, who apparently were already racially mixed, possibly due to the mingling of mongoloid peoples from Southeast Asia and caucasoid stocks from Indonesia, South Asia, or even the Middle East. Ever since the first Haoles (non-Polynesians) arrived, miscegenation of many different peoples has characterized life on the Hawaiian Islands. The survivors of two Spanish ships wrecked in the mid-sixteenth century fathered many children on the islands. Captain Cook, who arrived in 1778, found that Hawaiian hospitality included openness to both sexual relations and marriage with outsiders. After 1778 the Haoles never stopped coming, first for a waystation in the fur trade, next for sandalwood, then for whales, then for sugarcane, pineapples, and other agricultural products, and finally as tourists. Many white traders and planters took Hawaiian wives. Congregational missionaries arrived from New England in 1820, and some of their children eventually became partners in racially mixed marriages.

The escalating demand in the 1850s for labor in the sugar cane fields could not be met by the native Hawaiians, who were unused to monotonous field work and whose numbers were being drastically lowered by the diseases brought from the outside world. The planters first imported large numbers of workers from China, later several thousand Portuguese and other Europeans, and still later far larger numbers of Japanese. By 1900 the Japanese had become the largest ethnic group, comprising 40 percent of the population, while Hawaiians and part-Hawaiians were about 25 percent (Day, 1960:233; Howard, 1980:450). After the turn of the twentieth century several thousand Puerto Ricans and Koreans were imported, more Portuguese, and finally Filipinos (Berry, 1965:139–40). Probably at least half of these Puerto Ricans and some of the Portuguese had African black ancestry, in varying degrees. The small number of blacks in the islands between World Wars I and II were treated with respect, as equals (Adams, 1969:82). In recent decades many immigrants have come from the United States mainland, the Philippines, South Asia and East Asia, the Pacific Islands (Tahiti, Samoa, Tonga, Fiji, and others), Mexico, several European nations, the Middle East, and elsewhere. In response to the 1980 census, about 33 percent of the population designated "white" as their racial identity, less than 2 percent "black," and about 67 percent "other."

When Captain Cook arrived, there were about 300,000 Hawaiians. At the low point in 1910 there were only 38,547 native Hawaiians and part-Hawaiians combined. By 1930 there were more part-Hawaiians than unmixed ones, and in 1960 nearly nine times as many. The part-Hawaiian category was dropped in the 1970 census. A health survey conducted by the State of Hawaii in the mid-1970s found 151,652 Hawaiians and part-Hawaiians, making them the third largest population in the state (18.3 percent), behind the whites and the Japanese. However, this was based on having at least one native great-grandparent, which means being one-eighth Hawaiian or more, so that probably most of these people were part-Hawaiians. When it comes to self-designation, one person of mixed background might claim the Hawaiian identity while another with more native heredity does not. Moreover, many people on the islands change their ethnicity as they move from one situation to another (Howard, 1980:449–51).

The contest among Great Britain, Japan, and the United States as to which outside power would "protect" the Hawaiian Islands became intense during the last quarter of the nineteenth century, and the native rulers were caught in the crossfire. Queen Liliuokalani was deposed in 1893 by a series of relatively nonviolent maneuvers that were controlled by white economic interests tied to the United States. A republic was established in 1894, headed by Sanford B. Dole, who was the first governor when Hawaii became a territory of the United States in 1900 (Day, 1960:199–232). The native Hawaiians had already lost much of their land to Haole interests, and they continued to lose more. The generous chiefs, traditionally more concerned about good social relations than material goods, made land concessions too often and too cheaply. Today segments of the native and part-Hawaiian population have high rates of unemployment, poverty, and disease. In the 1970s a revival of traditional culture began, and there have been grievances about the economic, educational, legal, and political problems of the native and mixed Hawaiians, and charges of ethnic prejudice and discrimination, past and present, at the hands of wealthy whites and other groups.

Despite the eventual wresting of political and economic power from the original Hawaiians, and some undeniable tensions among the ethnic groups, the history of the islands has generally not been racist. The competitive struggles and occasional conflicts have essentially been those of class, and both individuals and entire ethnic groups have been able to ascend the ladder and vie for economic and political power. There has been no systematic racial segregation and discrimination, either de jure or de facto, and people generally are scornful of anyone who exhibits racial prejudice. Hawaii has been considerably Americanized, yet other traditions thrive, and members of all groups are shown respect in the *aloha* tradition. There is peaceful coexistence of groups with different cultures (cultural pluralism) and much social participation within the confines of the different ethnic communities (structural pluralism).

At the same time, there is much blending of the various ethnic traditions (cultural assimilation, of the melting pot variety), along with participation by members of all ethnic groups in both organized and informal activities in the common life of the community (structural assimilation). People from all groups interact not only in school, work, and other public settings, but also in small friendship groups and in recreational activities. Police officers, school administrators, government officials, business employers or managers, or professionals may all come from any ethnic group and often have racially mixed ancestry. Ethnic and racial intermarriages are quite common, and many people can identify ancestry in several different groups. It is considered bad manners to express disapproval of miscegenation (Berry, 1965:138–39; Adams, 1969:82). The tolerant, equalitarian balance of pluralism and assimilation is extended to racially mixed persons, whose status is not lower or higher than that of anyone else in Hawaii and whose upward mobility is not restrained by racial considerations.

The favorable treatment of the racially mixed is probably in part a result of their large numbers in Hawaii and also of the multiplicity of the parent groups. However, the crucial determinant seems to have been the tolerant, equalitarian traditions of the original Hawaiians, combined with the small numbers of the first Haoles and their desire to reap economic benefits rather than exterminate, enslave, or rule the natives. The Hawaiians were not conquered, relocated, or immediately subjugated, and they remained strongly organized until the end of the nineteenth century. They did not feel inferior, and it was beneficial for Haoles to deal with them as equals. White settlers were treated as esteemed consultants on the ways of outsiders and often married the daughters of Hawaiian chiefs. Thus, the first racial hybrids were highly respected, and this model has had a lasting impact. It is still prestigious to be part-Hawaiian. The pattern of ethnic and racial tolerance and respect was accepted by later arrivals, eventually including the missionaries (Berry, 1965:141–42; Adams, 1969:84–90).

It seems reasonable to assume that most recent white migrants to Hawaii from the mainland United States are at first inclined to perceive and treat the small African black population as they did back home, but also that this outlook usually changes because it conflicts so sharply with the general pattern of race relations on the islands. Earlier in the century, at least, white newcomers typically accepted the island pattern within a few months of their arrival (Adams, 1969:86–87). Many of the Pacific Island peoples are relatively dark-skinned, and the class status of the mixed people seems to be unaffected by color or other racial traits. Whether blacks are becoming part of this pattern or an exception to it in recent years is not clear and is in need of study. Perhaps the percentage of those with African ancestry who checked "other" rather than "black" in the 1980 census is higher than on the mainland, but it is also possible that recent black migrants tend to support the one-drop rule and resist total amalgamation and assimilation in Hawaii, as they generally do back home. On the mainland the one-drop rule applies to no group other than blacks, and that is still presumably the law of the entire United States. It remains to be seen whether that rule will prevail in Hawaii or whether persons with black ancestry will blend into the melting pot the same way other racial and ethnic groups have in the islands.

SAME STATUS AS THE SUBORDINATE GROUP: THE ONE-DROP RULE

We come now to the sixth status, the one occupied in the United States by all persons with any black ancestry. The one-drop, or hypo-descent, rule assigns all such persons to the status of the subordinate group, which in this case means blacks. Consider the instance of Harry S. Murphy, who alleged in 1962 that he, not James Meredith, was the first black to be admitted to the University of Mississippi, where he attended for nine months without attracting any attention because he looks white. In Latin America, Murphy would most likely be defined as white, but certainly not as black—which there usually means unmixed black (Harris, 1964:56). Noting the social conditions under which the other types of status have emerged and operated helps to place our own in better perspective.

We have traced the emergence of the one-drop rule in the United States, and its competition for a time with a status rule that is similar to the one for mulattoes in the British West Indies (see Chapters 3 and 4). We have also noted that American slave owners wanted to keep all racially mixed children born to slave women under their control, for economic and sexual gains, and that to define such children as anything other than black became a major threat to the entire system. It was intolerable for white women to have mixed children, so the one-drop rule favored the sexual freedom of white males, protecting the double standard of sexual morality as well as slavery. After the Civil War, because of the great fear of miscegenation involving Southern white women, mulattoes were increasingly alienated from whites. Instead of developing into a status group between black and white, representing either the third or fourth type discussed above, the lighter mulattoes provided the foundation for the upper-upper class in the American black community. The whites had left no alternative—a person either passed as white or remained black (Ottley, 1943:168–69). Even so, some ambiguities remained for a time.

Much of the repressive control of slavery was revived in the Jim Crow system, under which the one-drop rule was crystallized. The rule came to be accepted nationwide, by blacks as well as whites, in law as well as in custom. The Black Renaissance of the 1920s, and also the one nearly a half-century later, symbolized and enhanced the identification of mulattoes of all shades with black pride. The Jim Crow system was brought down in the 1950s and 1960s, and some gains were scored against de facto segregation as well, but the one-drop rule only grew stronger. The irony is that this is the rule that emerged to protect slavery and later to bolster Jim Crow segregation. There was no other rational argument for defining as black a half-white person, or one much more white than half but with at least one black ancestor, except that such a rule supported slavery and the Jim Crow system. In the words of a well-known anthropologist (Harris, 1964:56), "We have gone so far as to create Alice-in-Wonderland kinds of Negroes about whom people say, 'He certainly doesn't look like a Negro!' "

The Mississippi Chinese and their racially mixed offspring provided an interesting test of how the one-drop rule operates in the South. Their experience began during Reconstruction after the Civil War (Loewen, 1971), in the area of the Yazoo-Mississippi Delta in the northwestern part of the state, a flat plain 60 miles wide and 180 miles long that was cleared after the Civil War. Most of the sharecroppers brought in were blacks, but whites feared the newly won voting power of the former slaves, who were voting Republican. Chinese workers were recruited partly because they were not expected to become interested in citizenship and voting, but also because they had proven their capacity for hard work in building the railroads in the West. Most of the Chinese still in the delta in 1970 were descended from those who were recruited in 1869 and 1870.

The Mississippi whites at first perceived the Chinese essentially the same way they saw blacks, since most of them came in as sharecroppers. But within the first year, the Chinese began to leave the cotton fields to become grocers in the crossroads trading centers, and their economic status began to rise. During the next several decades their economic position improved considerably, raising their overall status as an ethnic group in the community. For a time they were considered neither black nor white and were relegated to an ambiguous, in-between status. In fact, during the 1930s and 1940s there was a system of triple segregation for the public schools of Cleveland, Greenville, and a number of other delta towns, with separate buildings for the whites, the blacks, and the Chinese. By the 1950s the buildings for the Chinese were abandoned and the children were admitted to white schools. Then the Chinese were also permitted to use other white public facilities, while the Jim Crow laws were still in effect. They felt the ambiguity of a status that seemed almost white but tenuous, and they still experienced discrimination. For example, Chinese teachers were not hired for white schools.

The experience of these Chinese Americans stands in sharp contrast to that of the Mexican Americans in the delta. The Chinese Americans first crossed one castelike color line and later another. The Mexican Americans had also been recruited as sharecroppers during Reconstruction, but they were never able to rise above that status. In 1970 the Mexican Americans were still below the color line, defined in Mississippi as blacks. School desegregation had been ordered by then, after the key Supreme Court decision of 1969 (see Chapter 4), but blacks and Mexican Americans were still heavily segregated in 1970, and Jim Crow was not yet dead.

The Chinese made the move into the crossroads grocery business to improve their economic position, which they could not do as sharecroppers. Although most had been village farmers in China, hard work in family commercial enterprises was traditionally valued in the areas from which they had migrated, along with the sharing of capital within the extended family. However, the delta Chinese could not have assumed the role of a middle minority if a special niche had not opened up in the structure of compulsory segregation in the sharecropping system. The whites did not want to sell groceries to blacks or do the manual labor of unloading wagons and stocking shelves. Most of the former slaves knew only farming and had no experience in small business. There were also some Lebanese, Syrians, Jews, and Italians who became small merchants in the delta, but usually in the larger towns. The delta Chinese were able to seize the rural opportunity when it opened up because they were on the land when the economic gap occurred.

Their small numbers helped the Mississippi Chinese to use their rising economic status to pull the group as a whole above the color line. Also, they remained nonpolitical and were motivated to succeed within the system rather than try to change it. As cultural outsiders they could appear not to understand the racial etiquette very well and be allowed some deviation from it. They remained flexible and alert to opportunities. Although there were tensions, and white opposition to their rise in group status, they avoided overt conflicts. Keeping much of their own culture, they developed a lifestyle visibly different from that of the black sharecroppers, being careful to speak, walk, and even dance more like the whites. They established homes away from the stores, became acquainted with white ministers, bankers, and wholesalers, and slowly persuaded the white community to open its schools, hospitals, and other white facilities to them.

We can now understand how miscegenation affected this remarkable process. Most of the delta Chinese recruits were single men, and at one time as many as one-fourth of them were married to black women. Then, observing that marrying blacks and having mixed children was a barrier to their rise in status as a group, the Chinese deliberately rejected further sexual contact and marriage with blacks. They stopped associating with Chinese who married blacks, unless the latter were willing to abandon their black families. Not accepted by the Chinese or the whites, and accepted only partly by the blacks, all but twelve of these mixed families had moved out of the delta by 1970. By then the Chinese as a whole were also leaving, but 90 percent of the remaining 1,200 were still in rural grocery stores. This status gap was disappearing, however, as the mechanization of agriculture brought the sharecropping system to its end. This middle minority was the target of some threats and violence in the crisis over desegregating the schools, which hastened their exodus from the delta. Their amazing feat of rising as a group above the color bar had been bought at the cost of rejecting their fellows who would not leave their black wives and mixed offspring. Following the one-drop rule, black-Chinese children and their descendants had to be defined as blacks.

We have seen that the one-drop rule does not fit in the Hawaiian Islands, yet the addition of the fiftieth state has not yet posed a serious national challenge to that rule. The rule also does not fit Cuban or Puerto Rican immigrants with some black ancestry, a situation not really resolved. Further ambiguities and strains are discussed in Chapter 7. The challenge of the Phipps case (*Jane Doe v. State of Louisiana*) has been answered by the courts with a clear reaffirmation of the one-drop rule. Despite some issues, this rule is unquestioned today by most whites and blacks in the United States. Comparisons with the ways racially mixed persons are classified in other societies highlights the uniqueness of the one-drop rule and helps us understand how it emerged and how it works. The lack of such a rule for all racial minorities other than blacks in the United States is discussed next.

STATUS OF AN ASSIMILATING MINORITY

We have not yet accounted for the status of those persons in the United States who are partly descended from American Indians, Japanese Americans, Filipino Americans, or one of the other racially distinctive minorities besides blacks. They represent the seventh type of status of racially mixed people, that of an assimilating minority, one that is being incorporated into the life of the dominant community. We must distinguish this one-way process from the melting pot form of assimilation, as in Hawaii, although both types involve the gradual loss of a group's original identity. In the melting pot process all groups contribute more or less equally to the emergence of a new culture and social organization and to a new group identity shared by everyone. The melting pot ideal is a blending of the best qualities of the merging groups into a new way of life, a goal that was strongly rejected in early-twentieth-century America (see Chapter 2). Throughout American history the pressure has been heavy for the native Indians and all newcomer groups to adopt the dominant Anglo-American ways and beliefs. There has been some two-way assimilation, through which pizza and other cultural traits from immigrant cultures have become part of the national life, but the non-Anglo groups have done most of the assimilating. The children of immigrant groups have been expected to get to school, learn English and eliminate the accent, learn Anglo-American history and patriotism, work hard, and drop the old-country ways as soon as possible.

Racially mixed persons in the United States, except for those with black ancestry, generally have been treated as assimilating Americans after the first generation of miscegenation. The children of the first generation of mixture most often have been treated as members of the lower-status group but sometimes have had an in-between position, or even a bottom-of-the-ladder status when both parent groups have rejected them. However, when the proportion of racial minority ancestry becomes one-fourth or less, these mixed persons are accepted as members of an assimilating minority. Thus, for example, someone whose lineage is one-fourth or less Chinese American or Mexican American (with Indian ancestry) is most likely to be accepted the same way an assimilating immigrant from Europe is. Such a person may be openly proud of having ancestry that is part American Indian, Filipino, Japanese, Guamanian, Korean, or Vietnamese, just as any assimilating American may be proud of lineage that is part Irish, German, Swedish, Italian, or Polish. Whether the intermarried progeny of the dark caucasoid peoples of South Asia are to be accorded this status will not be clear for another generation or two.

Both unmixed members of these non-African racial minority groups and their half-white offspring have had to work exceptionally hard to overcome discriminatory barriers to economic achievement and upward class movement. Their descendants who have three-fourths or more European ancestry very often experience the kind and level of prejudice so well known to European immigrant groups, but generally no more than that—that is, no racism. They do not have to hide their racial minority background if it is one-fourth or less, so there is no need to pass as white (see Chapter 1). As persons being assimilated into the dominant Anglo-American community, they find relatively little opposition to intermarriage with whites. There is no one-drop rule to deter their further miscegenation or their full assimilation into the dominant community. The implicit rule is that those with one-fourth or less ancestry from a non-African racial minority are defined as assimilating Anglo-Americans.

This seventh status rule may be distinguished from the fourth, although they may appear to overlap. Under both types of status the dominant group accepts intermarriage, and ultimately full assimilation, when persons with racially mixed ancestry meet the economic, educational, and other desired social class criteria. The specifications about race, however, are different. Under the Iberian variant of the fourth status rule, the person need not appear white and may even be fairly dark and have a considerable and unspecified proportion of African black ancestry, if the class attributes are satisfactory. Under the Northwest European variant, full assimilation may occur when the mixed person has known black ancestry but appears white. The seventh status rule, while silent on the question of racial appearance, permits intermarriage and full assimilation when the proportion of the person's racial minority ancestry does not exceed one-fourth.

CONTRASTING SOCIALLY CONSTRUCTED RULES

Rules for determining the group identity of racially mixed persons designate their status in the community. In this chapter the unique rule for determining the group identity and status of persons with black ancestry in the United States is compared with six other status rules at different times and in different places. A brief summary here highlights the differences. In several of the illustrations discussed, a racial hybrid group has shifted from one status to another in response to major changes in economic activities or political power. For example, the Métis of Canada and the Eurasians of India dropped from a middle position to a status subordinate to that of both parent groups. Amerasians in Korea and Vietnam have had a bottom-of-the-ladder status all along. The Mestizos of Mexico and the mulattoes of Haiti rose from an in-between position to a political status superior to that of both parent groups.

When a group with an in-between position has special occupations and mediates between the groups above and below it in status, it is a "middle minority." Many racial hybrid groups with an intermediate status have been middle minorities, meeting occupational needs the dominant community is unable or unwilling to fill and often achieving considerable economic success in spite of much discrimination. The loss of these special occupations can have drastic effects on the group's status, as the Métis learned. The comparative success of the middle minority is resented by lower-status groups, who often vent their hostility on the former when a crisis comes. Although the dominant community values having a buffer group, it rarely protects the middle minority in a crisis. Thus the middle minority is politically powerless, and it is especially vulnerable if it is a racially mixed group.

In the Republic of South Africa, both the Coloureds and the Asians have been buffer groups between the whites and unmixed blacks. The Coloureds are predominantly mulattoes, who would be defined as blacks in the United States, but they also include Eurasians and African-Asians. Largely Westernized, they have for centuries identified with the dominant white community. However, the establishment of the Apartheid system in 1948 imposed severe restrictions on the Coloureds and the Asians, as well as the blacks, including massive relocation in order to comply with the Group Areas Act, and the Coloureds have become more and more alienated from the whites and increasingly sympathetic to the blacks. After having experienced educational and economic gains and rising expectations, they met sudden, major setbacks in status—a recipe for strong political protest. Growing Coloured support for anti-Apartheid protest makes their buffer role less effective and white control more difficult to maintain.

In Brazil and other countries in lowland Latin America and the West Indies, the Mestizos and mulattoes originally were buffer groups between whites and unmixed blacks and Indians. In time the middle-minority position gave way to a fourth type of status—a flexible, highly variable position that depends more on class than on race. Whites are at the top of the class structure (except in Mexico and Haiti), unmixed blacks and Indians are at the bottom, and mulattoes and Mestizos make up most of the multilayered middle class. The ladder from the lower to the upper class has many rungs, and economic success and education outweigh color and other racial traits in determining a person's position. There are many terms of color reference, lightness being preferred, but the term applied may reflect a person's wealth and education more than actual physical traits.

On the Iberian islands in the Caribbean, as elsewhere in Latin America, light mulattoes and Mestizos may be absorbed by marriage into white families if they meet the class criteria, even when they have some visible negroid traits. For intermarriage to occur with whites on the Northwestern European islands in the Caribbean, mulattoes must appear white, although they may have some known black ancestry. Thus, even in the British West Indies there is no one-drop rule—and no concern about passing as white because only the racial appearance counts. This is the implied rule in Northwestern Europe, while the Iberian variant seems to prevail in Southern Europe.

The Hawaiian Islands represent a fifth type of status for racially mixed people, one in which class position has not been significantly affected by racial traits. The native Hawaiian tradition of tolerance and respect for other ethnic and racial groups continues to prevail and be applied to large numbers of people with mixed backgrounds. Although there has been class conflict, upward class mobility has not been restricted by discrimination against racial groups as such or against the racially mixed. The balance between melting-pot-style assimilation and equalitarian pluralism has meant equal opportunity for the races, including racial hybrids. Although Hawaii has been the fiftieth state since 1959, the one-drop rule is out of place there, and the extent to which it is being applied to (and by) persons of black ancestry remains to be seen.

The sixth type of status of the racially mixed is that of the subordinate parent group, the position of all persons in the United States with any known black ancestry, who are defined as blacks by the hypo-descent, or one-drop, rule. The same light mulatto defined as black in the United States might be classed as "coloured" in Jamaica and white in Puerto Rico. Sixty percent or more of the migrants from Puerto Rico are perceived in the United States as blacks, yet most of those 60 percent are racially mixed and were known on the island by one of the many color terms other than black, and many of them as white.

Until the 1850s the one-drop rule competed with an in-between status rule for free mulattoes in the Charleston and New Orleans areas (Chapter 3). The one-drop rule was acknowledged throughout the United States by mid-century and was later solidified under the Jim Crow system in the South, which revived a large measure of the repressive control of slavery (Chapter 4). The system of Apartheid in South Africa was also created to maintain white political control, but there only unmixed Africans are defined as blacks, so that the Coloureds are a buffer group. In both systems the resort to repressive measures by the whites has alienated the racially mixed people from the whites. In the United States, mulattoes of all degrees of mixture have come to identify strongly with blacks and to be proud of their black ancestry. Thus, we have the paradox of strong support by a large population of racially mixed people for a one-drop rule that emerged to protect slavery and Jim Crow segregation.

The seventh type of status is occupied by racially mixed Americans who are partly descended from Japanese Americans, American Indians (including Mestizos from Mexico), or any of the other racially visible minorities with the exception of blacks. This is the status of an assimilating minority, a minority being absorbed into the dominant Anglo-

American community, in contrast to the melting pot type of assimilation. When one-fourth or less of a person's racial ancestry comes from one of the nonblack racial minorities, that person is generally accepted as an assimilating person—not someone who is passing as white but someone who may take pride in a certain fraction of minority ancestry. The one-drop rule and the related concept of passing as white pertain only to blacks in the United States and the American status rule for mulattoes is also very different from the rules for racially mixed persons in other places and times.

S I X

BLACK ACCEPTANCE OF THE RULE

Racially mixed populations do not always readily accept the status assigned to them by the larger society. For example, the Métis fought back when they were pushed down from the middle-minority position to the bottom ethnic status in Canada (see Chapter 5). Given that the one-drop rule was developed and enforced to protect slavery, and later to strengthen the Jim Crow system, it might not seem surprising if the mulatto population had resisted the rule that classifies them as black. Instead, we have seen that blacks in general, including lighter mulattoes, have given increasing support to the rule since the 1850s, especially since the 1920s. In this chapter we examine the reasons why blacks support the rule so strongly, note the instances of rejection of the rule by some of the people defined as black, and attempt to explain why these exceptions do not seriously threaten the general pattern of black acceptance of the one-drop rule.

ALEX HALEY, LILLIAN SMITH, AND OTHERS

In the book *Roots*, and the television series based on the book, Alex Haley's true story inadvertently provided dramatic evidence that American blacks have accepted the one-drop rule (Haley, 1976). Blacks and whites alike rejoiced with Haley over his discovery of the village of Juffure in The Gambia, West Africa, the place where his ancestor, Kunta Kinte, was captured into slavery as a youth. Probably few have wondered why Haley did not pursue his white ancestry with as much diligence as he looked into his African ancestry. He knows painfully well about some of his ancestry from the British Isles, but how astounding it would be if he were to investigate that side of his genealogy! We are all so accustomed to the one-drop rule that it seems quite natural for Haley to identify only with his African roots.

Kunta Kinte was unusually determined in his efforts to keep his African name and identity alive in his family—most slaves were not able to do so. From the beginning the English colonists stripped the Africans of their personal and cultural identities, forcing them to take English names, to speak English, and to abandon African religious practices. Elizabethan English had defined blackness as evil, and African blacks were presented in writing and drama as ignorant heathens. The Church of England forbade the use of the "heathen" names, but to the African slaves the family name indicated clan identity and thus also tribal status and cultural style. Increasingly racially mixed, but defined as black regardless of the amount of white ancestry, the slaves were denied both an African identity and a white identity. As the names, languages, habits, memories, and legends of scores of different tribal cultures faded away, a new black American culture emerged, with only remnants of the ways of Africa.

After centuries of suppression of the African past, the story of Kunta Kinte came as a great symbolic victory to the black community. Black pride is now often expressed by emphasizing African names and styles and rejecting European names and ancestry. The "X" in some Black Muslim names symbolizes the broken past, which is why Malcolm Little replaced his English surname with an "X" (Boskin, 1976). This contrasts with the mulatto elites' custom of tracing their ancestry to the founding fathers or other illustrious white families, a practice that is now unpopular.

Singer Roland Hayes often referred to his mixed ancestry, which was half or more African black, part Indian, and presumably part white. He received many questions about his remarkable tenor voice, asking why it was so different and how he could produce such "deep purplish tones." After thinking about this, he often spoke of his voice as colored, or nonwhite, or black, but never as Indian, or white, or racially mixed (Helm, 1942:45–46, 118). In keeping with the remainder of this chapter, Hayes very likely would have identified himself and his voice as black even if his ancestry had been predominantly white or Indian. In the words of the old man quoted at the beginning of Chapter 1, "black people are all colors," and what makes a person black is the way one thinks, feels, believes, and the way one looks at life.

A telltale sentence appears in Lerone Bennett's valuable book *Before the Mayflower* (1962:249). Bennett writes, "Several well-known Negroes were products of unions between Negro men and white women" and then gives some examples. To any American, white or black, this would seem to be a perfectly reasonable statement, given the one-drop rule. As the federal courts have said, everyone knows that a person with any black ancestry in the United States is black. Yet it would make as much sense from a genetic standpoint to say that the child with a black parent and a white parent is white as to say it is black. More logically, the child is racially mixed, and predominantly white unless one parent is unmixed African. A person who is half or more white could not be defined as a black in Latin America, the Caribbean, the Republic of South Africa, and other places (see Chapter 5). Bennett's statement illustrates beautifully how uniformly black writers, and American blacks in general, accept the one-drop rule.

We have already noted that the one-drop rule is accepted by light mulattoes—including some who could easily pass as white, such as W.E.B. Du Bois, Adam Clayton Powell, Jr., Lena Horne, Vanessa Williams, Robert Purvis, and Homer Plessy. To those we might add such other well-known persons as Andrew Young, Julian Bond, Whitney Young, Muhammad Ali, and a number of black entertainers. One of the most remarkable examples is Walter White, longtime president of the NAACP. White's ancestry apparently was at least sixty-three sixty-fourths white, yet when he married a white woman the black press erupted in outrage. Mulatto leaders joined forces with other black leaders during the Black Renaissance of the 1920s, and in this spirit the black press clearly supported the one-drop rule absolutely. White's marriage portended virtually no miscegenation, but he had married outside the ethnic group he was leading. One need not look black in order to be a black, following the one-drop rule. This instance highlights the contrast with

Latin America, and even the British West Indies, where it is racial appearance that counts rather than ancestry.

Try to imagine the scene when John Davis stood before the Conference of Negro-African Writers and Artists in Paris in 1956 as head of the American delegation (see Chapter 1). He did his best to answer the chairperson's query as to why he considered himself black since he looked white. He was black, he said, by involvement, experience, and by choice (Baldwin, 1962:19). In short, however little he might be black genetically, he had been socialized to the black identity, so that his thoughts, feelings, and loyalties were those of a black. His appearance and actual genetic makeup were irrelevant, strange as that may sound to the rest of the world. He might have added that Americans with any black ancestry, even those who appear white, have lived with the one-drop rule all their lives and usually just take it for granted.

Roi Ottley noted the frequency of intermarriage between Chinese Americans and blacks in Harlem, and the invariable community definition of the mixed children as black. Commenting further, he wrote (1943:54): "In Harlem, as elsewhere in the United States, . . . the child of a red, yellow or brown person, no matter how little his appearance resembles that of a Negro, is considered *Negro.* And indeed no psychic injury is done the child. Some of the best-adjusted people I know are the progeny of such unions." This statement is more than recognition of the one-drop rule; it is an argument that the rule is good policy. Furthermore, it expresses a sentiment that has persisted among blacks since slave days: that the black community must extend care and affection to all children with any black ancestry, including those who look white. The old saying "We take care of our own" shows how completely the black community accepts the one-drop rule.

Informal adoption practices have been widespread in the black community since slave days, and, whether they are cultural survivals or not, they parallel the extended family customs in the tribes of West Africa. Ninety percent of all black children born out of wedlock in recent years are informally adopted by grandparents, uncles, aunts, or other relatives, while two-thirds of the illegitimate white children are formally adopted by nonrelatives. The black families most likely to adopt a child informally are families least likely to be approved by adoption agencies because they consist of grandparents, are headed by females, are elderly or poor, or are families that have children of their own (Hill, 1977:1–2, 29–32, 86).

In 1883 Angelina Weld Grimké, who appeared almost white, was born to Archibald and Sarah Stanley Grimké. Sarah Grimké's white, midwestern parents could not tolerate her marriage to Archibald, who was black. After the mixed marriage broke up, Angelina lived with her mother, Sarah, but that arrangement did not last and Sarah took steps to send the girl to live with Archibald. Sarah wrote to her former husband that Angelina needed the love and sympathy that only "one of her own *race*" (emphasis hers) could provide and that the child was getting old enough to understand how people in general reacted to a mixed child (Grimké, 1889). Biologically the child was much more white than black, so the "own *race*" to which her mother referred was the socially constructed category of black. To believe that a child who is partly black, genetically, can receive proper nurturing only in the black community seems natural enough to whites and blacks alike in the mainland United States, but not in Hawaii, Latin America, the Caribbean, France, Uganda, the Republic of South Africa, or other places (see Chapter 5). What seems natural in this regard depends on the social rule that governs the status of a racially mixed child in a given time and place. It seems natural for a group to care for a child that society assigns to it.

Lillian Smith, author of *Strange Fruit* (1944) and other books, recounts a startling experience with the one-drop rule during her early childhood in Georgia in the early twentieth century, when Jim Crow segregation was being built into a powerfully oppressive system. A little white girl was observed playing in the yard of a black family that was new in town, and a group of local white clubwomen decided they should do something about it. The black family's house was a crumbling shack, and the people looked ill. It was assumed that the white child had been kidnapped, and the black parents became evasive when questioned about her. The town marshal and the clubwomen took the child, Janie, and placed her in the Smiths' home, pending an investigation. Little Janie became Lillian Smith's roommate and playmate, and they quickly became quite close.

Three weeks later a message came from the orphanage for black children, resulting in much whispering and staring and finally in Mr. Smith's announcement that Janie had to return to the black family. When Lillian asked why, her mother explained that Janie was "colored," but Lillian insisted that the child was white and had good manners. Her mother said they had been mistaken and that it did not matter how Janie looked or acted. A "colored" child, she said, could not live in their home and could not even come to play. Mrs. Smith told Lillian she was too young to understand and not to bring up the subject again. When Lillian tried to explain to Janie, the girl asked whether Lillian was white and wondered why they could not live or play together (Smith, 1963:24–28). The orphanage and the black family had followed the one-drop rule, and continued to do so when the interfering whites hastened to obey the rule after discovering their error.

How do children, especially black children, learn about the rule and come to accept it? There is much evidence that both black and white preschool children generally notice variations in skin color, but more often than not they are unable to associate these differences with racial categories. When three- and four-year-old children are able to sort physiognomic traits into race groups, they apparently rely more on hair form and hair color—and perhaps more on eye color—than on skin color (Sorce, 1979:33–41). Perceived physical differences must be interpreted, and years of learning are generally required to grasp the complex way society classifies the races. Most very young children, black or white, have not yet learned how to apply the one-drop rule, especially in families that shield them from it. Many parents avoid the hard questions about racial classification and do not want their children to face racial prejudice and discrimination until they have to.

TRANSRACIAL ADOPTIONS AND THE ONE-DROP RULE

In the mid-1960s there was a great increase in transracial adoptions, which were used chiefly to reduce the nonwhite population in public institutions. This required adoption agencies to modify their historical guidelines for close matching of the physical, cultural, and emotional traits of children with those of the adoptive parents. It had been common for agencies to try to match even hair and eye color. Generally the black children placed with white families from the mid-1960s on had predominantly white racial traits and were often described as "racially mixed" or "biracial." In a little over a decade about 15,000 black children were adopted by white families.

In 1972 the National Association of Black Social Workers passed a resolution against the adoption of black children by white parents. Their stand was similar to that of the American Indian organizations that had become strongly opposed to the adoption of their children by whites, considering those children lost to their own communities. Such adoptions were called paternalistic and even genocidal. At a time when pride in the black identity was strongly emphasized, there was also concern because the "mixed" adoptees in white families are more likely to have problems of racial identity than those in black families. In the latter, no one questions the child's identity as black. The resolution by the National Association of Black Social Workers was a ringing endorsement of the one-drop rule. Although other black organizations did not publicly support this cause (Day, 1979:99–100), the strong opposition by black social workers sharply reduced the adoption of black children by whites, almost ending it by the mid-1970s. By 1987 at least thirty-five states had a policy against cross-racial adoption.

It is evidently common for white adoptive parents to minimize racial traits and to accept the "biracial" adoptees into their families as just children needing love and care. Apparently the majority of these white parents prefer to describe their adopted children by some term other than black—and often as "racially mixed"—a rejection of the one-drop rule. Many seem to assume that their child will not be subject to the rule, especially if the child looks almost white, and that people will simply accept the child as another human being. However, neither the white community nor the black will allow the "mixed" child to be an exception to the one-drop rule. At school, and in the community at large, the child will be defined as black. "Racially mixed" is not an accepted racial category in the United States for a child who has any black ancestry at all. One is either white or black.

Studies of very young black children adopted by white families, especially preschoolers, have shown that a relatively low percentage of such children have problems with racial identity. For example, in a study of forty-four black and forty-four white preschool children, all adopted by white parents, it was concluded that the transracial adoptions generally were as successful as the inracial adoptions. However, about half of the adoptive parents of the black children thought there might be racial identity problems later on (Zastrow, 1977:83–86). In a study of 125 black children who had been in white adoptive homes at least three years and had reached the age of six years or more, the average age was 8.8 years. About 77 percent of the adoptions in the latter study were judged to be successful, but 24 percent of the parents said their adopted children had exhibited confusion, embarrassment or anger about their racial identity. The researchers noted that they had obtained no responses concerning identity directly from the children and that more problems with race might emerge as the adoptees got older (Grow and Shapiro, 1974:iii–iv, 188).

When researchers interview black adoptees who are beyond early childhood, they often elicit much more hostility and ambivalence toward transracial adoptions than is reported in studies of the parents of small children. The majority of the white adoptive parents apparently resent the issue of black identity and try to minimize it, considering parenthood and families more important than race. They prefer to talk about human identity, to send the black child to predominantly white schools, and in effect to raise the adoptee as white. Black critics charge that these white parents refuse to acknowledge the racial differences and thus teach the child to ignore his blackness (Ladner, 1977: chap. 7). However, the studies also show that some white adoptive parents make strong efforts to teach the child to have a black identity and that some even move into black neighborhoods and change their lifestyles in order to do so. The trouble is, say the critics, that even the white adoptive parents who make such efforts cannot have much success because they are not black. Further, even when the child does adopt a black identity, he or she may be rejected by black families because the adoptive parents are white. Most whites do not see the wide range of racial traits prevalent in the black community and have not had to face the full implications of the one-drop rule.

A thirty-six-year-old black college professor who was interviewed in depth about his adoption by white parents said he would rather have been adopted by a black family. Only black parents, he said, can empathize with the child as a black person. The black child in a white family has no black role-models and is socialized to think as a white, especially if adopted before three years of age. It can be shattering for a child to grow up not realizing that he or she is defined as black by the community. Although this man was adopted at the age of thirteen, he too had problems with his racial identity. Although his parents shielded him from hostility as much as they could, his Black Muslim friends ridiculed him for having white parents. He said the "freedom rides" and the urban black protests of the 1960s first started him thinking seriously about his blackness. Then he went through a period of rejecting all whites, even concluding that much of what his adoptive parents had done for him was only to help relieve their white guilt feelings. Although reconciled with his adoptive parents, he has continued to resent the fact that he was denied an opportunity to learn the survival skills a black person needs (Ladner, 1977:149–55).

In a study of 388 transracially adopted children in 204 white families, the ages of the children ranged from three to eight years at the time the data were obtained. The majority of the adoptees were black, but some were American Indian, Asian, or Hispanic. The researchers found that the children generally lacked a clear sense of racial identity, and exhibited little ambivalence about race (Simon and Alstein, 1977:71–162). However, in a follow-up study of 133 of the original families seven years later, a major increase was found in the children's sense of racial identity, in their ambivalence about race, and in emotional and behavioral problems. The percentage of these ten- to fifteen-year-olds who identified themselves as black was much higher than when the children were younger (Simon and Alstein, 1981:13–19). Evidently experiences at school and in other public situations had increasingly confronted them with the fact that children and adults outside the family defined them as black persons. Even so, the majority of these older children seemed well adjusted.

In a study of sixty adopted black children who ranged in age from ten to twenty-six—thirty of them in white families and thirty in black—the mean average age of the black children in white families was 13.5 years. Only ten of the thirty adoptees with white parents identified themselves as black, six identified as "mixed," one as white, and thirteen tried to avoid a racial identity altogether and indicated they were "human," "part white," or simply "American." Eighteen of the sets of white parents preferred a color-blind approach, while twelve acknowledged the child's black identity. Half of these latter twelve had moved into black neighborhoods. Roughly 75 percent of these black adolescents (and older) apparently still tended to identify themselves the same way their adoptive parents did. The children who preferred a human identity to a racial one generally were the adoptees of the white parents who persistently had held to this stance, but apparently five had accepted the one-drop rule while their parents had not (McRoy and Zurcher, 1983:126–36).

Sometimes the apparent dissent of white adoptive parents may be more a matter of perception of the "mixed" child's features than of conscious opposition to the one-drop rule. That is, some parents and other family members simply see the child as an individual, not as someone who is racially different from themselves. Although typically there is more white than black ancestry in these cases, outsiders can see some negroid traits that the family does not perceive. Anthropologist Ashley Montagu reported on five instances in which he was consulted by such families, all of them upset because friends and neighbors were saying the child in question was black. Four of these adoptees were thirteen months old at the time of consultation, but one had reached the age of twenty-one and all had been adopted a few weeks after birth. In all five cases the child was clearly a light mulatto, but the families could not believe it when Montagu told them that. The consultation about the twenty-one-year-old was sought by her six white siblings, who all their lives had fought against having their adopted sister treated as a black. She had been discriminated against at school and elsewhere, and the siblings wanted to know if there could be a grain of truth in the label of black. All they could see were small individual differences among the seven of them (Montagu, 1977:743–44).

Montagu suggests further that full readiness to accept people with different racial characteristics from one's own can cause a person to cease to perceive as different even marked variations in skin color, hair texture, or nose shape. Although the percentage of whites in the United States who are capable of this degree of color blindness may not be large at present, generalized attitudes toward racial groups apparently can influence both the perception and the interpretation of physical differences. It is therefore not surprising that most American blacks, who are accustomed to accepting as fellow blacks persons whose racial traits range all the way from African black to European white, can identify readily with this entire continuum of people as members of their "own race." Again we must note that there is a good deal of color awareness among blacks in the United States and that both the darkest blacks and the lightest mulattoes have often had major problems in the black community. Even so, the relationships between racial attitudes and perceptions of physical differences may help explain the high level of acceptance of the one-drop rule by American blacks. Their attitudes reflect discriminatory treatment by whites of all blacks—light, brown, or dark.

REJECTION OF THE RULE: GARVEY, AMERICAN INDIANS, AND OTHERS

Social and legal rules rarely work perfectly or have total support. Despite general acceptance, there have been challenges to the one-drop rule within the black as well as the white community. Many Hispanic Americans with black ancestry resist the rule if they can. We have also seen that some black children adopted by white parents persist in resisting the nation's rule. The strong competition of another rule until the 1850s, especially in South Carolina and Louisiana, left lingering questions and ambiguities that were not completely resolved in the 1920s. There were challenges in court to the one-drop rule after the Civil War, and some later, and the Phipps case (*Jane Doe v. State of Louisiana*) revived the issue in the 1980s (see Chapter 1). Many older Creoles of Color still prefer to be called Creoles or colored rather than black. Biologically, they insist, they are only part African black, and their history is not black history. At this late date, many cleave to the in-between status and try to avoid the one-drop rule (Dominguez, 1986:163–64).

The derisive term "high yaller" indicates that very light mulattoes have often been considered illegitimate and trashy if they cannot demonstrate respectable family connections. Although this implies a rejection of the one-drop rule, the meaning seems usually to be that such persons are indeed black, but very "low-down" blacks. Similarly, since the 1960s, light mulattoes who have been put on the defensive by vigorous expressions of black pride have been made to feel they must take pains to emphasize their respectability and their blackness or they will barely be tolerated in the black community. The choice is between fighting discrimination within the black community that has raised them or attempting to "pass" into a strange and threatening white world (Williamson, 1980:190). This is a severe test of the one-drop rule, indicating grudging acceptance of it by the black community in this context.

A striking statement of rejection of the one-drop rule was made in one of my classes on minorities in the fall of 1978, where a panel of students was describing selected personal experiences with discrimination. One student, who might be described as a very light mulatto, said:

> I am part French, part Cherokee Indian, part Filipino, and part black. Our family taught us to be aware of all these groups, and just to be ourselves. But I have never known what I am. People have asked if I am a Gypsy, or a Portuguese, or a Mexican, or lots of other things. It seems to make people curious, uneasy, and sometimes belligerent. Students I don't even know stop me on campus and ask, "What are you anyway?"

As this panelist tried to describe her feelings of group marginality, a young black woman student (who appeared to be about half white, biologically) raised her hand and asserted strongly, "You don't have any problem. You are black." There was a murmur of approval and nodding of heads, especially among the black students, but the panelist replied softly, "No. No. Not just black. I am the other things too. All of them."

After class the black students showed great concern that this panelist either did not understand or did not accept the American definition of a black person. Her parents had sought to avoid the one-drop rule by emphasizing individual worth and the apparently equal fractions of the four ancestries, a position that would be quite normal in Hawaii. But this view would be acceptable in the forty-nine mainland states only if none of the four ancestries had been black. The other black students were frustrated and disturbed by this questioning of the one-drop rule, which had provided them with a clear guide to their own group identity. Some even suggested to me that the panelist was a traitor, trying to "deny her race." For persons whose appearance indicates some black ancestry, her sense of social marginality is unusual in the United States. Her parents were unusual in teaching their children to adopt an interracial and interethnic identity rather than just a black identity.

Marcus Garvey's Harlem-based black separatist movement in the 1920s was aimed at discrimination against blacks, but it also challenged the one-drop rule. As an unmixed black from Jamaica, Garvey considered mulattoes to be "coloreds," not blacks. He demanded that mulattoes be segregated so that they could become a buffer group between whites and blacks, and that miscegenation cease. He threatened to dismiss any member of his association who married a white, and he required his officers to be pure African. He ridiculed Du Bois, White, and other "near-white" leaders of the NAACP, and their integrationist program. Believing that blacks were God's chosen people, and that Jesus Christ himself was black, he demanded racial purity (Ottley, 1943:73–74; Cronon, 1955:172–93). Garvey even met with Ku Klux Klan leaders, who openly supported his outspoken views on miscegenation. This liaison with the KKK was attacked in bitter editorials by A. Philip Randolph (Anderson, 1972: chap. 9).

Garvey's movement was well timed to make a major contribution to the Black Renaissance of the 1920s, but not at all well timed in two fundamental respects. He openly denounced discrimination against blacks, helped make blacks and their achievements dramatically visible in New York, and did much to spread the concept and feeling of black pride. However, the building of pride in the new American black identity was destined not to be limited to unmixed blacks, as Garvey wanted, but extended to everyone with any black ancestry. Moreover, Garvey's separatist strategy was rejected, along with his views on racial purity. Both the leaders of the Black Renaissance, and the vast majority of the black population, were inhospitable to Garvey's view that they were not really blacks. By that time the one-drop rule was well established in both the white and the black community, and the Black Renaissance helped make it even firmer by aligning mulattoes more closely with the black community. In the end, only Garvey's strong sense of black pride was well received in the black community, while his definition of who is black and his separatism were strongly rejected.

A frequent theme in the literature of the Black Renaissance of the 1920s was the feelings mulattoes have about their mixed parentage, as expressed in this poem by Langston Hughes (1970:158):

CROSS

My old man's a white old man
And my old mother's black.
If ever I cursed my white old man,
I take my curses back.

If ever I cursed my old black mother
And wished she were in hell,
I'm sorry for that evil wish
And now I wish her well.

My old man died in a fine big house.
My ma died in a shack.
I wonder where I'm gonna die,
Being neither white nor black?

These lines should be interpreted as an expression of the experience of many people in the black community, not as a repudiation of the one-drop rule. The majority of mulattoes in the United States at present do not have a white parent, since the white ancestry is usually further back, but many do have. Such persons have thoughts and feelings about the white parent, even if the child was the product of sexual exploitation and no family relationship developed. The feelings of marginality are engendered by the knowledge of white parentage and by the individual's traits.

However, firm support for the one-drop rule in the community makes it clear that the person's group identity is black. Such expressions as Hughes's poem about an important aspect of life in the black community helped strengthen the alliance between the lighter mulattoes and blacks in general, thus reinforcing the one-drop rule.

The rule has been resisted by a great many mulattoes who are part American Indian or who have been protected by the Indian tribes. Black-Indian miscegenation began on a large scale in colonial times, when both groups were held as slaves or indentured servants. Some Indian bands were absorbed by the black population, while some tribes took in large numbers of blacks. Tribes often welcomed maroons (runaway slaves) and freedpersons, and some owned black slaves, with whom they intermarried. In wars with the whites, Indians often spared all the blacks and welcomed them to intermarriage and the Indian way of life. Blacks were numerous among the Seminoles and Creeks of Alabama, Georgia, and northern Florida, often living in separate villages (Bennett, 1962:268–71).

The eastern states have many small, isolated communities of racially mixed people who evade the one-drop rule and the black identity. At the middle of the nineteenth century there were some two hundred such places, most of them with a long history. "American Mestizos" is a general term that has often been applied to these communities. In general the residents appear to be predominantly white with some American Indian ancestry, and many have features that appear to be negroid. These groups have denied, notably during the Jim Crow era, that they have any black ancestry in order to avoid the segregation laws, the racial etiquette, and other discrimination. South Carolina has many of these groups, known there as Brass Ankles, Red Legs, Yellow-hammers, or Turks. At the junction of Virginia, Kentucky, and Tennessee they are called Melungeons. They are known as Red Bones in Louisiana, Croatans in North Carolina, Guineas in West Virginia and Maryland, Wesorts in southern Maryland, Issues in Virginia, Jackson Whites in New York and New Jersey, Moors and Nanticokes in Delaware, Creoles or Cajuns in Alabama and Mississippi, and Carmel Indians in Ohio.

These so-called American Mestizo groups have protected themselves from the one-drop rule by remaining as isolated as possible, which has become more and more difficult. Within their own communities they are presumably all equal, whatever their racial composition, and they are very cautious in their dealings with the outside. In recent decades some have resolved their dilemma by passing as white, some have migrated to other regions where they are not known, some have been recognized as Indians, and some have adopted the black identity. Many of them, however, continue to try to avoid being defined as blacks by remaining isolated and wary, a lifelong preoccupation in a land with a rule that defines all persons with any black ancestry as black (Berry, 1963:193–95).

BLACK ACCEPTANCE: REASONS AND IMPLICATIONS

The several instances of rejection of the one-drop rule noted in this chapter stand out because of their relative rarity. Deviation from the rule is very conspicuous, as illustrated by the experiences of my student, of Marcus Garvey, of many white adoptive parents of black children and some of the adoptees, and of many Hispanic Americans, and by the need for isolation of the American Mestizo groups. The typical response to such deviation in the black as well as the white community is strong affirmation of the one-drop rule. Blacks are just as anxious as whites to instruct the young and the deviant about how the rule works and how important it is to follow it.

Emile Durkheim, the French sociologist, argued (1960:102) that deviant acts and statements call attention to a violated rule, activate the supporting beliefs and feelings, and thus strengthen the consensus in support of the rule. Consider the sense of outrage black social workers express about white parents who adopt black children and then minimize or ignore the nation's definition of who is black, and consider Randolph's great anger at Marcus Garvey for saying that most Negroes in the United States are mulattoes and should be segregated from the "true blacks." Does this kind of response to deviance mean that the one-drop rule can never be changed? This difficult question is explored further in Chapter 8.

Blacks in the United States need to learn the necessary survival skills, and that requires a good understanding of the one-drop rule and how to cope with it. Blacks did not invent the rule, but they had to learn to live by it in order to survive slavery, the Jim Crow system, and the spread of the rule that would become national custom and law. Blacks and whites alike had to learn to treat all mulattoes, including blond, blue-eyed slaves, as blacks before the American Revolution. After slavery was ended, whites made it clear that mulattoes of all descriptions would be defined as blacks, not as whites or as some sort of in-between group. Light mulattoes became leaders in the black community, with which they identified even more strongly when hostility against them reached its peak in the first decade of the twentieth century. At this time, the light-skinned W.E.B. Du Bois attributed his move from a professorship at Atlanta University to become a militant black leader to the large number of lynchings from 1885 to 1909, when the Jim Crow system was being developed (Bennett, 1962:279–80). Light mulattoes were as likely as darker blacks to be lynched for violations of the master-servant etiquette.

We have seen that mulatto identification with the black community became stronger than ever during the Black Renaissance of the 1920s and that the one-drop rule was then firmly established. Both black pride and the one-drop rule received powerful reinforcement during the 1960s, and since then lighter mulattoes have often felt pressure to demonstrate their black pride and loyalty. Greater educational and economic opportunities have meant upward mobility and increased effectiveness for many, and the black community resents the potential loss of its more talented leaders through total integration into white institutions, and certainly through passing or intermarriage with whites. Black pride in the contributions of outstanding blacks in American history includes pride in the achievements of many light mulattoes.

The strong attitude in the black community against passing as white, and the apparent infrequency of permanent passing by those who could do so, suggest how strongly self-perpetuating the one-drop rule is. A person who has always been part of a black family and community cannot turn away from them without experiencing extreme stress and major difficulties. Those who do pass are acknowledging the one-drop rule but escaping its effects, not openly challenging it. The self-perpetuating effect of the rule is also suggested by the black hostility engendered when a prominent, white-appearing "black" marries a white person, as illustrated by the experiences of Walter White and Lena Horne. These reactions indicate the resolute insistence that anyone with even the slightest trace of black ancestry is black, and a traitor to act like a white.

This firm stance is based on more than the tendency to defend a traditional rule. Whites defined the black population of the United States by establishing the one-drop rule, and apparently the whites' original reasons for doing that are now irrelevant to most blacks. The whites forced all shades of mulattoes into the black community, where they were accepted, loved, married, and cherished as soul brothers and sisters. A sense of unity developed among a people with an extremely wide variation in racial characteristics. People in the black community resent the adoption of black children of any description by white families, and they do not want to lose members of their own families, neighborhoods, churches, or other associations through any means, particularly the most cherished and gifted ones, who enrich their lives and enhance group pride.

Blacks in the United States are certainly aware that most of them have racially mixed ancestry, and many must also know that the one-drop rule emerged to protect slavery and that it was consolidated in order to bolster Jim Crow segregation. However, black protests and political demands for equal opportunity have not included a challenge to the long-standing definition of who is black. Black pride is an expression of group solidarity that plays down racial and class diversity and focuses on the symbols of blackness. It must be acknowledged that the one-drop rule has some inherent problems and that color differences have caused some division within the black community since slave times. Transracial marriages and adoptions stir the feelings and minds of observers as well as participants, and a number of other factors cause both blacks and whites to raise questions about the one-drop rule. Yet the overwhelming reality is that most blacks in the United States have taken the one-drop rule for granted for a very long time, feel that they have an important stake in maintaining it, socialize their children to accept it, and rally to its defense when it is challenged.

SEVEN

AMBIGUITIES, STRAINS, CONFLICTS, AND TRAUMAS

We have seen that applying the one-drop rule has resulted in defining as black a population that ranges all the way from unmixed African blacks to people who appear to be white. The rule thus produces ambiguities, strains, conflicts, and traumatic experiences—costs to society that weigh more heavily on the black community than on the white. The different rules adopted in different societies and times to determine the status of a racially mixed population all cause problems of some kind, some of them more severe than others. The problems caused by the one-drop rule are complex, and some of them are painfully distressing, but the public level of concern about them has not been high because the rule is generally taken for granted in both the white and the black community.

THE DEATH OF WALTER WHITE'S FATHER AND OTHER TRAUMAS

One evening at dusk in Atlanta in 1931, Walter White's father was struck by a car as the driver sped up to beat a stoplight that was changing to red. The unconscious victim, who appeared to be white, was rushed to the white section of the Henry W. Grady City Hospital, where the best doctors began working frantically to save his life. Neighbors who had witnessed the accident notified the family. Walter's brother-in-law, whose skin color was light brown, went to the hospital to inquire. Not finding the victim in the dilapidated colored section of the hospital, he surmised what had happened, located his father-in-law in the white section, and identified him. Horrified, the attending whites asked, "Have we put a nigger in the white ward?" They then snatched the gravely wounded man from the examining table and, in a heavy rainstorm, hurried him across the street to the "colored" ward (White, 1948:135–38).

Walter White rushed by train from New York to find his father conscious but badly injured and receiving inadequate care in the crowded, unsanitary hospital ward. During the seventeen days there before he died, White's father tried to impress on his son that he should love the whites rather than hate them, no matter what happened. White could feel only hate at that time, an emotion fanned by his having to sit up all night on the train back to New York because known blacks, while allowed to be porters in the Pullman cars, could not be paying customers (Cannon, 1956:4–9).

Earlier in the Jim Crow era, Lillian Smith experienced another traumatic incident, which must have been even more of a shock for the black family and Janie, the small girl who appeared to be white, than it was for her little white friend Lillian (see Chapter 6). In both cases whites hastened to remedy the violation of the one-drop rule, as if the "black" presence had been contaminating the building, the furniture, even the air. Ending the close contact as soon as possible seemed much more important than the feelings and welfare of the people involved. Genetically, in both instances, the individual at the center of the incident was far more white than black, yet the apparent fear of being polluted by that trace of blackness was very strong. The socially constructed status category of blacks had to be respected and restored lest the racial etiquette and the entire system of racial segregation be put in jeopardy. To a Latin American, who would be concerned about racial appearance rather than known black ancestry, these responses would have seemed psychotic.

Traumatic experiences, along with ambiguities and strains of status relationships, began during slavery. Evidently many mulatto slaves, especially house servants who saw their white relatives daily, were uncertain about their status. There was the unusual but disturbing possibility of being freed, and even of being declared legally white, although usually the one-drop rule prevailed. There were also fears of total rejection by white relatives, especially of being sold outside the family. There were instances in which slave girls preferred to be whipped rather than submit to the master's sexual demands, on the ground that submitting to one's father would be incest and a sin (Helm, 1942:45–46).

In a captivating and poignant autobiography, Ossie Guffy tells about her experiences as a young black woman nearly eighteen years old living near Cincinnati in the late 1940s. Struggling to support two small children on her own, she was angry to find that a young white man named Augie was living next door, and still angrier when he spoke to her in a familiar way. He had a difficult time convincing her he was black until he introduced her to his mother, who was even darker than Ossie. Augie twitted Ossie about her prejudice against whites. They fell in love, Ossie became pregnant, and then Augie disappeared. His mother explained that she had helped him pass, marry a white woman, and "live on the other side of town, where he belongs," but offered to give Ossie substantial financial assistance (Guffy, 1971:91–98). These experiences, which were consequences of the one-drop rule, were probably as traumatic for Augie and his mother as they were for Ossie.

Being able to pass as white has constant potential for ambiguities, strains, and surprises, although not always so traumatic as those above. Those who pass have a severe dilemma before they decide to do so, since a person must give up all family ties and loyalties to the black community in order to gain economic and other opportunities. Probably most of those who pass are white on the outside but black on the inside, and for them adjustment to life as whites must be extremely difficult. Imagine what it must be like for them to listen to expressions of racial prejudice and to witness acts of discrimination against blacks. The stresses of passing as white call attention to the difference between the biological and social definitions of who is black. Those who agonize over whether to pass are already mostly white genetically, and perhaps entirely in some cases.

Thus, the struggle is mainly about permanently leaving the social status category, the community, that is called black.

Interracial marriages in the United States experience numerous uncertainties and severe strains (see Chapter 4). A major problem is the way the community classifies and treats the children of such marriages. A great many intermarried parents, primarily the white parents, apparently hope and believe that people will overlook the racial mixture and just treat the child as a human being. Even children who are well prepared to be defined as black can experience some problems, but those who are not so well prepared are likely to get some rude shocks as they get older. The problem is similar to that experienced by many of the black children adopted by white parents who reject the black identity as long as possible. In Chapter 6 we noted a black professor's strong resentment of his white adoptive parents for not helping him accept the black identity and learn the necessary survival skills. Even when white adoptive parents encourage the black identity, the child is likely to be rejected by black children because of the white home.

The one-drop rule is also the source of another strain on the white parent in an interracial marriage: the submergence of the white ancestry in the public definition of the resulting child as black. It is as if the child has only African ancestors, as if the white parent's family and white ancestry do not exist. Typically the child has more white ancestry than black, yet the white lineage is supposed to count for nothing. This strain is accentuated when grandparents or other family members or friends refuse to accept the child. Although the white parents of racially mixed children may experience some special satisfactions in addition to the usual joys of parenthood, probably few are adequately prepared for their resentment of the rule that in effect cuts the child off from the white side of the family tree and its heritage.

COLLECTIVE ANXIETIES ABOUT RACIAL IDENTITY: SOME CASES

Under a one-drop rule, uncertainty about the racial identity of many individuals is shared on both sides of the color line, and in both communities this can mount to the proportions of collective hysteria. The first two traumatic experiences cited above show marked anxiety on the part of the whites who inadvertently violated the one-drop rule. And as noted earlier, the collective anxiety of whites about the number of mulattoes, about blacks passing as white, and about miscegenation involving white women reached a peak early in the twentieth century as the Jim Crow system was being developed. There was much apprehension about the unknown amount of black ancestry in the white population of the South, and this was fanned into an unreasoning fear of invisible blackness. For instance, white laundries and cleaners would not accommodate blacks because whites were afraid they would be "contaminated" by the clothing of invisible blacks. In the Jim Crow system, acting like blacks or voluntarily associating with them came to be considered proof of blackness even in the absence of known black ancestry. The "white nigger" concept, which was based on perceived attitudes and social participation rather than on black appearance or lineage, omits biological evidence as the basis for the social definition of who is black (Williamson, 1980:98–108). This phenomenon is reminiscent of the collective hysteria about the "secret Jews" in Spain during the Inquisition and the fear of witchcraft in Renaissance Europe and New England.

Greater enforcement of the one-drop rule by whites after 1850, and the resulting increase in the identification of lighter mulattoes with blacks rather than with whites, resulted eventually in the "high yellow" stereotype. Light-skinned persons who have not been able to demonstrate descent from a respectable mulatto family have faced prejudice and discrimination from the black community as well as the white. Evidently one reason for this antagonism has been resentment of the traditionally high status and exclusiveness of the mulatto elites in the black community. Blacks in general exhibit much pride in the achievements of lighter mulattoes, particularly those who have struggled for black causes, but there is also much ambivalence and anxiety over the question of group loyalty. During the 1930s and 1940s, some blacks were even heard to deprecate the great "Brown Bomber," Joe Louis, saying that he was "too white."

The slogan "Black is beautiful" helped promote black unity in the 1960s and 1970s and put pressure on light mulattoes to prove their loyalty and their pride in the black community. It was then that the term "black" rapidly replaced "Negro," and also that "Afro-American" was strongly promoted as the preferred ethnic term. Although many people defined as black by the one-drop rule do not look very black or African, the "Black is beautiful" slogan was not meant to exclude them, but rather to encompass all members of the racially diverse black community. There was much open criticism of the traditional mulatto elitism and the widespread use by blacks of skin whiteners and hair straighteners to conform to white standards of beauty. Attention was called to the irony of whites' spending money for suntans and curled hair while blacks bought skin bleaches and hair straighteners. At least for a time, many light mulattoes felt strong pressure to affect "Afro" hairstyles. Ironically, this came at a time when many such persons had arrived at a strong commitment to the black identity, in response to the civil rights protests of the 1950s and 1960s. Research has shown that the sense of self-worth of many light mulattoes has declined since the 1960s, affecting their marital choices, and that the preferred skin color has become light brown. Although most light mulattoes apparently have chosen to try to cope both with these pressures imposed by the black community and with discrimination by whites, rather than risk trying to pass as white, the dilemma many of them face has been described as tragic (Williamson, 1980:190–92).

Divisions in the black community over variation in color were stressed by many of the people Gwaltney interviewed in his anthropological study published in 1980 (one of those interviewed was quoted at the beginning of Chapter 1). These themes were addressed spontaneously, not in response to fixed questions but in free-flowing interviews in which people were asked to talk at length about their experiences as black persons. The interviewer was black and blind, and he obtained permission from each subject to tape the conversation. Summaries and exerpts from three of these interviews follow.

A thirty-six-year-old black woman teacher who is blond and looks white volunteered that she had had mixed feelings about her appearance all her life. As a child she was taught by her aunts to take pride in her caucasian features and in belonging to the "better class of colored people." She was also taught to develop cultural pursuits and to take responsibility for "less fortunate members of the race." She exulted in being able to say to darker children such things as "Was my face red!" or "I blushed all over." She was not supposed to play with children who were quite dark. She learned to tell jokes about black, white, and brown people. Later she learned that the dark-brown people made jokes about the so-called yellow people and that many of them refused to eat with the latter. Brown parents would not let their children play with the "low-down" yellow children. When one of her girlfriends married a German, the bride's dark-brown father refused to accept the marriage and insisted that his daughter was dead. This interviewee generalized that black people are unreasonable about color differences and that they really have no choice but to learn to be a more united community (Gwaltney, 1980:84–86).

Gwaltney interviewed another, younger black woman who also looks white, who said that the greatest problem in the black community is that a great many blacks do not think clearly about color (Gwaltney, 1980:77–79). She believes blacks and whites alike "do not even see straight" when they talk about skin colors and that both groups see her differently when they find out she is a black. Here is some more of what she had to say:

> See, people have gotten colors all mixed up with ideas about what is good or bad or nasty or clean. . . . You know, my mother said that a lot of her own relatives did not want to eat her cooking because her skin was light. I mean, a lot of people think that light people are all—well, that they are not clean cooks. It works both ways—not the same thing, but every group has these stupid things about color. . . . My mother used to tell me about the blue veins, and when I was in high school some girls were really interested in that. If the skin is—well, if it is less dark you can see your veins. And this small thing was made so big that it split up friendships and made people hate and envy each other. My father told me about those paper-bag tests and comb tests that you had to pass to get into some of the clubs that they used to have in Louisiana. . . . They used to put a brown paper bag in the bend of your arm, and if your skin was the same color or lighter, then you could join. . . . Or maybe you could come in and eat or do whatever they did in those clubs. Sometimes there would be a man who would run a comb through your hair, and if it went through easily—you know, if your hair wasn't too curly—then you could get in. (Gwaltney, 1980:80)

This woman said that although she has never tried to pass as white she has often been accused of it by other blacks. When she got a job at a hospital, a black high school acquaintance took pains to inform her new work associates that she is black. On the other hand, she is severely criticized for associating with dark blacks. Once when she attended a movie with a neighbor boy who was very dark, her girl friends teased her, saying they didn't know she "dealt in coal." When the boy learned of this he was hurt, would not listen to her explanation, and never spoke to her again. She also felt confused when her brown-skinned uncle used to say, "Black is evil, yallah so low-down, look here, honey, ain't you glad you brown?"

Finally, the same young woman said that conflicts over color differences in the black community are very difficult to deal with because nobody talks about the problem. Once, at a community program where blacks and whites were discussing problems of race relations, she was asked to point out a specific problem. She wanted to mention the greatest problem for her, color divisiveness among blacks, but she said nothing because the blacks would have considered it wrong to mention it in front of whites. She said the black community should judge all people by their actions, not their skin color. If it is wrong for whites to make other people miserable because of something so unimportant and involuntary as color, it is wrong for blacks to do so too (Gwaltney, 1980:80–82).

Rather than criticize both blacks and whites for color discrimination, some "blacks" who appear white focus all their hatred on the white community. One woman Gwaltney interviewed was considered too dark by her father's side of the family. She said:

> Too many blackfolks are fools about color and hair. . . . My uncle is a preacher and he says that white people are born evil. He'll tell you in a minute that the Bible says that the wicked are estranged from the womb. Now, as far as he is concerned, when you say "the wicked," you have said "the white race." He cannot stand white people, and although he is a man with good common sense most of the time, you cannot make him see reason about this race thing. He looks as white as any white person, but you'd better not tell him that unless you are ready to go to war. He won't even call them men. He says, "The beni did this" or "The beni have said so-and-so." (Gwaltney, 1980:71–72)

This uncle's daughter had married a white man five years before and had two children, but the uncle ignored his grandchildren and acted as if his daughter had died. He and his daughter had been very close, and although she still came often to see him he totally ignored her. One time she brought his favorite pie to a party, but he would not touch it, and he informed a young girl relative that his daughter was dead. The woman doubted that her uncle would ever speak to his daughter again. The other relatives had also resented the marriage, and the woman expressed their feelings when she said, "I mean, why should this ordinary white boy walk in here and take a queen?" Nevertheless, they had maintained social relations with this cousin, saying her marriage was her own business. Only the cousin's father remained adamant (Gwaltney, 1980:74).

PERSONAL IDENTITY: SEVEN MODES OF ADJUSTMENT

Problems of personal identity, especially for very light mulattoes, are apparent in the above experiences and at many places throughout this book. These personal dilemmas are the internalized counterparts of the ambiguities and strains involved in occupying a marginal status in the pattern of race relations in the United States. There have been conflicting perceptions of light mulattoes and conflicting role expectations, especially in the black community. It is the one-drop rule that does not permit individuals to be classified as racially mixed and that instead defines as members of the black community persons who actually have an extremely wide variation in racial traits. Without this rule the dilemmas that light mulattoes who are adopted by white parents are in concerning their identity would be quite different, and probably much less severe than they often are. The same might be suggested for many children of interracial marriages and for persons with known black ancestry who appear white. Conferring the status of black on all persons with at least one black ancestor seems to resolve questions about racial identity surprisingly well for most, but not for all. Many continue to feel the uncertainties of the classic "marginal man" (Stonequist, 1937) and to have distressing, contradictory experiences.

Light mulattoes adjust to the problems of marginality in various ways. (1) They may become preoccupied with expressing strong hatred of all whites, an aggressive pattern that often seems to suggest ambivalent feelings about oneself and the black community. (2) They may accept the black identity but worry about color discrimination and conflict within the black community and hope that color differences can be minimized. Both these modes are illustrated in the interviews cited above. (3) They may make a conscious commitment to the black identity, to embrace the symbols of blackness, and to work hard to prove their pride in being black. (4) They may become strongly committed to reducing discrimination by the white community against all blacks, as illustrated by the work of Du Bois and White. (5) They may accept and make use of the marginal status position, adopting a marginal identity rather than a black identity, perceiving and dealing objectively with the black and the white communities both while not being fully a part of either, and often being a liaison person between the two. (6) They may suppress the dilemma and reject any kind of racial identity, focusing instead on a professional identity or some other absorbing role—for example, being a teacher, doctor, reporter, husband or wife, parent, church or community worker, chess player, supporter of women's rights, or participant in an environmental or peace movement. (7) They may decide to pass as white, experiencing all the stress and risks involved in assuming a white identity. Sometimes a person will switch from one mode of adjustment to another, and sometimes adopt more than one style at a time.

For the majority of the lighter mulattoes, it appears, the constant reinforcement of the American definition of black by both the white and the black community provides a basis for a clear sense of group identity. Increased black pride may have reduced the number who feel marginal, although many of those who do experience marginality feel it intensely. More confidence in black political participation and in maintaining a strong black culture as means of gaining greater opportunities has strengthened the basis for a sense of black identity. However, for an undetermined number of persons whose ancestry is mostly white but who are blacks by definition, marginality and dilemmas of identity are continuing realities.

LENA HORNE'S STRUGGLES WITH HER RACIAL IDENTITY

The life of singer Lena Horne reveals a long and complex struggle with her sense of self, primarily involving her racial identity (touched on briefly in Chapter 1). She was born in a small neighborhood of upper-middle-class blacks in Brooklyn in 1917, to parents whose families had traditions of high respectability if not mulatto elitism (Horne, 1965:1–3; Buckley, 1986). Her parents separated when she was three years old, and she continued to live in Brooklyn with her father's parents until she was seven. Her stern grandmother worked for many black political causes but would never talk about slavery, racial discrimination, or the black identity. Young Lena was not allowed to play with the white children in the area because they were "dirty Irish" (Horne, 1965:7–11).

From age seven on she had some jolting experiences with color when her mother placed her in a series of private homes. In Miami the black children referred to her as yellow. When she lived with her blond uncle in rural Georgia she was called a "yellow bastard" by black schoolchildren and asked why she was so light—although the black girls and women in that community used hair straighteners and skin-whitening beauty aids. She learned that skin color alone was not the problem, because the very light children of a respected local family were not teased, but it was assumed that she was the illegitimate child of an irresponsible white man (Horne, 1965:21–32).

When Lena's mother was remarried, to a white Cuban, their black friends were quite hostile. Lena was startled at the strong anti-white attitudes blacks expressed about this. Her stepfather showed contempt for blacks for not taking more action to fight the discrimination by whites. This marked the beginning of a long period of marginal existence for Lena, in which she saw little of her black friends and relatives and felt neither black nor white. At age sixteen she began working for the Cotton Club in New York, which caused a stir back in the proper middle-class neighborhood in Brooklyn. She wanted to earn money because she thought it might bring her personal respectability and solve her identity problems (Horne, 1965:45–46).

When Lena Horne was getting her start as an entertainer, the typical response was that she neither looked nor sang like a Negro. Her agent tried to get her to solve the problem by learning some Spanish songs and passing as a Latin white. Other members of her family could have passed as white but had not, and she had been taught that was a terrible thing to do. She never seriously considered passing, but began to worry about her racial identity. Was she a middle-class Brooklyn "colored" girl, a rootless child, a black who could fake it as a blues singer or as a Spanish lady? Her dilemma deepened when she got a job with a white band, Charlie Barnet's, and caused the band endless problems in negotiations with racially segregated nightclubs and hotels. Often a hotel would say she could perform there but not stay overnight. These segregated facilities were nationwide, not just in the South.

Love songs were what Lena Horne did best, and she has been called the "first Negro sex symbol." As she struggled with her career and her sense of identity, a number of black entertainers helped her begin to build a black (then "Negro") identity. Paul Robeson talked with her very deliberately about identity and became especially important to her in this respect. Later, in the 1950s, she would be banned from radio and television for several years, partly because of her friendship with Robeson and his associations with Communists. When such entertainers as Tallulah Bankhead repeatedly told her that she had no Negro features, she felt resentment and became convinced that she was Negro and not white (Horne, 1965:106–29).

When Miss Horne took her first screen test, she failed to get a Negro part because she looked like a white person trying to act like a black. This distressed her greatly, and she was even more embarrassed when they tried makeup to help her look darker. Her father objected to her playing the part of maids, and the Negro actors at Metro-Goldwyn-Mayer (MGM) held a protest meeting, saying she was being used as a tool by the eastern NAACP. The Negro bit-part actors had a stake in the status quo in Hollywood, and some of them accused Miss Horne of trying to pass after she got her first small movie part. She appeared in a number of films, always in those earlier years as a singer only, and generally her songs were eliminated for Southern audiences. Count Basie and others tried to persuade her to stay in movies so that whites could see a black woman as a woman, and thus pave the way for others (Horne, 1965:136–44).

The singing engagement that first brought Lena Horne to national attention was in 1940 at the Savoy-Plaza Hotel in New York. The hotel denied her a room there, except for a dressing room, and she registered at the Hotel Theresa in Harlem. One night after collapsing on stage while performing at the Savoy-Plaza, she was carried to a room upstairs. A doctor said she should not be moved, but she insisted on being taken to her own hotel, shouting, "I don't care if I'm dying. Don't leave me where I'm not wanted!" So they took her to the Hotel Theresa, and even though the Savoy-Plaza pleaded with her to change hotels after the much publicized incident and accept accommodations at the Savoy, she continued to return to the Theresa every night after performing (Horne, 1965:147–48).

When Lena Horne met Zulme O'Neill, later Mrs. Cab Calloway, she asked what that "white bitch" was doing hanging around a black man at a party for black soldiers during World War II. She was informed that Miss O'Neill was not white, had graduated from Howard University, and had joined Gunnar Myrdal's research team to study the Jim Crow system in the South. Miss Horne apologized, saying she thought only white people couldn't tell "what we were," and they laughed about it and became good friends. During the war years she participated in political causes for blacks, as her grandmother had done in Brooklyn. When she and her daughter moved into a white neighborhood in Hollywood, petitions were circulated to force them to move out, until this activity was stopped by Humphrey Bogart, Peter Lorre, and others (Horne, 1965:148–57). Horne gave United Service Organization (USO) shows at military camps, suffering through segregation to do so, until at Fort Riley, Kansas, she saw German prisoners of war sitting in the front row at the separate show for blacks. After protesting publicly, she resigned from the USO tour. She also took a stand against segregated housing for wounded Japanese American soldiers living in Hollywood. She had become aware that a "name" has far more influence than an average person, and she considered it her duty to speak out (Horne, 1965:174–78).

Lena Horne's second marriage, to bandleader and composer Lennie Hayton, was kept secret for more than three years because Hayton was white and she feared being called a "white Negro." When the marriage was announced in 1950, many friends and most members of her family stopped speaking to her, black news reporters often asked hostile questions about her marriage, and she received hate letters from both whites and blacks. A typical letter from a black said: "You are one of *us*. Why should you marry one of them?" In her view, black men especially resent such a marriage, taking it as another put-down. When looking for a place to live, the Haytons experienced three kinds of discrimination: against blacks, Jews, and mixed marriages (Horne, 1965:193–241).

The constant incidents involving racial prejudice and segregation wore Lena Horne down, although her agents and her manager-husband, Hayton, protected her as much as possible. She especially hated performing in Las Vegas. Usually she would fight back, often refusing to perform. She mistrusted whites and avoided parties. She liked singing in Europe much better and considered becoming an expatriot in order to feel freer. Once, when she was performing in Miami, she and her husband were nearly arrested for renting a bungalow in violation of a suburb's segregation law. She was put on a union blacklist for performing for allegedly leftist political action groups and for being friendly with Paul Robeson, and she could not get radio or television work in the 1950s until her name was removed from the list in 1956. She had a bit part in a film in 1956. At the end of 1957 she began the successful eighteen-month New York run in the musical *Jamaica* (Horne, 1965:235–55).

Lena Horne experienced a letdown after the musical ended, but felt somewhat better when she joined the National Council of Negro Women and Delta Sigma Theta, a black service sorority. She discussed the problems of blacks and women with Eleanor Roosevelt. Increasingly she felt that she had been estranged from blacks, and she experienced a growing sense of "racial anger." She felt that she had been used as a token symbolic "first" in films, while constantly being discriminated against as a black. She began to identify with the student sit-ins and other civil rights protests by young blacks.

Finally Miss Horne's feelings exploded in 1960, in an incident at a restaurant in Beverly Hills. A white man who wanted dining service was told they would get to him as soon as they finished waiting on Lena Horne and her party. The man replied that she was "just a nigger" and asked where she was. She stood up and answered him, began throwing things at him, and managed to hit him. She had always been afraid that blacks would consider such a reaction as just a publicity stunt on her part, but the ensuing national publicity brought an outpouring of letters and other expressions of identification with her by blacks from across the country. This made her feel she had finally been accepted by her "own people," and she realized that she had always wanted this acceptance.

When Attorney General Robert Kennedy invited her to attend a meeting on the civil rights crisis in Birmingham, Alabama, in 1963, she wondered whether a "symbolic first" had the right to be a black protest leader. Her husband convinced her that she did have that right, just as a black. Later she was apprehensive about singing at an NAACP rally in Jackson, Mississippi, wondering if Southern blacks would really accept her. They did accept her, though, and she began to sing protest songs at rallies sponsored by other civil rights organizations. She met and worked with Medgar Evers, Martin Luther King, Jr., and other major black protest leaders. Finally, she was no longer just one of the "Negro firsts," not just "a freak Negro who didn't sing like one." Her sense of self was stronger than ever, she was now secure in her black identity, and she could finally express love (Horne, 1965:267–87).

In 1965 Lena Horne quit the regular nightclub circuit, tired of singing white songs in expensive white places, dressed in white gowns. She began speaking tours for the National Council of Negro Women and the Delta Sigma Theta sorority, and she made an autograph tour to promote her autobiography. Her first television special was in 1967, and in 1968 she had a dramatic role, not a bit part, in the movie *Death of a Gunfighter*. There was no mention of color in her love affair with a white man in this film—quite a triumph over her early film experiences in the 1940s.

The black protests of the 1960s were repressed violently by the white community, and brutality both by white vigilantes and by police officers was constantly on the television news. These developments had a profound effect on Miss Horne and seemed to force her to identify even more with blacks. She had met NAACP leader Medgar Evers in Jackson, Mississippi, not long before he was shot and killed in 1963. Malcolm X was killed in 1965, and Horne was devastated when her husband said, "Those rabble-rousers always kill each other." She then insisted that she and her husband separate for a time, to allow her time to think about her black identity. Although most blacks had not accepted the black nationalist goals of the then mainstream Black Muslims, or even the less separatist goals of Malcolm X, they identified strongly with the latter's powerful expressions of black determination and unity. Miss Horne felt alienated from liberal whites, to whom she had always been grateful for accepting her. She now even saw her white husband as an adversary, and their separation lasted for three years, which he spent arranging music scores in Hollywood while she remained in New York working for civil rights causes.

In 1970 she lost both her father and her son, and her husband died in 1971 (Haskins and Benson, 1984:161–63). Three years after Hayton's death, Horne was persuaded to begin singing again, first on a British tour with Tony Bennett, which was repeated in the United States and Canada, with no hotel problems. However, Miss Horne refused to sing in Boston during the mid-1970s crisis over the strong white reactions to the mandatory busing of schoolchildren to achieve racial balance. She did more singing on the road, became an important figure in the second Black Renaissance, and made a film with Diana Ross in 1978. She has since received several honors, including a special Tony award for the 1981–82 special television program and two drama critic awards (Haskins and Benson, 1984:201).

After the 1960s the black community became Lena Horne's most important audience. No longer was she following either a marginal or a suppressive mode of adjustment to her problems of racial identity. During the 1970s she moved through a period of hatred of whites to assume some civil rights leadership, and then to a strong emphasis on expressing the symbols of black pride. Her black identity had become firm enough by the 1980s that she no longer seemed bitter about the way she had been treated by her light mulatto family or about discrimination against lighter blacks by darker ones. She had become able to accept whites too, so long as they approved of her message of black pride. She has described herself as a "late bloomer" in developing a firm black identity and a comfortable sense of self, and without the events of the civil rights movement it might not have come about. At one time or another she apparently experienced all the modes of adjustment noted earlier except for the seventh, passing as white. Her life story demonstrates how difficult it can be for light mulattoes to cope with the problems of racial identity under the one-drop rule.

PROBLEMS OF ADMINISTERING THE ONE-DROP RULE

Although the one-drop rule is supported by a strong consensus, applying the rule causes numerous problems and results in some litigation too. We have seen that mistakes in racial classification caused great anxiety as Southerners enforced the laws of Jim Crow segregation. And Lena Horne's story demonstrates that even a very light black can mistake another light black for a white. The deviations from the one-drop rule (Chapter 6) pose some difficult administative problems. For example, in the mid-1960s to the early 1970s many adoption agencies used the label "racially mixed" to refer to lighter mulatto children when they were trying to get large numbers of those children adopted by white families. This administrative avoidance of the one-drop rule probably contributed to rejection of the rule by many white adoptive parents, and thus to delay and stress in the child's acceptance of the black identity. The rule says that children with any black ancestry are to be defined and treated as black persons, not just as human beings without a racial identity, or as mixed people of varying colors. This is often a delicate issue for adoption personnel, particularly for those who are not sympathetic to the one-drop rule.

Flagrant abuse of bureaucratic authority in administering the one-drop, or one black ancestor, rule came to light in Louisiana in recent decades. In the offices that keep vital statistics for Louisiana cities and the state, certain persons have unofficially been known as "race clerks" because of their zeal in trying to make sure the one-drop rule is strictly enforced. These clerks flagged the records of white families whose racial purity is questionable, a practice that was ordered stopped in 1977, at which time there was a list of 250 suspect families. The state's official list of black surnames had been considered more authoritative than birth certificates, church records, or statements by members of a person's community. When race clerks had not been able to persuade a family to come in to discuss it, they had often simply changed birth certificates. In 1976 the state office spent some 6,000 person-hours checking race cases. The champion of these Louisiana race clerks, the deputy registrar in the Office of Vital Records for the City of New Orleans, was fired in 1965 for insubordination. For fifteen years she had been the city's self-appointed arbiter of who could have a "white" birth certificate and who could not, and thus of who could marry whom. She simply refused to issue a copy of a birth certificate if she saw anything in the file that made her at all suspicious. In her last five years in the office she had ignored at least 4,700 applications for certified copies of birth certificates and at least 1,100 applications for death certificates (Trillin, 1986:69–70; Dominguez, 1986:36–51).

Difficulties in racial classification are also encountered in programs of racial desegregation and other efforts to combat discrimination. A program to achieve racial balance in a school district, whether by busing or some other means, requires knowledge of which families are black, and administrators of public housing projects or of budgets for education, recreation, or health programs designated for minorities must be able to identify black families. Affirmative action for school admissions or job hiring and promotions depends on knowing who is black, who is Indian, who is Hispanic, and so on. Such programs are based on deliberate treatment of racial and ethnic categories so as to overcome discrimination against them, rather than on a color-blind policy. A great many programs require demographic information about racial and ethnic groups, and the counting process depends on clear rules of classification.

All efforts to determine the racial composition of a neighborhood, city, state, or the entire country entail the difficult task of identifying all persons who have any known black ancestry regardless of physical appearance. After experimenting with various other operating instructions for more than a century, the U.S. Bureau of the Census adopted the practice of racial self-designation in 1960. This change apparently has not caused any significant shift in the total number of black people reported, due to general acceptance by blacks of the one-drop rule. Those with black ancestry who reject the one-drop rule do not find "mixed" or "human" in the list of racial categories and may check "other" or leave it blank. Presumably those who pass as white check "white," and it is very difficult to estimate their numbers in recent decades. The dependence of all enumerations of blacks in the United States on the one-drop rule must be remembered in interpretations of population growth and migration and in international comparisons of black populations. Other nations count differently, because their definitions of who is black are not the same.

Partly because of the one-drop rule, the typical list of minority groups constructed for administrative purposes is an unsatisfactory mix of race and ethnicity. The "Asian" listing is highly ambiguous, both racially and culturally. "Hispanic" is a cultural, not racial, designation; a Spanish-speaking person may be of any race or racial mixture. Large numbers of Hispanics with some black ancestry have succeeded in defining themselves as Hispanics or Latinos, thus evading the one-drop rule, at least in some situations. Often this definition is accepted for school, affirmative action, or other administrative purposes. On many admissions and application forms, Puerto Ricans are not given the choice of checking "white" or "black," on the assumption that most of those with African ancestry will check "white" (Dominguez, 1986:272–73). In this regard the self-designation of race in the census results in ambiguity. Until 1980 the Census Bureau counted as Puerto Rican the first two generations of immigrants, others being counted as either whites or blacks (Wagenheim, 1975:9; Bahr, Chadwick, and Stauss, 1979:27, 77). In 1980 the Census Bureau asked all those with "Spanish/Hispanic descent" to indicate whether their ethnicity was Puerto Rican, Cuban, Mexican, or "other," partly in order to estimate the incidence of black ancestry among those checking "white" or "other" on the race question (Lieberson and Waters, 1988:6–8, 15–18).

The so-called Mestizo groups (see Chapter 6) have posed problems not only for census enumerators but also for public administrators and law enforcement officials in the East and the South. A varied mixture of black, American Indian, and white ancestry, they have had to live in relatively isolated, small communities in order to evade the one-drop rule. Their entire lifestyle has been designed to avoid the black identity. Tribal American Indians with some black ancestry have also resisted the one-drop rule, and this often becomes an administrative issue in the

South when they leave the reservations. There are variations in both the tribal and the state definitions of who is an American Indian.

A growing administrative and social problem is the racial classification of the dark-skinned caucasian peoples from India and elsewhere in South Asia. The number of Asians from many countries now coming into the United States is much larger than it was before 1965, when the restrictive national origins immigration quotas were abolished. When Hindu poet and savant Rabindranath Tagore visited California before World War II, hotel managers discriminated against him as a black (Ottley, 1943:56). At the Atlanta airport in the 1950s, the UNESCO representative from India was directed to the segregated waiting room for blacks. South Asians have often been treated as blacks in the 1970s, 1980s, and 1990s, in actions designed to maintain the de facto racial segregation in housing in California and elsewhere. For many years the federal courts kept ruling that people from India are not caucasian, but finally held that they are. More recently, Indian spokespersons have contended that "Asian American" should be included as an affirmative action category in combating discrimination in employment, promotions, and school admissions (Rose, 1985:197–98).

Canada includes all East Asians and South Asians in the category "nonwhite." The terms "coloured" and "black" in Great Britain are applied not just to persons of African descent but also to people from India, Pakistan, and Bangladesh. In Great Britain a marriage between a Pakistani or Indian and a European is defined as interracial (Schaefer, 1980:228–32). Probably the term "Asian" suggests "nonwhite" to many if not most Americans, and apparently many consider South Asians to be blacks. After all, the logic might run, the United States defines as blacks many persons whose skin color is lighter than that of most people from India or Pakistan. The same issue has arisen over the perception and treatment of immigrants from the Pacific Islands. Most Americans have been carefully taught that there is no in-between, that all people who are not East Asian or American Indians must be either white or black. Such perceptions affect administrative and legal decisions as well as more informal relations among groups.

Lawsuits testing the legality of the one-drop rule have been infrequent ever since the federal courts so unequivocally endorsed the well-known custom of defining anyone with even a single black ancester as a black person. The Phipps case (*Jane Doe v. State of Louisiana*) was big news nationally in 1983, largely because of its rarity. When the state presented genealogical evidence that allegedly showed Mrs. Phipps and her siblings to be three thirty-seconds black, the courts of Louisiana at all three levels, and the U.S. Supreme Court, left the "traceable amount rule" (the one-drop rule) undisturbed. Brian Bégué, Mrs. Phipps's lawyer, argued before the appellate courts that the one-drop rule violates equal protection of the law because "If you're a little bit black, you're black. If you're a little bit white, you're still black" (Trillin, 1986:76–78).

In Hawaii there is potential for conflicts in law and in policies of public administration over the one-drop rule, because the rule is contrary to the traditional perception and treatment of racially mixed people on the islands (Chapter 5), but perhaps the current experiences of persons with some black ancestry are not uniformly consistent with the tradition. Relevant issues might arise concerning black military personnel or their families, the actions of tourists, or practices in establishments controlled by mainland interests. If mainland custom and law are applied, the one-drop rule might be challenged in court as unsuitable to Hawaiian life. An appeal to courts on the mainland would present the federal judiciary with an even more difficult test than the Phipps case. Could Hawaii perhaps become an official exception to the one-drop rule, even though it is a part of the Union, or might challenges from the islands help to nullify or modify the rule in the rest of the states.

MISPERCEPTIONS OF THE RACIAL IDENTITY OF SOUTH ASIANS, ARABS, AND OTHERS

Misperceptions of racial differences appear to derive at least in part from living in a society with a one-drop rule. Physical features are so important as indicators of ethnic identity that they are often accentuated. When racial differences between two ethnic groups are small or nonexistent, it is common for physical differences to be exaggerated or even created by hairstyles, dress, jewelry, scars or other bodily decoration, and even alterations of physical traits. Visible physical traits become symbols of taste, beauty, refinement, courage, and loyalty to the group. Perceptions of and beliefs about the physical differences, whether the traits are natural or created, are affected by cultural differences and experiences with the groups concerned (Royce, 1982:148–52).

Skin color has been a salient physical feature in intergroup relations, especially in the modern Western world, and it is often used to refer to clusters of traits. The colonial powers encountered darker peoples of different shades around the world and developed the idea that the darker the skin the lower the status and quality of the group. The same concept had emerged much earlier in Hinduism, after Aryan-speaking peoples from Iran and Afghanistan conquered the darker peoples of India. However, light skin is by no means universally valued, as seen in the outlook of the Chinese and Filipinos and in the phrase "Black is beautiful" (Royce, 1982:152–54). We have seen that light brown rather than black has evidently become the preferred color among American blacks, including the ones who are very light, and in Hawaii there seems to be no generally preferred color.

Social distance tests, showing how closely white Americans have been willing to associate with members of some forty ethnic groups, showed remarkable stability from 1926 to 1966. Consistently at the bottom of the list were Hindus, Koreans, mulattoes, Chinese, Turks, Negroes, and Filipinos, and then Japanese and Serbo-Croatians. Social distance was fairly highly correlated with perceived skin color, with such groups as Italians, Portuguese, and Poles in the middle of the list, and English, white Americans, Canadians, and Scots at the top (Bogardus, 1968:152–56). Evidently a good many of the groups on this color continuum are not considered to be white by a large number of Americans, so that only the very whitest populations are seen as white. It would appear that Grant (1916), Stoddard (1920), and other Anglo-Saxon and Nordic supremacists early in the century had some influence on American perceptions of and beliefs about race. Earlier, in the nineteenth century, it was widely believed in England and the United States that the Irish are a dark and inferior race. (Like other Celtic peoples, the Irish are actually Mediterranean whites, similar to the Spanish, Southern French, Italians, Greeks, Jews and other peoples around the Mediterranean, except that Celts more often have blue eyes.) There is recent evidence that many caucasoid groups, including Turks, Iranians, Italians, and Arabs, are not perceived as white by students in Canadian schools (Daniels, 1981:353–56).

Many blacks apparently share the misperceptions of race held by so many whites in the United States, and have some of their own. It seems plausible to suggest that the broad range of physical variation in the black community is a major influence on perceptions of race, especially those of blacks. One consequence of this is the common failure to realize that both the blacks and the whites of South Africa define most of the population called black in the United States as "Coloured," not black. Under the Apartheid system, Coloureds and unmixed blacks are residentially segregated from each other, and problems can arise when leaders of the American black community seek to visit black leaders in South Africa.

There are other misperceptions with important implications for life in the United States. Included among the interviewees in Gwaltney's anthropological study was a seventy-eight-year-old black woman. After describing many mulattoes, blacks, and other dark types she had seen in Morocco and other countries in which she had traveled, she said:

> A lot of them don't want to admit their color because they are afraid that these whitefolks over here would give them a hard time. Now they are right about that. . . . I was in the hospital not long ago and I met this doctor that they said was an Arab. Well, he was darker than many people in my own family. I was proud to see one of the race better hisself. But, you know, that devil didn't want to hear a thing about his color. They had a lot of doctors from India and Jordan working there too. Now, a lot of the colored people didn't want to have anything to do with them because they said if they will pass like that, maybe they are not really doctors, either. . . . There was a young Iraqian doctor there and he was darker than me, but he sure did everything he could think of and then some to show how white he was supposed to be. I don't trust anybody who would deny their color like that. (Gwaltney, 1980:90)

Apparently many American blacks and whites alike assume that almost any dark shade of skin color must be the result of miscegenation with African blacks. This elderly black woman also seemed to assume that all presumably mixed persons everywhere should be defined as black, using the American one-drop rule. Many Moroccans are indeed mulattoes, but many are unmixed Arabs or Berbers. Most people from India are certainly dark, but they are so-called Hindu caucasoids, not part African. Most Arabs are Mediterranean whites, although many in Iraq are descended in part from Hindu caucasoids from India or Pakistan, as are other Arabs and many Iranians, especially along the Persian Gulf. Also, however, some slaves from African tribes have been absorbed into the populations of the Arabian Peninsula.

Another person the black anthropologist Gwaltney interviewed was a black sailor about sixty years old. Gwaltney informed the man that anthropologists classify the people of India and Egypt as caucasians and asked him what he thought about that. The man replied that Gwaltney's anthropological colleagues had lied to him, and said further:

> Well, then, most of them anthropologists ain' never been to Alexandria, Egypt, or Madras, India, cause . . . they got some stone black citizens in both of them towns, not to mention the places in between 'em! Hell, no, they ain' white, an' if you could see 'em you sho' wouldn't be askin' no question like that. A whole heap of folks I saw in Alexandria and other places in Egypt was just as black or blacka den me and mo' than a few was blacka den you, and Jack! That is black enough! (Gwaltney, 1980:91–92)

A white student of mine who had seen blacks at work on the docks in Cairo once said much the same thing. I replied that I too had observed dockworkers in Arab ports in North Africa, and offered a very different interpretation. I explained that there are indeed Nubian tribal peoples who come from the Upper Nile to work as dockhands and as servants in Cairo and Alexandria, but that they are a proud, endogamous people who will not intermarry with the white Arabs. Only in westernmost Africa has Arab-black miscegenation been extensive. My student had not made a distinction between the blacks and the suntanned Arab and Coptic workers. He had simply lumped all Egyptians into the same racial category. I suggested that this would be similar to seeing black workers at such ports as Tampa, New Orleans, or Galveston and concluding that all Americans are blacks.

This same perception of Arabs has been prominent in the crises and changes among the Black Muslims. From 1934 on, Elijah Muhammad's teachings as leader of the "Lost Nation of Islam" included the belief that the Arabs and South Asians are blacks. A good part of his message about the historical supremacy of blacks over the barbaric whites was based on Muhammad's spread of Islam in the seventh century and the several centuries of political dominance and brilliant intellectual leadership by the Arab empires. The Black Muslim practice of dropping their slave names and taking Arabic names is based on the fact that many of the slaves were brought to the United States from areas where the Arabs and Islam had prevailed. Elijah Muhammad opposed the strategy of racial integration in the belief that mixing with whites weakens the natural superiority of blacks—themes that are very similar to those of the earlier Marcus Garvey movement. Although many of these teachings were at variance with the world Islamic movement, the prescribed moral behavior closely followed the Koranic code (Lincoln, 1961:10–16, 68–124, 218–19; Essien-Udom, 1964:28).

Malcolm X became very critical of these separatist teachings, and in 1964 he broke off from what was then the Black Muslim mainstream to form the Organization of African-American Unity. He argued that limited cooperation with whites is both possible and necessary, so long as blacks maintain group pride, control their own organizations, and participate aggressively in politics. This conviction was due in part to the good treatment he had received from whites during a visit to North African countries. He emphasized that he had found the Arabs to be whites, not blacks, and that there was a wide range of color in Egypt. Malcolm X was shot and killed in February 1965, probably by followers of Elijah Muhammad (Sizemore, 1973:321–24; Malcolm X, 1965).

Elijah Muhammad sent his sons to Cairo to study Islamic theology and law. When he died in 1975, his son Wallace assumed leadership, but he guided most of the Black Muslims away from extreme separatism and toward orthodox world Islam and adopted a new name for the organization, The American Muslim Mission. Wallace maintained that his father's anti-white teachings had been anti-Islamic, that the Arabs are whites and not racist, and that the original Muhammad was the last major prophet. The general thrust of Wallace Muhammad's teaching has been similar to that of Malcolm X. Louis Farrakhan has rejected this turn away from separatism and has led his smaller Nation of Islam in the path he believes is true to the teachings of Elijah Muhammad. Farrakhan's public comments in support of the Rev. Jesse Jackson's presidential candidacy in 1984 and 1988 were in the spirit of the separatist tradition, although that position is firmly rejected by Jackson, a Baptist minister.

SAMPLING ERRORS IN STUDYING AMERICAN BLACKS

Scientists in various fields are not immune to misperceptions of race, and very often their misperceptions have affected the design and interpretation of studies of racial differences. One basic problem—the confusing of race with culture (see Chapter 2)—is compounded by a second one, the wide genetic variation in the population defined as black under the one-drop rule. Even when very strict experimental controls of other variables are used in typical medical, psychological, or other studies, most of the black subjects are racially mixed. Some have mostly African ancestry, some mostly white, with a continuum of fractions in between. Sometimes the results are qualified by brief, summary descriptions of the appearances of the black subjects, but more often there is no mention of physical variation. The knowledge and cautions of physical anthropologists and geneticists are often ignored.

It is easy for scientific researchers as well as people in general to be lulled into indifference to the racial variation in the American black community. The first mulattoes during slavery were half black and half white, but ongoing miscegenation and the use of the one-drop rule made lighter and lighter mulattoes seem black, until only the very lightest ones seemed marginal. It is common now to hear someone say, "One parent is black and the other is white, so the child is half-and-half." This describes the child's marginal social group status, but one such child may have a parent whose ancestry is three-fourths African black while another child's parent's ancestry is one-fourth black. The ancestry of the first child would be three-eighths African, the second one-eighth, and the lineage of neither would be "half-and-half." According to the one-drop rule, both simply are black, and both are likely to be used as "black" subjects in much scientific research, along with others at different points on the racial continuum. The black sample may be taken from a black residential area or be based on the judgments of clerks or professionals at a clinic or counseling center or on the racial self-designations of students or medical patients. In any case, the black subjects are typically chosen by using the social definition of race, rather than a genetic definition, but that is appropriate only when the purpose is to study blacks as a social status group or community rather than as a biological category.

The study of racial differences in performance on standardized tests, especially intelligence tests, has been highly controversial, but the criticisms are usually limited to confusing race with social class and other cultural differences. Whether the black test subjects are obtained from conveniently available school classes or from all the classes in a school district or city, or are chosen by a representative sampling procedure, they are racially heterogeneous. Aggregate percentage adjustments of test data for estimated variations in racial ancestry, such as those made by Arthur Jensen (1969), are most unsatisfactory. It is extremely rare even to acknowledge the problem. The unit of analysis in studying race and intelligence is the human individual. To avoid gross aggregate errors, it is necessary to measure the independent variable—race—for each individual, as well as what is presumed to be the dependent variable—the intelligence quotient (IQ).

Another illustration of this problem may be found in studies of responses to pictures of members of different groups. Often there is no explanation of why certain pictures of black persons were chosen, while in other cases they are deliberately selected to reflect the range of traits in the black population. In one study of racial and ethnic designations and preferences of children, responses were obtained to pictures of two black, two white, and two Mexican American children. One of the two black children appears to be mixed but predominantly African, while the other looks mostly white. The pictures are said to be "representative" of the racial groups concerned. Although the researcher acknowledges that the facial expressions, hairstyles, and dress of the children in the pictures may have affected the responses, there is no comment on the large physical differences between the two "black" children (Rohrer, 1977:25–26, 31–32).

Even though most American blacks are racially mixed, only about one-fifth of the genes of the black population as a whole are from white ancestors, and probably fewer than that are from American Indians. For a substantial majority of American blacks, the proportion of African ancestry would probably range from somewhat more than half to more than nine-tenths. Therefore, one might ask, is it not useful to study differences between whites and a population that is predominantly of African origin, especially for a trait such as sickle-cell anemia, which has almost as high an incidence among American blacks as among West Africans? Better yet, why not compare whites with those whose genes came only or almost entirely from Africa, or compare groups that have different amounts of African traits with each other? If it is important to determine racial differences with some precision, how about requiring that certain gene markers of African populations be identified before individuals are included in samples of blacks?

The problem is even more complex than so far suggested here, because genes are randomly distributed in individuals, and gene frequencies therefore do not necessarily correspond to proportions of ancestry.

Thus, some persons with a given fraction of African ancestry have many more "negroid genes" than others with the same lineage, and the smaller the fraction the more probable it becomes that the individual has inherited no genes at all from African peoples. For an unknown number of persons with some known African ancestry, then, the social definition of who is black is entirely fallacious biologically. Selection of black research subjects on the basis of African black appearance might be more justifiable in studies of racial differences than including all people with any known African black ancestry.

The direction of the error introduced by including individuals with many "white genes" in samples of blacks is that racial differences are found to be smaller than they should be, rather than larger. When significant racial differences are found, it is necessary to ensure that they are due to race and not to cultural differences of the sampled populations. When the research aim is to study American blacks as a social status group or community rather than as a biological category, the black community should be sampled in all its racial diversity. In all research designs and interpretations having anything to do with race, it should always be clear whether the definition of who is black is the social or the genetic definition. Not to be clear about the definition, and about the corresponding procedure for selecting blacks to be studied, contributes to the already massive confusion of race with culture.

BLOCKAGE OF FULL ASSIMILATION OF BLACKS

A final area of strain, and sometimes even trauma, is the blocking of blacks from full assimilation except through the stressful means of passing as white. Although the one-drop rule has certainly not prevented miscegenation, most of it illicit, it renders all persons with even invisible amounts of *known* black ancestry socially unassimilable, since their public identity remains black. In the 1950s and 1960s black leaders concluded that complete assimilation of blacks as a people into white community life is neither possible nor desirable. The general black rejection of total separatism in favor of the strategy of integration into the dominant educational, economic, and political institutions has been designed to obtain greater equality of opportunity, not total assimilation. However, some of those who look white consider full assimilation as their personal route to equal treatment. If these individuals are not deterred from passing as white, and thus avoiding the one-drop rule, they must keep their traces of black ancestry secret permanently.

For members of racially visible minority groups other than blacks in the United States, such as American Indians or Korean Americans, miscegenation can lead to upward social mobility and full assimilation into the dominant community (see Chapters 1 and 5). Those racial minorities are not subject to a one-drop rule, and those persons whose ancestry is one-fourth or less from one of those groups are able to become fully assimilated by intermarrying with whites without having to pass as white. Full assimilation is the path to equality followed by immigrant groups from Europe. But this path to equality is barred for blacks by the one-drop rule, since a person remains a black no matter how small the fraction of African ancestry, and the only option is the drastic step of passing as white. For those who do pass, the anxiety about the risks and the sense of loss of family, friends, and the black community must be great, even for the relatively small number who are not "black on the inside." The white community pays a price for the one-drop rule in its anxiety about passing. As the black community in the 1960s became convinced that full assimilation is neither possible nor desirable, internal strains and conflicts developed over how much integration into the white community should be sought. Although the one-drop rule is the ultimate barrier in the white obstacle course to the full assimilation of blacks, it is but one part of the total pattern of unequal treatment.

COSTS OF THE ONE-DROP RULE

Although whites invented and have determinedly enforced the one-drop rule, both by custom and by law, the rule is now strongly reinforced by social controls within the black community. Informal but powerful social pressures deter those who could pass from doing so, and punish those who marry whites. The rule has come to be considered essential to maintaining pride in the black ethnic identity. The deviations from the rule call symbolic attention to it, thus apparently reinforcing it. Despite this high level of support in both the white and the black community, the one-drop rule has its costs—ambiguities, strains, conflicts, and traumas. The uncertainties and problems are due in large part to the wide physical variation in the community defined as black by the rule.

The inability to tell that some persons who look white have some black ancestry can result in personal traumas and deep dilemmas concerning personal identity. Both black families and white ones are torn apart over interracial marriages, sometimes when the "black" partner appears to be totally white. There has been collective white hysteria about "invisible black blood," and divisiveness in the black community over color differences among blacks. The lightest mulattoes feel pressure to prove their blackness. In enforcing the one-drop rule there are also administrative tangles, legal battles, and misperceptions of the racial identity of very large populations in Asia and the Middle East, by American whites and blacks alike. Even much scientific research involves misperceptions of race, or at least the failure to take adequate account of the wide physical variability of the population defined as black in the United States. These difficulties contribute to a very fundamental one, the confusion of race with culture. Finally, for those who choose the road to full assimilation in their quest for equal treatment, the one-drop rule exacts heavy personal costs for passing.

All rules for determining the status of racially mixed populations are subject to administrative and other problems. Certainly the first three status rules discussed in Chapter 5 may incur tensions, oppression, and violent conflicts. Color is relatively unimportant under the fourth and fifth rules (Latin America and Hawaii), especially the latter, yet there are complex problems of social class. In the United States, the experience of nonblack racial minorities under the seventh rule is a rocky version of the path to equality taken by immigrant groups. Assuming the continuation of the sixth rule for American blacks, perhaps the right question is: Can our problems with the one-drop rule be solved or at least ameliorated?

EIGHT

ISSUES AND PROSPECTS

"You have only to look at us to know that miscegenation was part of our background and history, no matter how we decide to deal with it. It's the last big taboo, and I think both blacks and whites have to face this" (McHenry, 1980:38). This statement was made by Barbara Chase-Riboud, an American black woman who married a Frenchman and who has lived in France as a sculptor most of her adult life. She also does drawings and has published two volumes of poetry and an award-winning novel about Sally Hemings, Thomas Jefferson's alleged slave mistress (Chase-Riboud, 1979). In the interview quoted above, Chase-Riboud said that most Americans, both black and white, tend to deny that the lives of black Americans and white Americans have been interlocked. She suggested that Alex Haley's book and television special *Roots*, may have prepared the way for Americans to talk more openly about miscegenation. We need only add that a full discussion of this subject requires adequate treatment of the nation's rule for defining who is black.

The main aim in the present book has been to provide an understanding of the development and effects of the one-drop rule—with necessary emphasis on the connections with miscegenation—not to advocate replacing the rule. Particularly among whites there has been an inadequate understanding of the rule, and both whites and blacks have shown little awareness and concern for some often severe problems engendered by it. Both blacks and whites have lacked perspective on how our definition of black differs from the definitions used in other countries. When difficulties arise—for instance, over the racial classification of Puerto Rican immigrants or other matters—they are likely to be poorly understood. We have been more provincial than we realized. Even if no changes in the rule are possible or desirable, there might be ways to avoid some of the more distressing effects of its application.

A MASSIVE DISTORTION? A MONSTROUS MYTH?

When the term "Brown America" gave way to "Black America" in the 1960s, and the term Negro gave way to black, the nation became more racially polarized than it had ever been (Williamson, 1980:3–5). The paradox is that many members of the community defined as black do not look very black—and some not at all—and studies show that the skin color most preferred is "light brown." One important result of the renaissance of black pride has been to dramatize the disparity between the social-cultural and scientific definitions of who is black. To the uninitiated the nation's definition is astonishing and illogical as a biological classification. Visitors from other countries, and foreigners who see our images on the screen and read our magazines and books, are often amazed to see people who look white being called black. Immigrants, and even children, are similarly astounded when our social definition of who is black so often denies the physical evidence before their eyes.

Such statements as "He certainly doesn't look like a black" indicate that we have indeed created Alice-in-Wonderland blacks in the United States (Harris, 1964:56). Borrowing another image from an old story, the child sees that the emperor is naked but everyone else is pretending the great one is fully clothed. How often do our children say, or think, "But that person is white, or maybe a little bit black and mostly white, so why is everybody pretending she (or he) is black?" Since our definition departs from both common-sense observations and scientific classification, it must often seem hypocritical to children and adults alike. Hypocritical may seem too strong a term, but other potent ones come to mind too, such as massive distortion, monstrous myth, or Big Lie. The myth causes traumatic personal experiences, dilemmas of personal identity, misperceptions of the racial classification of well over a billion of the earth's people, conflicts in families and in the black community, and more.

How do we answer our children and our international visitors? What does perpetuation of such a conceptual distortion do to our mental health? Apparently it is common for black parents to answer simply that black people come in all colors and that appearance is not so important as one's feelings, beliefs, and loyalties. Black children are taught black unity, but they also learn about divisions in their community over variations in color. The teaching that it is very wrong for anyone born and socialized in the black community to "deny his or her color" reinforces the one-drop rule. Only large-scale miscegenation over many generations could have produced the broad and continuous range of racial variation in the black community, yet blacks understandably do not like to talk about this. It was strong white enforcement of the one-drop rule that placed all persons with any black ancestry within the black community, yet black parents generally take the rule as a fact of life and ignore its origins.

White parents have an even harder time explaining the one-drop rule, partly because they and their children see less of the spectrum of racial variation in the black community. Whites are less likely to be aware of the historical facts about miscegenation, to realize that most persons defined as black in the United States are racially mixed and that some "blacks" even look white. There is also less white awareness that most of the white-black sexual contacts have not involved marriage but have been illicit and largely forced onto black women. Whites are also less likely to realize that, ever since 1850 or so in the United States, the mixing of the genes of the populations from Europe and Africa has resulted more from mulatto-African black and mulatto-mulatto unions than from direct contacts with whites. Consequently, whites tend to be less aware of the discrepancy between the social-cultural and genetic definitions of who is black in the United States.

Most parents, white and black, evidently teach their children informally that color is not the only indicator of blackness, that one must also look at the hair, nose, and other physical features. More often than not, though, the indicators of blackness are emphasized without explicit reference to the realities of miscegenation, including the fact that the genetic makeup of a person whose racial identity is uncertain is mostly white (caucasoid). Surprise is the typical response of white college students and adults when the one-drop rule is explained and illustrated. Many white parents emphasize the danger of a sexual union between a white person and an almost-white person by asserting the fallacious but still widely held belief that any resulting children can be "coal black." The idea that even a trace of blackness is contaminating can be communicated without actually putting it into words. And some white parents, especially the supporters of white supremacist groups such as the Ku Klux Klan or Aryan Nations, still teach their children the full set of classic racist beliefs about miscegenation (see Chapter 2).

Apparently neither black nor white parents emphasize that the one-drop rule emerged to protect slavery and later became crucial in building and maintaining the Jim Crow system of segregation. It served to keep mulattoes in slavery or in the black community by defining as blacks all children born to a mother defined as black, and it facilitated the sexual exploitation of black females by white males and the repressive control of black males in the interest of protecting "white womanhood" (Chapters 3 and 4). By defining all mixed children as black and compelling them to live in the black community, the rule made possible the incredible myth among whites that miscegenation had not occurred, that the races had been kept pure in the South. Senator Theodore Bilbo of Mississippi, although conceding that white males had put a lot of "white blood into black veins," blatantly insisted that no race mixing of any consequence had occurred because white women had kept the white race pure (Bilbo, 1947:57–58). Along with the master-servant racial etiquette and the systematic use of coercion, including terror, the one-drop rule operated to keep all persons defined as blacks "in their place" throughout the Jim Crow era. In the cities the rule has meant the de facto segregation from whites of all persons with any apparent or known black ancestry. Ironically, unity and pride in the black community have promoted support for this rule of slavery and segregation by influencing the lightest mulattoes to remain loyal and not pass as white or marry whites. Even parents who understand these historical developments well find these hard things to tell their children, white or black.

CLUES FOR CHANGE IN DEVIATIONS FROM THE RULE

Do the deviations from the one-drop rule (Chapter 6) portend any attempts to change it? To answer that question, we need first to ask whether there is any prospect that the competing rule during slavery might be revived. That rule, which became quite firm only in the Charleston and New Orleans areas, said that mulattoes have an in-between status and that only unmixed Africans are blacks (Chapter 3). It gave way to the one-drop rule as the South tried to save slavery and mulattoes became alienated from whites and increasingly aligned with the black community. By the 1920s the one-drop rule was supported so strongly by both whites and blacks that Marcus Garvey's view that only unmixed Africans are blacks provoked hostile responses from mulatto leaders of the black community. Since then, most light mulattoes have taken pride in their black identity, and since the 1960s the pressure on them to retain their pride in that identity has been great. It now seems extremely unlikely that a rule that assigns mulattoes a status different from that of unmixed blacks could ever again receive general support in Louisiana or South Carolina, or anywhere in the United States.

Many white adoptive parents and racially intermarried couples depart from the one-drop rule by defining their black children as racially mixed, or just "human," rather than black. However, black social workers succeeded almost completely in stopping whites from adopting black children in the mid-1970s, considering the practice harmful to the development in the child of a firm black identity. Although the rate of black-white marriage has increased somewhat in the last two decades, it remains low. Some intermarried parents teach their children to identify as much with their other ethnic ancestries as with the black one, but both the black and the white community generally treat such children as blacks anyway, not as part English, German, Irish, or whatever. Thus these deviations affect relatively few people directly and do not jeopardize the one-drop rule.

We have seen that many of the Spanish-speaking people who have some black ancestry identify themselves as Hispanics or as whites rather than as blacks, an exception known to census enumerators, school officials, and other public administrators. This deviation from the one-drop rule seems to be accepted as a practical compromise, although the black community is much puzzled by it and critical of any people who would deny their color. There are also many people with some black ancestry among American Indian populations, and among the so-called American Mestizos in two hundred or so small, isolated southern and eastern communities, who reject the black identity and the one-drop rule. These exceptions generally seem to be considered nuisances rather than dangerous deviations, and official action to enforce the one-drop rule in these situations is not very determined. These are tolerated, patterned deviations.

Challenges to the rule in court have been rare, especially in the twentieth century. As the Phipps case demonstrates, the rule still seems to be well settled in both state and federal law in the United States. That case has aroused widespread interest, however, and could encourage other legal tests. Cases could come from the Hispanic community, where racial classification often has been a local issue. Before long, Hispanics will become the nation's largest minority group, and they are already increasingly active in politics and in court. Legal challenges to the federal rule might come from Hawaii, where the one-drop rule is contrary to the traditional pattern of race relations. However, the probability of major judicial or legislative challenges to the rule for the nation as a whole seems small. Overall, both individual and patterned deviations from the one-drop rule are likely to continue to symbolize and strengthen it more than pose significant challenges to the rule.

CLUES FOR CHANGE IN COSTS OF THE RULE

Perhaps the costs of the one-drop rule to persons, families, and society as a whole hold clues about the prospects for the future. The black community bears a disproportionate share of these costs, especially for the dilemmas of personal identity, traumatic personal experiences, divisiveness over color differences, family conflicts, and, for those who want to risk that route, the blockage of full assimilation except by passing as white. The consequences of misperceiving the racial classification of South Asian and Middle Eastern populations, and of errors in sampling the black population in scientific studies, are borne by blacks and whites alike. Administrative problems and collective hysterias have been experienced in both the white and the black community, but more in the former. While these are all significant matters, no one of them alone seems likely to become the basis for action to bring about change. If taken all together, however, these problems could constitute grounds for some serious thought about the effects of the rule.

The misperception of the racial identity of South Asians, Middle Easterners, and the darker Pacific Islanders, by both whites and blacks, may become a national issue because of the larger numbers of immigrants from Asian countries since the abolition of the national origins quotas in 1965. Discrimination in housing and other discrimination by whites against immigrants from India and some adjacent nations indicate that there is a widespread belief that such people should be treated as African blacks. Many members of the black community are resentful because the South Asians do not identify with them. Although the latter have been classified as caucasians by scientists and the federal courts, public perception of South Asians as nonwhites creates potential conflicts and the presumption that they are subject to the one-drop rule. If South Asian immigrants go to court over the matter, they are most likely to seek to be declared an exception to the one-drop rule, not to challenge the rule itself.

In the aftermath of the civil rights movement, collective white anxiety about black-white miscegenation and passing as white has not been marked, although in the 1980s and 1990s there has been a resurgence of activity by the Ku Klux Klan, small Nazi organizations, and other white supremacy groups. These groups see the increased number of immigrants from South Asia and East Asia as part of the nonwhite threat, and they are horrified by the only modest increase in the rate of black-white marriages. Concern about the responses and threats of white supremacy groups has been increasing in the white community, although so far it has not become a major public issue. Anxiety among blacks about intermarriage, and about passing as white, has at times reached a level that prompts some of the lighter blacks to see the resulting pressures as a serious problem.

Administrative difficulties in implementing the one-drop rule are not generally perceived as public crises. The Census Bureau expedient of having people designate their own race or ethnic group is also practiced quite widely in schools, public health and welfare agencies, and hospitals. Generally this is not seen as a problem, since most persons with black ancestry follow the one-drop rule. Southern legislatures have taken some pains to get the rule enforced when American Indians with black ancestry leave the reservation. Law enforcement officials in the South and East have not been greatly concerned about the exceptions to the rule in the many small "American Mestizo" communities, since these places remain quite isolated from the rest of the population. The zealous enforcement of the rule in the designation of race on birth records produced a public issue in Louisiana, at least for a time. Administrative problems are indicators of potential public concern over the one-drop rule, then, but are unlikely to precipitate major national issues.

Of the five problems that affect mainly blacks, the two that seem most likely to arouse the black community to the need for action are conflicts within it over color differences, and conflicts within black families. In addition to causing pain and suffering to many persons, these conflicts disrupt black unity and embarrass the black community. However, even though these conflicts are a consequence of the one-drop rule, any suggestion now of changing the rule would impair black unity, not enhance it. Blacks seem more likely to activate their churches and other agencies that seek to resolve conflicts, and to encourage unity among "blacks of all colors." The promotion of black pride has been intended to minimize color and class differences in the black community, not to exacerbate them. At present such pressing problems as drug abuse, crime, and the high rates of teenage pregnancies are high on the agenda of the black community. Even if the level of black concern about conflicts over color differences were to rise considerably, it is highly improbable that the remedies proposed would include changing the rule responsible for the spectrum of color variation in the black community.

The personal traumas, problems of identity, and dilemmas over passing as white are felt keenly by the light-colored persons concerned but do not seem to arouse the general concern of the black community. While the light blacks who experience these problems receive some sympathy, they are often targets of hostility from other blacks. Lena Horne experienced discrimination from both the white and the black community, including members of her own family. Pressures from the black community are especially strong when a very light person passes or marries a white. Such social controls apparently help deter passing and intermarriage and reinforce the one-drop rule, while the persons concerned often experience agonizing dilemmas and feelings of resentment.

Here the value of ethnic unity comes into conflict with an American value much prized by whites and blacks alike, the freedom to make personal choices about one's life. Punitive actions by whites or blacks against passing and intermarriage inhibit that personal freedom, causing forced choices that are painful to make and subordinating love and personal marital choice to loyalty to the ethnic community. Because passing, intermarriage, and the goal of total assimilation are all overwhelmingly rejected in the black community, by most of its lightest members as well as the darker ones, the pressure on deviant individuals can be intense. Despite some gains, blacks as a whole are a long way from having equal opportunities in the United States, and those relative few who consider improving their life chances by passing or intermarrying find the black community ready to punish them heavily for it. Here the black community is enforcing the one-drop rule almost as determinedly, if not so violently, as Jim Crow terrorist enforcers ever did. Because the white community too stands ready with strong punitive measures, the risk of passing as white is great.

We have seen that it is the way people think, feel, and believe, not how they look, that makes them members of the black ethnic community. Along the entire color continuum, in response to common experiences that include systematic discrimination by whites, nearly all persons with some black ancestry have internalized the black identity. The pressure not to deny their color is put especially on those whose ancestry is mainly white, at least some few of whom have developed a white identity and thus are not black either biologically or in ethnic identification. Through no fault of their own as individuals, the experiences of some have been different from almost all other persons with known black lineage, and "on the inside" they have not become members of the black community. Examples include some of the children adopted by white parents, a large number of Puerto Ricans, Cubans, and other immigrants from the Caribbean area, residents of the isolated Mestizo communities, and some intellectuals and artists.

There are also several other modes of adjustment to this problem of personal identity (see Chapter 7). Some simply wish to be independent, marginal but loosely connected to both the black community and the white, an adjustment that often has advantages in interracial marriages and in academic or other professional communities (Willie, 1975). This latter pattern is preferred by some blacks who have been raised by white adoptive parents, so that they are not forced to reject either the white or the black community. This is an individualistic variation of the mode that the more traditional Creoles of Color are still trying to perpetuate. However, there is very low tolerance for deviations from the one-drop rule in our nation's polarized pattern of black-white relations.

POSSIBLE DIRECTION: WHICH ALTERNATIVE?

Whites are not alone in taking the one-drop rule for granted. Not only have black civil rights efforts not included attempts to change the rule, but the very thought of changing it is seen as a threat. Blacks continue to push for an end to discriminatory practices that deny them equal opportunities, and also to worry about severe internal problems in their communities. Rising black unity at the end of the 1960s meant supporting as much institutional integration as necessary to gain equal treatment but rejecting more complete integration and the eventuality of total assimilation into white community life (Chapter 4). The type of intergroup accommodation envisioned is equalitarian pluralism, a mosaic of mutually respectful racial and ethnic groups with equal status. Black rejection of the goal of full assimilation is based partly on the knowledge that whites will not accept it—the one-drop rule standing as the ultimate barricade. It is based also on the desire to maintain black culture, including some ethnic organizational patterns. The selective pattern of separation, however, would be voluntary rather than mandated and enforced by whites.

Given the origins of the one-drop rule in white racist beliefs and overwhelming power domination, how do we explain the acceptance and even strong support of the rule in the American black community today? The answer is that under the rule all racially mixed progeny have been assigned the same social status as unmixed blacks, the eventual result being an ethnic community composed of all persons with any known African black ancestry. The common experiences shared in this black community provide the basis for ethnic unity and pride and for political and other organized efforts to protect and help its members. The suggestion today that the one-drop rule is an arbitrary social construction that could be changed sounds to the black community like a dangerous idea. If one result of such a change would be to cause some lighter-colored persons to leave the black community for the white community, the former would lose some of its hard-won political strength, perhaps some of its best leaders, some members of its churches and other community institutions, some business and professional people, and some customers and clients. American blacks now feel they have an important vested interest in a rule that has for centuries been a key instrument in their oppression.

Whites, especially those who have not lived in the South, typically have only a vague understanding of how the one-drop rule has operated, and there have been no initiatives to eliminate it. The mere suggestion would no doubt increase awareness of the rule and arouse widespread fears of a drastic rise in miscegenation. Replacing the rule would require a marked decline, to a very low point, of white prejudice and discrimination against blacks. The last whites to accept a major change in the rule would be those most bent on perpetuating racist beliefs and practices. Realistically, then, it would seem that if any modification of the rule is possible, it must be perceived as a minor exception, such as the existing patterned deviations.

Although the purpose here is not to propose changing the one-drop rule, a brief further exploration of the likelihood of change will bring the current scene into sharper focus and help us to anticipate future developments. If the rule were to be modified even slightly, what direction would the change probably take? Might the rule be modified to move it toward one of the world's other status rules for racially mixed people (see Chapter 5)? We can eliminate fairly quickly the first two types, those in which the status of mixed populations is either lower or higher than that of both the parent groups. The historical circumstances of such bottom-of-the-ladder hybrid groups as the Métis in Canada, the Ganda of Uganda, the Eurasians, and the Amerasians in Korea and Vietnam are very different from those of American mulattoes under slavery, Jim Crow, or the conditions of today. The ultimately superior political position of the mulattoes of Haiti and the Mestizos of Mexico also has no possible parallel in the United States.

As for the middle-minority position that has occurred in many times and places, we have already noted that the potential seems to be nil for a revival of the niche occupied by mulattoes during slave times in South Carolina and Louisiana. That exception is the only instance in the United States in which mulattoes have occupied a buffer position between blacks and whites. For over a century now, the nation's light mulatto leaders, whatever their particular style, have performed as leaders of blacks rather than of a middle group, and they have tended to hold high rank in the class structure of the black community. In recent years they have been clasped more tightly than ever in the embrace of black pride, emphasizing the polarization of the groups defined as blacks and whites in the United States. We have only to recall the sharp distinction in the Republic of South Africa between unmixed blacks and Coloureds to realize what a different pattern has developed under the one-drop rule.

The definition of the racial status of mulattoes on the mainland of the United States seems much less likely to move in the direction of the Hawaiian pattern than that of either the Latin American or the Northwestern European variant in the Caribbean. Being proud of all one's ancestries is the antithesis of the one black ancestor, or one-drop, rule. Hawaii's balance between equalitarian pluralism and the melting pot type of assimilation is worthy of careful study, but anything even approaching that pattern on the mainland is not a realistic possibility in the foreseeable future.

Both in Latin America and in the United States, miscegenation has produced the complete range of racial traits from negroid to caucasoid to American Indian mongoloid, along with marked color consciousness, and the traditional association of higher status with lightness. The differences between the two patterns are great, however, including the high frequency in Latin America of marriage between whites and lighter mulattoes with visible negroid traits, and the very low rate in the United States. Many Latin American mulattoes, and not just the lightest ones, are considered whites, while most others are designated by one or more of the many terms for gradations of color. These reminders ought to suggest the low probability that racially polarized North America might move in the direction of the pliant racial patterns of Latin America, where class is more important than racial traits.

Although the major outlines of the two variants of the pattern in the Caribbean are similar, the Northwest European variant is more similar to the pattern in the United States than the Iberian variant is. The main difference between the two Caribbean variants is that the Northwest Europeans, including the British, have not married mulattoes with visible African traits as the Iberian whites have. There has of course been illicit black-white miscegenation, or there would be no mulattoes on those islands, but the British, the Dutch, and the French have readily associated with and married mulattoes who have known black ancestry but who appear white. Thus even the British in the Caribbean have been concerned with racial appearance rather than with ancestry and have not had a one-drop rule. It is worth remembering that in South Carolina and Louisiana it was generally acceptable for whites to marry known mulattoes, even those with visible African traits, until the 1840s. Also, in Europe there is no general opposition to intermarriage with persons with known black African ancestry, and in Southern Europe they need not even appear white.

The Northwest European variant in the Caribbean is closer to the pattern in the United States under the one-drop rule than the pattern under any of the world's other status rules for racially mixed people. Although racial intermarriage rates are quite low both on the Northwest European islands in the Caribbean and in the United States, collective hysteria about invisible blackness and the agonizing process of passing as white are avoided on those islands. Although white Americans generally would no doubt perceive the idea of adopting the Iberian variant in the Caribbean as a drastic deviation from the one-drop rule, it seems possible that many could accept the Northwest European variant, treating it as only a limited and beneficial exception. Such toleration might be possible especially for those who realize that the lightest blacks carry very few genes from African ancestors, in some cases none, and that many common beliefs about miscegenation are false and racist. Other whites, however, especially supporters of white supremacy organizations, would be as adamantly opposed to the Northwest European variant as to any other departure from the one-drop rule. White fears of massive miscegenation would be fanned, and this change would stand little if any chance.

Would the Northwest European variant of the Caribbean pattern be received in the black community any better than in the white? If it were accepted, pressures on light mulattoes to demonstrate their loyalty would lessen, and the relative few wishing to be fully assimilated by the white community would not have to abandon their families of origin, black friends, and the black community and secretly pass as white. Here we are dealing with the ultimate testing point of the one-drop rule, and with matters that arouse strong emotions in both the black and the white community. Acceptance of the Northwest European variant by the black community would require the belief that it would be but a minor exception to the one-drop rule, that very few persons would be lost to the white community, and that black unity would not be impaired. It seems highly unlikely that the black community would take this leap of faith, not so long as equal treatment of blacks is still a distant and elusive goal.

What about the prospect for assimilation by the dominant Anglo-American community, including full acceptance of widespread intermarriage between whites and one-fourth (or less) blacks? This process has helped the visible racial minorities other than blacks to climb the class ladder and achieve equal treatment. To whites this would seem to be an extreme departure from the one-drop rule, which is designed to prevent total assimilation of persons with invisible as well as visible black ancestry.

While some barriers to opportunities for blacks have been lowered, white opposition to informal social contacts has remained strong, so that public and on-the-job contacts have not led to much increase in after-hours socializing, sexual liaisons, or intermarriage. Churches remain as segregated as ever. Housing segregation has been increasing in urban areas, not declining, keeping blacks and whites largely separate in their private lives. In the black community, pressures for unity have also limited social contacts between blacks and whites. Total assimilation by the dominant community means loss of the minority group's identity, and counting that group as just part of one's ancestral background. Therefore, complete assimilation is firmly rejected by both the white and the black community.

PROSPECTS FOR THE FUTURE

We can only conclude that none of the world's known alternatives to the American definition of who is black now seems at all likely to be given serious consideration in the United States. Although the one-drop rule was developed to perpetuate the enslavement, segregation, and institutional exploitation of blacks, it is now firmly entrenched in both the black and white community and in American custom and law. We have seen, however, that there are significant deviations and even administrative exceptions and legal challenges to the rule. So far the deviations have provided symbolic support more than they have undermined the rule, and the court cases have strengthened the rule. Both the deviations and the lawsuits have enhanced public awareness of the painful costs the rule imposes on significant numbers of people.

If white support for the one-drop rule ever declines, blacks may become less adamant about demanding absolute enforcement. We have seen that most of the problems attending the rule put a heavy burden on the black community. Moreover, the black community is not so dependent on light mulatto leaders and role models as it was before the 1970s, now that significant numbers of blacks of darker hue are attaining important political and other positions and making educational and occupational gains. But unfortunately, blacks as a whole have lost many of the earlier political, legal, and educational gains, and the gaps between whites and blacks in percentage of employment and in average family income have increased. The black community seems to be concerned about some of the consequences of the one-drop rule, but though this concern might produce efforts to remedy the problems, proposals for even minor changes in the one-drop rule itself would most likely be seen as an unacceptable threat to the black community.

Although, in the light of history, there is bitter irony in the fact that blacks support the one-drop rule, there is no mystery about how that happened. The rule was created in the slave South, where miscegenation was widespread, to force all racially mixed individuals with any known black ancestry into the status of slaves. Later the rule buttressed the Jim Crow system and other patterns of segregation and discrimination, became accepted as the nation's norm, and was backed by law. Determined white enforcement of the one-drop rule brought persons with a wide range of racial traits together in the black community, and centuries of shared experience resulted in a common ethnic culture. Lighter-colored persons increasingly joined forces with darker ones for mutual protection in the latter half of the nineteenth century, sharing a common destiny and eventually pride in a common community. Initially the black community had no choice but to accept the one-drop rule and teach its children how to cope with it, but eventually this ethnic community came to favor the rule and help to enforce it vigorously to keep lighter-colored members from defecting to the white community.

Some scholars assert that widespread black-white intermarriage is the only way to solve the problems of black Americans (Henriques, 1975). Some believe that the gradual "browning" of the dominant white American population is inevitable, at least within 150 years or so, due partly to increased immigration from Asian nations and partly to more black-white intermarriage (Pear, 1984:28). Those who hold this view seem to overlook the fact that there has been considerable black-white miscegenation for centuries, mostly outside of marriage, and that the population defined as white is unaffected as long as the one-drop rule prevails. Those who pass as white have few genes from African forebears, in some cases none, and thus do not darken the white population. The rate of black-white intermarriage seems likely to remain very small, and the resulting children will be defined as blacks. Extramarital sexual contact between blacks and whites has remained at a low level, especially since the 1960s, and does not result in many children. A more plausible forecast would be that further browning of the population defined as black will occur and that the percentage of Americans with dark skin will show some increase as a result of immigration from both Asia and Africa. The extent of extramarital sexual contact and intermarriage between European Americans and immigrants from South Asia remains to be seen.

Many black scholars and other leaders have urged that the term "African American" be substituted for "black," to shift attention from the physical traits of a racial group to cultural experiences that people of African background have shared in their long history in America. The term suggests that African Americans will increasingly take their place in the nation as another ethnic group. Black leaders today generally envision African Americans as part of a pluralistic pattern of peoples rather than as an assimilating group that is in the process of giving up its ethnicity to a common "melting pot" or, as European immigrant groups have done, to become Anglo-American. That is, African Americans would remain a community with some institutions of its own and its own cultural identity, just as Mexican Americans wish to do.

Some who encourage the use of the term "African American" hope its use will reduce the importance of race in American life and even help bring about a color-blind society. This last would seem to be a vain hope, at least for some generations to come. The immediate effect of using the African American label is simply to substitute it for "black" as a designation of both racial classification and ethnic group identity. The one-drop rule remains, with an African American defined as someone with at least one African ancestor, rather than as a person with "even one drop of black blood." Genetically the rule retains its long-standing meaning, since the African ancestry referred to is that of black peoples, not of Arabs, Berbers, Copts, Afrikaner, or other African whites. Perhaps in time the American pattern of black-white relations will become less polarized, in which case African American would be a suitable designation to accompany that process.

It seems unlikely that the one-drop rule will be modified in the foreseeable future, for such a move would generally be opposed by both whites and blacks. This means that any efforts to mitigate some of the troubling consequences of the rule (Chapter 7) must be undertaken within the framework of the rule as it now stands. All of the rules used in societies around the world for defining the status of racially mixed populations have had their own special problems. Americans seem not to have worried much about the costs exacted by the one-drop rule.

Greater willingness to discuss the history of black-white miscegenation may well result in greater understanding of the uniqueness of the one-drop rule in the world and of how it singles out blacks in the United States in contrast to all other racially visible minority groups. In a nation founded on democratic ideals, sooner or later serious questions will be raised about a rule of racial classification that was created from racist beliefs and designed to deny equal opportunities to all persons who have any African black ancestry. However, unless the whole institutional pattern of discrimination against blacks declines drastically, most whites will not be inclined to accept a significant change in the one-drop rule, and in the meantime the black community also has a vested interest in maintaining that rule.

More visits to Hawaii, more international travel and communication, and more immigration from Asian and Latin American countries are bound to increase awareness that there are other ways to define the status and identity of racially mixed persons. Growing international involvement may also draw our attention to the socially constructed one-drop rule in the United States, a rule that violates genetic logic and often amazes our children, Latin Americans, Asians, Africans, and even the British, French, and other Europeans. Whether or not any change in the one-drop rule is ever possible or deemed desirable, we need a fuller and broader understanding of the American way of defining who is black. In our increasingly multiracial society, there will almost certainly be new crises in race relations, new perspectives and attitudes, new concepts and social practices, and appropriate changes in the nation's laws. Although the one-drop rule itself appears to be secure for the indefinite future, it is likely that ways to ameliorate the more serious problems stemming from it will be sought.

WORKS CITED

Adams, Romanzo. 1969. "The Unorthodox Race Doctrine of Hawaii." In Melvin Tumin, ed., *Comparative Perspectives on Race Relations*, pp. 81–90. Boston: Little, Brown & Co.

Anderson, Claud, and Rue L. Cromwell. 1977. " 'Black Is Beautiful' and the Color Preferences of Afro-American Youth." *Journal of Negro Education* 46 (Winter), 76–88.

Anderson, Jervis. 1972. *A. Philip Randolph: A Biographical Portrait*. New York: Harcourt Brace Jovanovich.

Bahr, Howard M., Bruce A. Chadwick, and Joseph H. Stauss. 1979. *American Ethnicity*. Lexington, Mass.: D. C. Heath & Co.

Baldwin, James. 1962. *Nobody Knows My Name*. New York: Dell Publishing Co.

Ballhatchet, Kenneth. 1980. *Race, Sex, and Class Under the Raj: Imperial Attitudes and Policies and Their Critics, 1793–1905*. New York: St. Martin's Press.

Banton, Michael. 1983. *Racial and Ethnic Competition*. Cambridge: Cambridge University Press.

Barrow, Brian. 1977. *South African People*. Cape Town: Macdonald South Africa.

Bennett, Lerone, Jr. 1962. *Before the Mayflower: A History of the Negro in America, 1619–1962*. Chicago: Johnson Publishing Co.

———. 1965. *What Manner of Man: A Biography of Martin Luther King, Jr.* Abridged ed. New York: Pocket Books.

Berlin, Ira. 1975. *Slaves Without Masters: The Free Negro in the Antebellum South.* New York: Pantheon Books.
Berry, Brewton. 1963. *Almost White.* New York: Macmillan Co.
———. 1965. *Race and Ethnic Relations.* 3rd ed. Boston: Houghton Mifflin Co.
Berry, Brewton, and Henry L. Tischler. 1978. *Race and Ethnic Relations.* 4th ed. Boston: Houghton Mifflin Co.
Bilbo, Theodore Gilmore. 1947. *Take Your Choice: Separation or Mongrelization.* Poplarville, Miss.: Dream House Publishing Co.
Blackwell, James E. 1975. *The Black Community: Diversity and Unity.* New York: Dodd, Mead & Co.
Blalock, Hubert M., Jr. 1967. *Toward a Theory of Minority-Group Relations.* New York: Capricorn Books.
Bland, Randall W. 1973. *Private Pressure on Public Law: The Legal Career of Justice Thurgood Marshall.* Port Washington, N.Y.: Kennikat Press.
Blassingame, John W. 1972. *The Slave Community: Plantation Life in the Antebellum South.* New York: Oxford University Press.
———. 1973. *Black New Orleans, 1860–1880.* Chicago: University of Chicago Press.
Blaustein, Albert P., and Clarence Clyde Ferguson, Jr. 1957. *Desegregation and the Law.* New Brunswick, N.J.: Rutgers University Press.
Bogardus, Emory S. 1968. "Comparing Racial Distance in Ethiopia, South Africa, and the United States." *Sociology and Social Research* 52 (January), 149–56.
Boskin, Joseph. 1976. *Into Slavery: Racial Decisions in the Virginia Colony.* Philadelphia: J. B. Lippincott Co.
Buckley, Gail Lumet. 1986. *The Hornes: An American Family.* New York: Alfred A. Knopf.
Burma, John G. 1946. "The Measurement of 'Passing.' " *American Journal of Sociology* 52 (July), 18–22.
Burman, Stephen. 1979. "The Illusion of Progress: Race and Politics in Atlanta, Georgia." *Ethnic and Racial Studies* 2 (October), 441–54.
Campbell, Mavis. 1974. "Aristotle and Black Slavery: A Study in Race Prejudice." *Race* 15 (January), 283–301.
Cannon, Poppy. 1956. *A Gentle Knight: My Husband, Walter White.* New York: Rinehart & Co.
Catterall, Helen T., ed. 1926–37. *Judicial Cases Concerning American Slavery and the Negro.* 5 vols. Washington, D.C.: Carnegie Institute of Washington.
Chamberlain, Houston Stewart. 1899. *Foundations of the Nineteenth Century.* 2 vols. Translated by John Lees. London: Bodley Head.
Chase-Riboud, Barbara. 1979. *Sally Hemings.* New York: Viking Press.
Coon, Carleton. 1962. *The Origin of Races.* New York: Alfred A. Knopf.
Cronon, Edmund Davis. 1955. *Black Moses.* Madison: University of Wisconsin Press.
Daniels, Doug. 1981. "The White Race Is Shrinking: Perceptions of Race in Canada." *Ethnic and Racial Studies* 4 (July), 353–56.
Davies, James C. 1971. *When Men Revolt and Why.* New York: The Free Press.
Davis, F. James. 1978. *Minority-Dominant Relations.* Arlington Heights, Ill.: AHM Publishing Co.
Davis, F. James, Henry H. Foster, Jr., C. Ray Jeffery, and E. Eugene Davis. 1962. *Society and the Law.* New York: The Free Press.
Davis, Kenneth. 1976. "Racial Designation in Louisiana: One Drop of Black Blood Makes a Negro!" *Hastings Constitutional Law Quarterly* 3 (Winter), 199–228.
Day, A. Grove. 1960. *Hawaii and Its People.* Rev. ed. New York: Duell, Sloan, & Pearce.

Day, Caroline Bond. 1932. *A Study of Some Negro-White Families in the United States.* Harvard African Studies No. 10. Cambridge, Mass.: Peabody Museum of Harvard University.

Day, Dawn. 1979. *The Adoption of Black Children: Counteracting Institutional Discrimination.* Lexington, Mass.: Lexington Books, D. C. Heath & Co.

de Gobineau, Joseph-Arthur. 1853–55. *Essai sur inegalité des races humaines.* Translated by Adrian Collins. London: Heinemann.

Dominguez, Virginia R. 1986. *White by Definition: Social Classification in Creole Louisiana.* New Brunswick, N.J.: Rutgers University Press.

Durkheim, Emile. 1960. *The Division of Labor in Society.* Translated by George Simpson. New York: The Free Press.

Eckard, E. W. 1947. "How Many Negroes Pass?" *American Journal of Sociology* 52 (May), 498–503.

Editors of Newsweek Books. 1974. *Thomas Jefferson: A Biography in His Own Words.* New York: Newsweek; distributed by Harper & Row.

Edwards, Gilbert Franklin. 1958. *The Negro Professional Class.* New York: The Free Press.

Essien-Udom, E. U. 1964. *Black Nationalism.* New York: Dell Publishing Co.

Forbes, Jack D. 1966. *Afro-Americans in the Far West.* Washington, D.C.: U.S. Government Printing Office.

Frazier, E. Franklin. 1957. *The Negro in the United States.* Rev. ed. New York: Macmillan Co.

Garn, Stanley M. 1965. *Human Races.* 2nd ed. Springfield, Ill.: Charles C. Thomas.

Gist, Noel P., and Roy Dean. 1973. *Marginality and Identity.* Leiden: E. J. Brill.

Glasco, Laurence. 1974. "The Mulatto: A Neglected Dimension of Afro-American Social Structure." Paper given at the Convention of the Organization of American Historians, April 17–20, 1974, pp. 23–38.

Goering, John M. 1972. "Changing Perceptions and Evaluations of Physical Characteristics Among Blacks, 1950–1970." *Phylon* 33 (September), 231–41.

Gordon, Milton M. 1964. *Assimilation in American Life.* New York: Oxford University Press.

Grant, Madison. 1916. *The Passing of the Great Race.* New York: Scribner.

Greenberg, Jack. 1959. *Race Relations and American Law.* New York: Columbia University Press.

Grimké, Sarah Stanley. 1889. Letter to Archibald Grimké, April 25, 1889. Box 3, folder 79, Archibald Grimké papers, Moorland-Spingarn Research Center, Manuscript Division, Howard University, Washington, D.C.

Grow, Lucille J., and Deborah Shapiro. 1974. *Black Children—White Parents.* New York: Child Welfare League of America.

Guffy, Ossie. 1971. *Ossie: The Autobiography of a Black Woman,* as told to Caryl Ledner. New York: Bantam Books.

Gwaltney, John Langston. 1980. *Drylongso: A Self-Portrait of Black America.* New York: Vintage Books.

Haley, Alex. 1976. *Roots: The Saga of an American Family.* New York: Doubleday & Co.

Harris, Melvin. 1964. *Patterns of Race in the Americas.* New York: W. W. Norton.

Haskins, James, with Kathleen Benson. 1984. *Lena: A Personal and Professional Biography of Lena Horne.* New York: Stein & Day.

Hellman, Ellen, and Henry Lever, eds. 1979. *Race Relations in South Africa, 1929–1979.* New York: St. Martin's Press.

Helm, Mackinley, 1942. *Angel Mo' and Her Son, Roland Hayes.* Boston: Little, Brown & Co.

Henriques, Fernando. 1975. *Children of Conflict: A Study of Interracial Sex and Marriage.* New York: E. P. Dutton.

Heuman, Gad J. 1981. *Between Black and White: Race, Politics, and the Free Coloreds in Jamaica, 1792–1865.* Westport, Conn.: Greenwood Press.

Hill, Christopher. 1964. *Bantustans: The Fragmentation of South Africa.* London and New York: Oxford University Press.

Hill, Robert B. 1977. *Informal Adoption Among Black Families.* Washington, D.C.: National Urban League Research Department.

Hoetink, H. 1967. *Caribbean Race Relations: A Study of Two Variants.* London and New York. Oxford University Press.

Holzman, Jo. 1973. "Color, Caste Changes Among Black College Students." *Journal of Black Studies* 4 (September), 92–101.

Hooton, E. A. 1948. *Up From the Ape.* New York: Macmillan Co.

Horne, Lena, and Richard Schickel. 1965. *Lena.* Garden City, N.Y.: Doubleday & Co.

Horowitz, Donald L. 1973. "Color Differentiation in the American Systems of Slavery." *Journal of Interdisciplinary History* 3 (Winter), 509–41.

Howard, Alan. 1980. "Hawaiians." In Stephan Thernstrom, ed., *Harvard Encyclopedia of American Ethnic Groups*, pp. 449–52. Cambridge, Mass.: Harvard University Press.

Howard, John. 1974. *The Cutting Edge: Social Movements and Social Change in America.* Philadelphia: J. B. Lippincott Co.

Hughes, Langston. 1970. *Selected Poems.* New York: Alfred A. Knopf.

Hunt, Chester, and Lewis Walker. 1974. *Ethnic Dynamics: Patterns of Inter-Group Relations in Various Societies.* Homewood, Ill.: Dorsey Press.

Jensen, Arthur R. 1969. "How Much Can We Boost IQ and Scholastic Achievement?" *Harvard Educational Review* 39 (Winter), 1–123.

Johnson, Charles S. 1941. *Growing Up in the Black Belt: Negro Youth in the Rural South.* Washington, D.C.: American Council on Education.

Johnston, James Hugo. 1970. *Race Relations in Virginia and Miscegenation in the South, 1776–1860.* Amherst: University of Massachusetts Press.

Jorge, Angela. 1979. "The Black Puerto Rican Woman in Contemporary American Society." In Edna Acosta-Belén, ed., *The Puerto Rican Woman*, pp. 134–41. New York: Praeger.

Killian, Lewis. 1975. *The Impossible Revolution, Phase II: Black Power and the American Dream.* 2nd ed. New York: Random House.

King, Martin Luther, Jr. 1967. *Where Do We Go from Here? Chaos or Community?* New York: Harper & Row.

Kroeber, Alfred L. 1948. *Anthropology.* New York: Harcourt, Brace & Co.

Ladner, Joyce A. 1977. *Mixed Families: Adopting Across Racial Boundaries.* Garden City, N.Y.: Anchor Press/Doubleday & Co.

Laue, James H., and Leon M. McCorkle, Jr. 1965. "The Association of Southern Women for the Prevention of Lynching: A Commentary on the Role of the Moderate." *Sociological Inquiry* 35 (Winter), 80–93.

Lelyveld, Joseph. 1985. *Move Your Shadow: South Africa Black and White.* New York: Times Books.

Lieberson, Stanley, and Mary C. Waters. 1988. *From Many Strands: Ethnic and Racial Groups in Contemporary America.* New York: Russell Sage Foundation.

Lincoln, C. Eric. 1961. *The Black Muslims in America.* Boston: Beacon Press.
Litwach, Leon F. 1961. *North of Slavery.* Chicago: University of Chicago Press.
Loehlin, John C., Gardner Lindsey, and J. N. Spuhler. 1975. *Race Differences in Intelligence.* San Francisco: W. H. Freeman & Co.
Loewen, James W. 1971. *The Mississippi Chinese: Between Black and White.* Cambridge, Mass.: Harvard University Press.
Lowenthal, David. 1969. "Race and Color in the West Indies." In Melvin Tumin, ed., *Comparative Perspectives on Race Relations,* pp. 293–312. Boston: Little, Brown & Co.
McHenry, Susan. 1980. " 'Sally Hemings': A Key to Our National Identity." *Ms Magazine* 9 (October), 35–40.
McRoy, Ruth G., and Louis A. Zurcher. 1983. *Transracial and Inracial Adoptees: The Adolescent Years.* Springfield, Ill.: Charles C. Thomas.
Malcolm X. 1965. *The Autobiography of Malcolm X.* New York: Grove Press.
Mangum, Charles Staples, Jr. 1940. *The Legal Status of the Negro in the United States.* Chapel Hill: University of North Carolina Press.
Marden, Charles F., and Gladys Meyer. 1973. *Minorities in American Society.* 4th ed. New York: D. Van Nostrand Co.
Martin, Tony. 1976. *Race First.* Westport, Conn.: Greenwood Press.
Martin, Waldo E., Jr. 1984. *The Mind of Frederick Douglass.* Chapel Hill: University of North Carolina Press.
Model, F. Peter, ed. 1983. "Apartheid in the Bayou." *Perspectives: The Civil Rights Quarterly* 15 (Winter–Spring), 3–4.
Montagu, Ashley. 1964. *Man's Most Dangerous Myth: The Fallacy of Race.* Rev. ed. New York: Harcourt Brace Jovanovich.
———, ed. 1975. *Race and IQ.* New York: Oxford University Press.
———. 1977. "On the Nonperception of 'Race' Differences." *Current Anthropology* 18 (December), 743–44.
Mörner, Magnus, ed. 1970. *Race and Class in Latin America.* New York: Columbia University Press.
———. 1967. *Race Mixture and the History of Latin America.* Boston: Little, Brown & Co.
Morris, Laura Newell. 1971. *Human Populations: Genetic Variation and Evolution.* San Francisco: Chandler Publishing Co.
Muir, Donal E., and C. Donald McGlamery. 1984. "Trends in Integration Attitudes on a Deep-South Campus During the First Two Decades of Desegregation." *Social Forces* 62 (June), 963–72.
Mullins, Elizabeth I., and Paul Sites. 1984. "The Origins of Contemporary Black Americans: A Three-Generational Analysis of Social Origin." *American Sociological Review* 49 (October), 672–85.
Myrdal, Gunnar, assisted by Richard Sterner and Arnold M. Rose. 1944. *An American Dilemma.* New York: Harper & Bros.
Newman, William M. 1973. *American Pluralism: A Study of Minority Groups and Sociological Theory.* New York: Harper & Row.
Nicholls, David. 1981. "No Hawks or Pedlars: Levantines in the Caribbean." *Ethnic and Racial Studies* 4 (October), 415–31.
Ottley, Roi. 1943. *New World A-Coming.* Cleveland: World Publishing Co.
Pear, Robert. 1984. "Immigration and the Randomness of Ethnic Mix." *New York Times,* October 2, 1984, p. A28.
Pettigrew, Thomas F. 1971. "Race, Mental Illness, and Intelligence: A Social Psycho-

logical View." In Richard H. Osborne, ed., *The Biological and Social Meaning of Race*, pp. 87–124. San Francisco: W. H. Freeman & Co.

———, ed. 1975. *Racial Discrimination in the United States.* New York: Harper & Row.

Pierson, Donald. 1942. *Negroes in Brazil.* Chicago: University of Chicago Press.

Pitt-Rivers, Julian. 1967. "Race, Color, and Class in Central America and the Andes." *Daedalus* 96 (Spring), 542–59.

Powell, Adam Clayton, Jr. 1971. *Adam by Adam: The Autobiography of Adam Clayton Powell, Jr.* New York: Dial Press.

Preston, Dickson J. 1980. *Young Frederick Douglass: The Maryland Years.* Baltimore: Johns Hopkins University Press.

Reed, T. Edward. 1969. "Caucasian Genes in American Negroes." *Science* 165 (August 22), 762–68.

Reuter, Edward Byron. 1918. *The Mulatto in the United States.* Boston: Richard G. Badger.

———, ed. 1934. *Race and Culture Contacts.* New York: McGraw-Hill Book Co.

———. 1970. *The American Race Problem.* 3rd ed., rev. by Jitsuichi Masuoka. New York: Thomas V. Crowell Co.

Roebuck, Julian B., and Marcus L. Hickson. 1982. *The Southern Redneck: A Phenomenological Study.* New York: Praeger.

Rohrer, Georgia K. 1977. "Racial and Ethnic Identification and Preference in Young Children." *Young Children* 32 (January), 24–33.

Rohrer, John H., and Munro S. Edmonson. 1960. *The Eighth Generation Grows Up: Cultures and Personalities of New Orleans Negroes.* New York: Harper & Row.

Rose, Arnold M. 1956. *The Negro in America.* Boston: Beacon Press.

Rose, Arnold M., and Caroline Rose. 1948. *America Divided.* New York: Alfred A. Knopf.

Rose, Peter I. 1985. "Asian Americans: From Pariahs to Paragons." In Nathan Glazer, ed., *Clamor at the Gates: The New American Immigration*, pp. 181–212. San Francisco: ICS Press.

Royce, Amya Peterson. 1982. *Ethnic Identity: Strategies of Diversity.* Bloomington: Indiana University Press.

Schaefer, Richard T. 1980. "Racial Endogamy in Great Britain: A Cross-National Perspective." *Ethnic and Racial Studies* 3 (April), 224–35.

Simmons, Peter. 1976. " 'Red Legs': Class and Color Contradictions in Barbados." *Studies in Comparative International Development* 11 (Spring), 3–24.

Simon, Rita J., and Howard Alstein. 1977. *Transracial Adoption.* New York: John Wiley & Sons.

———. 1981. *Transracial Adoption: A Follow-Up.* Lexington, Mass.: D. C. Heath & Co.

Sizemore, Barbara. 1973. "Separatism: A Reality Approach to Inclusion?" In Edgar C. Epps, ed., *Race Relations: Current Perspectives*, pp. 305–31. Cambridge, Mass.: Winthrop Publishers.

Smith, Lillian. 1944. *Strange Fruit: A Novel.* New York: Reynal & Hitchcock.

———. 1949. *Killers of the Dream.* New York: W. W. Norton. Rev. ed., 1962.

———. 1963. *Killers of the Dream.* Garden City, N.Y.: Anchor Books/Doubleday & Co.

Snyder, Louis L. 1962. *The Idea of Racialism.* New York: Van Nostrand Reinhold Co.

Solaún, Mauricio, and Sidney Kronus. 1973. *Discrimination Without Violence.* New York: John Wiley & Sons.

Sorce, James F. 1979. "The Role of Physiognomy in the Development of Racial Awareness." *Journal of Genetic Psychology* 134 (March), 33–41.

Stoddard, Ellwyn R. 1973. *Mexican Americans.* New York: Random House.

Stoddard, Theodore Lothrop. 1920. *The Rising Tide of Color.* New York: Scribner.

Stonequist, Everett V. 1937. *The Marginal Man.* New York: Charles Scribner's Sons.

Thernstrom, Stephan, ed. 1980. *Harvard Encyclopedia of American Ethnic Groups.* Cambridge, Mass.: Harvard University Press.

Thompson, Daniel C. 1963. *The Negro Leadership Class.* Englewood Cliffs, N.J.: Prentice-Hall.

Thompson, Leonard. 1969. *African Societies in Southern Africa.* New York: Praeger.

Toomer, Jean. *Cane.* 1923. New York: Boni and Liveright.

Trillin, Calvin. 1986. "American Chronicles: Black or White." *New Yorker,* April 14, 1986, pp. 62–78.

Tumin, Melvin M., ed. 1969. *Comparative Perspectives on Race Relations.* Boston: Little, Brown & Co.

Tumin, Melvin M., and Arnold Feldman. 1969. "Class and Skin Color in Puerto Rico." In Melvin M. Tumin, ed., *Comparative Perspectives on Race Relations,* pp. 197–214. Boston: Little, Brown & Co.

Udry, J. Richard, et al. 1971. "Skin Color, Status, and Mate Selection." *American Journal of Sociology* 76 (January), 722–23.

Van den Berghe, Pierre L. 1971. "Racial Segregation in South Africa: Degrees and Kinds." In Heribert Adam, ed., *South Africa: Sociological Perspectives,* pp. 37–49. London: Oxford University Press.

Vander Zanden, James W. 1972. *American Minority Relations.* 3rd ed. New York: Ronald Press Co.

Wagenheim, Kal. 1975. *A Survey of Puerto Ricans on the U.S. Mainland in the 1970s.* New York: Praeger.

Wagley, Charles, ed. 1963. *Race and Class in Rural Brazil.* 2nd ed. Paris: UNESCO.

Watson, Graham. 1970. *Passing for White: A Study of Racial Assimilation in a South African School.* London: Tavistock Publications.

White, Walter. 1948. *A Man Called White: The Autobiography of Walter White.* New York: Viking Press.

Williams, J. Allen, Jr., and Paul L. Wienir. 1967. "A Reexamination of Myrdal's Rank Order of Discriminations." *Social Problems* 14 (Spring), 443–54.

Williamson, Joel. 1980. *New People: Miscegenation and Mulattoes in the United States.* New York: The Free Press.

Willie, Charles V. 1975. *Oreo: A Perspective on Race and Marginal Men and Women.* Wakefield, Mass.: Parameter Press.

Wilson, William J. 1973. *Power, Racism, and Privilege.* New York: The Free Press.

———. 1976. "Class Conflict and Jim Crow Segregation in the Postbellum South." *Pacific Sociological Review* 19 (October), 431–46.

———. 1978. *The Declining Significance of Race.* Chicago: University of Chicago Press.

Woodson, Carter G. 1918. "The Beginnings of the Miscegenation of the Whites and the Blacks." *Journal of Negro History* 3 (October), 335–53.

Woodward, C. Vann. 1957. *The Strange Career of Jim Crow.* Fair Lawn, N.J.: Oxford University Press.

Zastrow, Charles H. 1977. *Outcome of Black Children–White Parents Transracial Adoptions.* San Francisco: R&E Research Associates.

INDEX